Proven Solutions for Improving Supply Chain Performance

A volume in
The Proven Solutions Series
C. Carl Pegels, *Series Editor*

Proven Solutions for Improving Supply Chain Performance

by

C. Carl Pegels

School of Management
University at Buffalo
State University of New York

INFORMATION AGE PUBLISHING

Greenwich, Connecticut 06830 • www.infoagepub.com

Library of Congress Cataloging-in-Publication Data

Pegels, C. Carl.
Proven solutions for improving supply chain performance / by C. Carl Pegels.
p. cm. – (Proven solutions series)
Includes bibliographical references.
ISBN 1-59311-316-1 (pbk.) – ISBN 1-59311-317-X
1. Business logistics. 2. Industrial management. I. Title. II. Series.
HD38.5.P44 2005
658.5–dc22

2004030907

Printed in the United States of America

CONTENTS

PREFACE

Scientific research of the supply chain has so far been rather sparse because of the supply chain's complexity. However, research of the numerous links that make up the supply chain has been rather extensive. And, of course, when we discuss the supply chain and its links, we focus on the management, control, and direction of the many facets of the supply chain.

Scientific research is published in academic research journals, which are typically only read by other scientific management researchers. Some of these research results may eventually find their way into management textbooks, but these textbooks generally only provide exposure to management students and their professors. This, of course, is not undesirable because management students will be future managers of business functions, including the supply chain. However, the potential immediate beneficiaries of the scientific research results, the current professional managers, seldom are exposed to or are aware of the benefits of the research.

The barrier that stands in the way of scientific management research and the professional supply chain manager is the language used to publish the research. Scientific management research utilizes extensive and sophisticated statistical tools with which the professional supply chain manager is generally not familiar. Because of this barrier publishers of scientific management journals seldom promote their journals to professional managers.

Another barrier standing in the way of the dissemination of scientific management research is the abundance of popular management literature written by the so-called management gurus. There is a veritable flood of

Proven Solutions for Improving Supply Chain Performance, pages vii–viii books on the market providing professional managers with enough reading material to keep their free time well occupied.

The problem with the popular management literature is that most of it is based on the writer's opinion, and their ideas have seldom been scientifically tested. The published material is often referred to as armchair wisdom. Even if the material is based on a successful case study, the case study typically consists of a sample of one, and as a result is not generalizable to other situations or organizations.

Proven Solutions for Improving Supply Chain Performance is a collection of about 175 descriptions of scientific management studies in the management of supply chains. Each one of the scientific studies is presented in readable and understandable form for individuals who probably have not had the statistical and scientific education and training to fully understand the underlying studies.

The research summaries can also be viewed as research translations that can be quickly understood by the nonscientific reader. Even if the reader is able to follow the original research studies, the summaries will enable individuals to quickly grasp the importance of each study.

The book is significantly different from the popular management literature, which is generally based on "armchair" theories that have little basis on fact, and seldom have been scientifically verified.

Although the book is targeted for the supply chain manager/administrator, it can also be used as a supplementary reader in such courses as Operations Management, Service Systems Management, Manufacturing Management, Purchasing Management, and, of course, in Supply Chain Management courses.

The primary sources for each of the research summaries are five academic journals: the *Journal of Operations Management* (elsevier.com/wps/find/journaldescriptions), the *Academy of Management Journal* (aom.pace.edu/amjnew), the *International Journal of Operations and Production Management* (oberon.emeraldinsight.com), the *Decision Science Journal* (decisionsciences.org), and the *Production and Operations Management Journal* (poms.org/pomswebsite/journal.html).

ACKNOWLEDGMENTS

I would like to thank all the students who contributed to the development of this book through the contribution of research translation drafts of individual published research papers. I also want to thank Valerie Limpert for an outstanding job of typing and proofreading several versions of the manuscript, and to my wife, Patricia, for providing moral support during the preparation of this book.

CHAPTER 1

HIGHLIGHTS OF RESEARCH RESULTS

The purpose of this book is to publicize the scientific management research, which has produced numerous tools, techniques, and approaches for managing the various aspects of the supply chain. Supply chain management has evolved over the past decade as the focus area for improving the flow of materials from suppliers to customers and for lowering the costs incurred in the supply chain.

The means of publicizing the above are numerous, easy-to-understand summaries of the research reported in scientific management research journals available at university and main city libraries and on the Internet.

The supply chain is rather complex and involves many participating activities and functions including personnel who perform the functions and activities to ensure proper functioning of the supply chain. As a result, research results that will be reported cover a variety of topics that impact on supply chain performance.

The easy-to-understand summaries of the research reports can also be typified as research translations or interpretations. Making the research understandable is the main objective of all included research summaries. The summaries are organized into 18 chapters, each covering eight or nine research papers.

Much of the popular management literature in book stores, in the top 10 business books, and on managers' bookshelves are so-called managerial "wis-

Proven Solutions for Improving Supply Chain Performance, pages 1–14

doms," which have no or little relationship to fact as determined by scientific, empirically based research. This book has been written to provide supply chain managers, and managers of those areas that comprise the supply chain, with a collection of managerial facts that have been tested out scientifically.

GRAPHICAL MODEL OF SUPPLY CHAIN

A graphical description of a typical supply chain is shown in Figure 1.1. Note that the main components of the supply chain are the main players, the inventory storage areas, and transportation. The main players consist of the suppliers, the manufacturer, the distributor, and the retailer. The inventory storage areas are required for temporary storage until the material can be transported to the next destination, or until it can be utilized by the next main player. The transportation is responsible for moving the goods to the next destination.

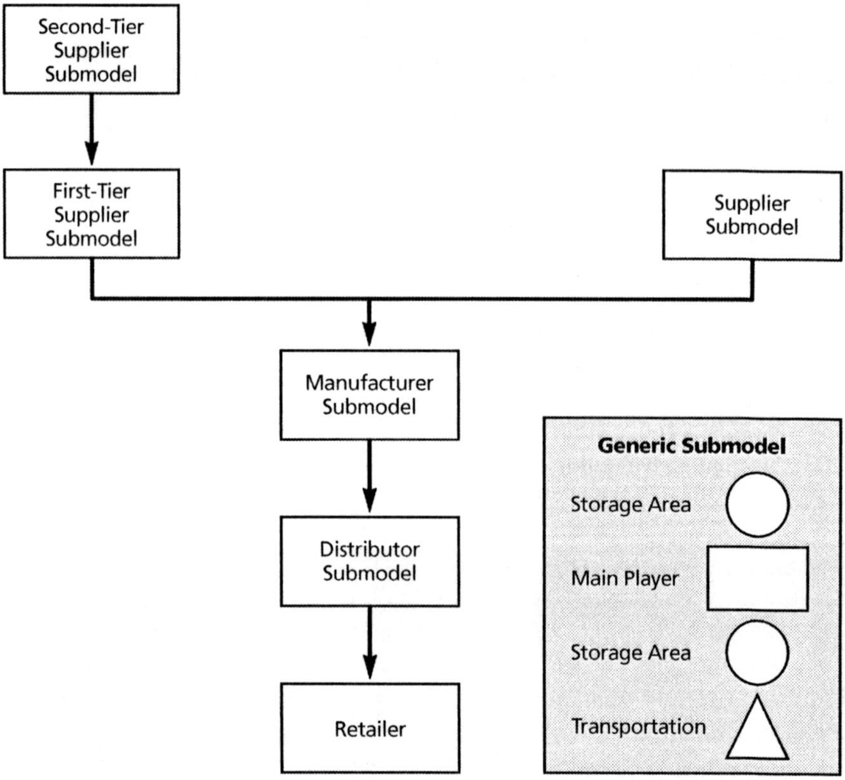

Figure 1.1. Model of supply chain.

What follows are brief descriptions of some of the more interesting studies largely based on the perceived interest level of supply chain and supply chain-related managers. The reports below are based on scientific research, and not on anecdotal stories.

SUPPLY CHAIN MANAGEMENT: STRATEGIC ISSUES

Several papers in this chapter are of particular interest. The first paper develops a model for supply chain design that is based on the experience IBM had in launching its IBM personal computer. The experience taught IBM a lot about supply chain design. The author ends up recommending a three-dimensional concurrent engineering model in the design of the supply chain. The three dimensions are product development, process development, and supply chain development.

The second paper addresses the issue of how a firm can move from vertical integration to supply chain integration. To accomplish the change the firm depended on supply chain integrators. The case study was based on the experience Hewlett Packard (HP) had in making the move to a supply chain-integrated firm. The approach used by HP produced a supply chain integrative model as a collaborative model of product development, design, and manufacturing.

The result is that HP generates design requirements while contract manufacturers do the detailed design and manufacturing.

The third paper reports on an investigation in the worldwide automobile industry. The study identified eight trends. The results showed that delivery speed and quality of supplier parts has improved, product life cycle has become shorter, production and product development are becoming more globalized, and outsourcing has increased. Also, the number of suppliers utilized had decreased, product development time had decreased substantially, suppliers have become substantially more involved in development time, and just-in-time deliveries had tripled over the past 15 years.

SUPPLY CHAIN MANAGEMENT: OPERATIONAL ISSUES

The first paper in this chapter of particular interest is on buyer–supplier relationships, also called buyer–supplier alliances. The researcher investigated four hypotheses and tested them with empirical data. The first confirmed hypothesis states that partner reputation will be positively related to alliance outcomes. The second unconfirmed hypothesis states that partner reputation will be positively related to alliance outcomes. The third confirmed hypothesis states that shared decision making will be positively related to alliance outcomes. And the fourth and last hypothesis, which was also confirmed, states that similarities between partners will be positively related to alliance outcomes. It was also confirmed.

The second paper proposed that 15 purchasing practices can be combined into five dimensions. The five dimensions were empowerment, employee competence, interaction frequency, interaction effectiveness, and buyer–seller relationship management. Three performance variables were then identified, consisting of market share, degree of achievement of total quality management (TQM) goals, and degree of achievement of customer satisfaction goals. The results of the study indicated that purchasing competence positively influenced TQM goals and positively influenced the achievement of customer satisfaction goals.

The third paper also addressed intercompany collaboration. It focused on integrating production schedules between buyer and supplier. The research determined that the total cost of the supply chain can be minimized but the supplier will benefit more than the buyer. This comes about because the buyer will have to maintain larger amounts of safety stock. However, if the above is known beforehand, the benefits of lower supply chain cost can be shared by both buyer and supplier.

SUPPLY CHAIN MANAGEMENT: INTERNATIONAL ISSUES

Of particular interest in this chapter are three papers. The first paper addresses the benefits gained from environmental progress of South East Asia's global suppliers. The empirical data for this study was obtained from the Philippines, Indonesia, Malaysia, Thailand, and Singapore. The researchers evaluated the relationships between environmental initiative, greening of suppliers, environmental performance, competitiveness, and economic performance. The results indicated that the greening of global suppliers in South East Asia has taken root and was proven beneficial to society but also to the initiators.

The second paper is a study on how 25 firms learned over time to successfully operate joint ventures. The experience that benefited the firms originated from operating wholly owned subsidiaries and joint ventures. The results also showed that experience gained from joint ventures in developed countries was more beneficial than experience gained from joint ventures in developing countries. The key idea gained from this study is that firms only absorb experience as it relates to what they already know in a related line of business and if the experience is related to the firm's knowledge base.

The third study looks at how differences in culture affect cross-border mergers. The results showed that there was a high correlation between the difference of culture and the performance of the companies after the acquisition. The more different the cultures were the better was the performance in terms of sales. Another variable that affected the success of the merger was the size of the acquisition. Smaller acquisitions performed significantly better than larger acquisitions.

JUST-IN-TIME MANAGEMENT

The first paper of interest in this chapter is a comparison with American manufacturing in 1850 versus just-in-time (JIT) methods used today at the beginning of the 21st century. Not realized by many is the fact that JIT methods share many characteristics with the methods used by the United States during the 1850s. However, the study shows that knowledge of work organizations, material scheduling, logistics, production techniques, facility layout, and location has advanced since the 1850s. How to increase productivity has advanced significantly, but focusing on what needs to be done has remained consistent.

The second paper looks at the critical issues in just-in-time manufacturing. The basis of the paper is a case study of six plants including numerous interviews in each of the plants. The study identified four initiatives that were essential conditions for successful implementation of just-in-time manufacturing. The four initiatives consisted of promotion of employee responsibility, provision of training, promotion of teamwork, and visible demonstration of management commitment.

The third paper looked at the impact of just-in-time methods based on economic theory. Based on economic theory there are four crucial inputs in manufacturing. They consist of labor, capital, energy, and materials. Forty firms participated in the study. The results indicated that there was a significant performance difference between just-in-time firms and non-just-in-time firms. Just-in-time firms generate 6 percent more output than non-just-in-time firms with the same inputs.

DEMAND FORECASTING

The first paper in this chapter of particular interest is a study of the effects of feedback on judgmental forecast accuracy. The researchers used an experiment with university students as subjects. The subjects were given a scenario where repetitive forecasts were to be made. Following each forecast, subjects were either given performance feedback in terms of how they could improve their subsequent forecasts, or only performance feedback. The results showed that the group that was given task feedback performed better than the group that was given only performance feedback.

The second paper is a study on the benefits of improved demand forecasting accuracy. Three sources of savings as a result of improved forecasts were identified. The first source of savings is in lower stock shortages, provided that management takes proper action in response to the improved forecasts. The second source of savings results from the firm's ability to buy more of their materials and supplies on a long-term contract basis. And the third source of savings results from improved localized forecasts allowing the reduction of company-wide inventory levels, thus lowering overall operating costs.

The third study looks at the benefits of retailer–supplier cooperation for highly varying demand items such as special toys and high fashion products. The results showed that early order commitment from retailers will reduce total supply chain cost. The overall conclusion that can be drawn from the study is that retailers will benefit from accurate demand forecasting models. Accurate forecasting allows retailers to place orders in time for the supplier to plan his output.

INVENTORY MANAGEMENT AND SCHEDULING

The first paper of particular interest in this chapter is a study of the critical factors of manufacturing requirements planning (MRP) implementation. The focus of the study is on identification of the critical factors. The results revealed that top management support is probably the most important factor to achieve success at MRP implementation. Other critical factors are accuracy of inventory records, market forecasts, capacity planning, and support from colleagues. The benefits of MRP implementation were found to be improved customer service, better production scheduling, and reduced manufacturing costs.

The second paper also addressed the same question as the previous paper. What are the benefits of implemented MRP systems? The findings showed that determinant variables such as data accuracy, participant support, degree of integration, and company size affect benefits on many different dimensions. These dimensions consisted of operational efficiency, customer service, interdepartment cooperation, and degree of integration.

The third paper focused on the impact of parts commonality. Because of the wide variety of products demanded by the market and produced by companies, there tends to be a proliferation of parts. The goal of parts commonality is to have as few parts as possible. This can be achieved by using the same parts in many different products. To achieve this goal, parts commonality should be a serious issue in product design. The overall benefit to the process is the reduction in parts inventory.

OUTSOURCING AND PURCHASING

Several papers in this chapter are of particular interest. The first paper investigates the impact of strategic sourcing and manufacturing technology on manufacturing flexibilities. Strategic sourcing includes the impact of supplier responsiveness and assistance in product design, production process, and product introduction cycle time. Manufacturing technologies refer to cellular manufacturing, just-in-time approaches, and integrated manufacturing. Manufacturing flexibility includes modification, volume, and new product development flexibility. The results showed that strategic sourcing had a significant impact on modification flexibility but not on the other two flexibilities. Advanced manufacturing technologies had a significant impact on volume flexibility but not on the other two flexibilities.

The second paper is a study of modular outsourcing in three automobile plants in Brazil and Poland. The paper revealed that modular outsourcing was undergoing a major change in the worldwide automobile industry. The most revolutionary change they found existed in Volkswagen's Resende plant in Brazil. In the Resende plant, Volkswagen has distributed the venture risk to the module suppliers. The suppliers provided capital to build the plant, get paid on final assembly of the vehicle, and share vehicle repair costs for each defective module they supply. There are 1,200 employees in the Resende plant, but only 200 are Volkswagen employees. The remaining 1,000 employees are on the suppliers' payrolls.

The third paper describes the major changes and benefits of electronic procurement for maintenance, repair, and operating (MRO) items. The study is based on the experience of 32 firms. The benefits of electronic procurement of MRO items were substantial. The major benefit was the cost of electronic procurement, which was only one-third of manual procurement. Another benefit was the improved visibility of all MRO transactions by individuals in the organizations, thus allowing close control. Also beneficial is the potential for reduction in the supply base, resulting in further cost reductions. Still another benefit is the open visibility of the entire MRO supply base. This provides opportunities to evaluate the cost of outsourced versus insourced MRO items.

BUYER–SUPPLIER RELATIONS

The first paper of interest is an evaluation of buyers' strategies to improve supplier performance in the manufacturing setting. The buyer typically uses four activities related to the supplier. They are supplier assessment, direct involvement, supplier incentives, and competitive pressure. The results indicate that supplier assessment and incentives are key enablers of supplier development. Direct involvement also plays a direct and critical role in achieving supplier performance improvement.

The second paper addresses purchasing/supplier involvement, purchasing strategy, and firm performance. For the study the researchers used subjective data obtained through a questionnaire survey, and objective data for firm performance. The results revealed that purchasing involvement with the supplier has a significant positive relationship with strategic purchasing. Strategic purchasing measures the degree of purchasing involvement with new product design and development decisions and strategic sourcing. Strategic purchasing in turn has a significant positive effect on financial performance.

The third paper addresses the impact of supplier selection and involvement on customer satisfaction and firm performance. The results revealed that supplier selection had a significant and positive effect on product quality, delivery service, and competitive pricing. Also supplier involvement had a significant and positive impact on delivery service and firm performance. And product quality had a significant and positive impact on delivery service and product variety. Also delivery service had a significant and positive impact on product variety and firm performance. And product variety had a significant and positive impact on competitive pricing and firm performance. Finally, competitive pricing had a significant and positive impact on firm performance.

TOTAL QUALITY MANAGEMENT

The first paper of special importance in this chapter covers total quality management (TQM) practices, performance, and customer satisfaction. The three propositions in the study stated that TQM practices have a strong impact on customer satisfaction, and have a moderate impact on plant performance. And plant performance has a weak impact on customer satisfaction. The results showed strong support for TQM practices and customer satisfaction, weak support for TQM practices and plant performance, and no support for plant performance and customer satisfaction.

The second paper asks the question if TQM adoption provides competitive advantage to the firm. The area of study was the hospital industry. The results indicated that hospitals with high structural control showed a strong relationship between TQM practices and financial performance. In contrast, hospitals with low structural controls did not show a significant relationship between TQM practices and financial performance.

The third paper is a study of the impact of quality improvement speed on quality-related costs. The results indicate that when the speed of quality improvement increases, the rate of growth in quality-related costs will decrease. Also, when speed of quality improvement increases, the rate of growth in future costs will not be affected. Slower continuous improvement in a learning environment may be the best approach to achieve quality improvements at manageable costs.

MARKETING AND SALES MANAGEMENT

The first paper of interest in this chapter focuses on the driver of customer satisfaction in Denmark. The study shows that a business strategy is successful if it creates satisfied and loyal customers mainly by having a good service-minded image. The research showed that for such areas as the cable TV industry and the supermarket industry, of the four drivers of customer satisfaction, consisting of expectations, image, product quality, and service quality, image is the most important.

The second paper is a study of computer-based intimate exchanges and self-disclosure. The study focuses on the question of whether people tend to disclose more information about themselves when a machine—a computer in this case—interacts in a human manner. The study is based on an experiment using 60 college students as subjects. The results suggest that computers can be used to simulate person-to-person interactions. The implications are that with the technique, using interactive computers, efficient customer profiling can be done, but it is also able to build long-term customer relationships and provide opportunities to build more personalized products.

The third paper is a study of how the firm's price and quality strategies for a product are related to the country in which the firm is marketing the product. A survey questionnaire was sent to CEOs in the United States, Japan, and countries in the European Union. The researchers then interviewed 120 MBA students at an American university. The product price and quality were defined in terms of economy, value, and premium, which measures a range from low price/low quality to high price/high quality. The research revealed that Japan has predominantly a superior value strategy, the European Union has predominantly a premium strategy, and the United States has predominantly an economy strategy. It is important that firms align their strategy based on the above results.

DOMESTIC MANUFACTURING

Evaluation of scheduling rules in a job shop is the focus of the first paper. The researchers focused on the question if common scheduling rules are more effective than a random assignment rule. The two common rules were the greatest total processing time (GTPT) rule and the least total processing time (LTPT) rule. The means of evaluation were simulation of several machines in a job shop. The results indicated that the two common rules did not perform any better than the random assignment rule.

The second paper is a study of flexible management practices and managerial performance. The study used a survey questionnaire addressed to manufacturing plant managers. The results of the study revealed that all manufacturing practices, except monitoring and delegating, are positively correlated with managerial performance. The results also indicate that relationship-oriented practices and participative leadership practices are more effective in managing work when the emphasis is high on flexibility.

The third paper is a study of flexibility as process mobility. The area of study focused on 52 U.S. plants in the uncoated fine paper industry. The most interesting result from the study is that flexibility is affected more by human aspects of the manufacturing plant than by technological aspects of the plant.

INTERNATIONAL MANUFACTURING

The first paper of interest in this chapter addresses the global spread of production. The paper addresses the migration of manufacturing from country to country. The researchers discovered that manufacturing is increasing in both developing economies as well as in developed countries. In addition, manufacturing has been growing faster than any other sector of the developed economies during the past few decades. However, the faster growth has been in output and not in employment. The authors conclude that manufacturing is still a major part of the way of life in developed economies.

The second paper is a comparison of American and European manufacturing practices. Manufacturing executives were surveyed from 20 countries including both developed and developing economies. The results showed that differences in manufacturing practices can largely be explained by regional or cultural differences, industry differences, and differences based on the degree of freedom in the market in terms of government regulations.

The third paper is a study of operations managers in Australia and Canada. Data for the study was obtained from surveys done in both countries.

The results revealed that operations managers in the two countries were quite similar. The most important areas of concern for the managers in terms of importance were cost reduction, productivity, and organization of work. The managers were generally satisfied in their jobs and with their compensation. Another important result revealed that the managers felt that technical skills were not sufficient to perform their jobs. Human resource skills were very important in the performance of their responsibilities.

TRANSPORTATION AND LOGISTICS

Several papers in this chapter are of particular interest. The first paper evaluates the use of electronic data interchange (EDI) on delivery performance. Data was collected from the World Class Manufacturing (WCM) project covering four countries including Germany, Italy, Japan, and the United States. The results of the study revealed that the EDI link between suppliers and buyers as well as the extent of the EDI usage improves on-time delivery performance, especially in time of production instability.

The second paper is a study of operational efficiency at major airports. Data was obtained from a mail survey to 80 major U.S. airports. The results revealed that airports that were hubs for major air carriers were those that were more efficient than nonhub airports. Also, airports not located in the Snow Belt were more efficient than Snow Belt airports. This study is important because government support for airports is highly dependent on airport efficiency.

The third paper is a study of delivery speed and reliability. Data was collected through surveys from manufacturing firms. The results indicated that delivery speed and delivery reliability are two unique manufacturing strategies within the make-to-order manufacturing environment. Delivery speed can best be attained through design interface, supplier interface, and process layout. Delivery reliability can best be achieved through meeting production plan and master scheduling goals.

PROJECTS AND TEAMWORK

The first paper of particular interest in this chapter is a study on personality heterogeneity in teams. Data were collected from 59 student teams. Each team conducted a semester-long process improvement project in a sponsoring organization. Five traits believed to be significant indicators of team performance were selected. They were conscientiousness, extraversion, agreeableness, neuroticism, and team orientation. The results revealed, among others, that greater diversity within a team in agreeableness and neuroticism resulted in lower team performance. Also, greater diversity among team members in extraversion resulted in higher team performance.

The second paper is a study of the effects of physical co-location on product development projects. If a project team is located in the same building, there are bound to be more face-to-face meetings than if it were not. The results revealed that physical co-location in teams that produces more face-to-face meetings enjoys better success in product development projects.

The third paper is an investigation into what the effective problem-solving tools are for improvement teams. The study was based on information gathered from 16 improvement teams. The results revealed that as many as 11 different problem-solving tools were used by each project team. However, the four most commonly used problem-solving tools were fishbone diagram, facility layout diagram, work flow analysis, and difficulty-impact grid.

HUMAN RESOURCE MANAGEMENT

The first paper of interest in this chapter is a study of procedurally-just performance systems. The data was obtained from an experimental study with managers as subjects. The results of the study indicated that there is a continuing unfairness in managerial decision making, much of it caused by personal bias. Managers who felt they had been evaluated unfairly by their superiors performed fairer evaluations of their subordinates. Also, managers who felt they had been treated fairly by their superiors performed unfair evaluation of their subordinates.

The second paper is a study of the effects of leaves of absence on career success. The data for the study was obtained from past surveys. The researchers compared the salary of someone, regardless of gender, who had worked continuously without taking any leaves of absence with the salary of someone else who had taken at least one leave of absence. The results indicated, not surprisingly, that the salary of those in managerial positions who had taken a leave of absence were less than those who had not taken time off from work. The largest implication of the study is for women with managerial positions who take leaves of absence for family reasons.

The third paper is a study of firm reputation and social attractiveness. The data was generated from a large list of firms for which reputation ratings were available. A group of knowledgeable students then rated the selected companies in terms of attractiveness as a potential employer. The results of the study showed that a firm's size influences its attractiveness, moderated by the applicant's self-esteem and need for achievement. The conclusion is that the importance of corporate image is an influence on prospective applicants' attraction to the firm.

ORGANIZATIONAL ISSUES

Several papers in this chapter are of particular interest. The first paper defines what the requirements are for a firm to be a good corporate citizen. The definition is based on a literature survey of a number of studies. One definition described a good corporate citizen as one that treats a mix of stakeholders well. Stakeholder groups in their definition included employees, customers, stockholders, and the community. Another group defined social responsibility as a firm's commitment to operate in an economically and environmentally sustainable manner while acknowledging the interests of a variety of stakeholders.

The second paper is a study of the multiple roles of managerial women. The study is based on a survey and interview of 61 female managers and executives, average age of 40 years, with responsibilities ranging from middle management to top-level executives. A follow-up study of 276 women was also undertaken. The results of the study show that women, and probably also men, who occupy multiple life roles outside of work are not only effective at work but the multiple life roles actually are an indicator of managerial effectiveness.

The third paper is a study of personal initiative and job success. The major question the researchers attempted to answer was if future behavior is a good indicator of past behavior. The study is based on data collected from a variety of sources, both national and international. To measure personal initiative, the interview to collect the data measured the following scaled items: general initiative at work, education initiative, interviewer evaluation of initiative, self-reported initiative, and spouse-reported initiative. The study revealed that well-measured past behavior is a good indicator of future behavior. The results are especially important because in today's economy personal initiative is very important.

FIRM PERFORMANCE

The first paper of particular interest in this chapter is a study of human resource management (HRM) systems and firm performance. The study is based on a review of eight papers published on the issue. The results showed that HRM systems affect firm performance but in many different ways. One point of importance is that HRM systems are administrative activities rather than a strategic function. HRM systems can be used to gain competitive advantage, provided the firm takes advantage of the many ways in which HRM can be utilized.

The second paper is a study of corporate performance's relationship with financial performance. The data was obtained from 67 firms that had been rated on the social performance criterion during the 1982–1992 period. The results indicated that there is a positive association between social and financial performance in large U.S. firms.

The third paper is a study of the effect of 360-degree feedback in managerial evaluations on firm performance. The 360-degree feedback evaluation program requires that managers evaluate their subordinates but subordinates in turn also evaluate their managers. The 360-degree feedback method is widely accepted as an effective performance management tool, although it is also questioned as to its effectiveness. The study was based on 750 publicly traded companies. The research revealed that unless everyone involved in the program is trained in the art of giving and receiving feedback, the process can lead to conflict among team members. The performance results revealed that firms with 360-degree feedback are valued 5.7 percent lower than firms that do not.

FUNCTIONALLY TRIGGERED PERFORMANCE

Three papers of special interest are summarized below. The first paper is a study of quality practices, quality performance, manufacturing performance, and business performance. A survey questionnaire was sent to 200 suppliers to the electronic sector in Ireland. The results showed that quality practices have a definite and positive impact on quality performance. Quality performance, in turn, has a direct and positive impact on manufacturing performance. And finally, manufacturing performance has a direct and positive impact on customer satisfaction.

The second paper is a study of the effects of firm characteristics and total quality management on financial performance. The empirical basis for the study are 435 quality award winners. The results show that the quality award-winning firms had a change in operating income that was 39 percent higher than nonaward winners. The results also showed that lower capital-intensive firms benefit more from implementation of total quality management than higher capital-intensive firms.

The third paper is a study of performance benefits from just-in-time implementation. Executives of 89 firms that applied just-in-time methods were surveyed to gain an understanding of the benefits of just-in-time adoption. The results showed that more than 61 percent of the responses were positive with firms experiencing benefits in quality improvements, time-based responses, employee flexibility, accounting simplification, firm profitability, and inventory reductions. Only 5 percent of the responses were negative with respect to changes after adopting just-in-time methods.

CHAPTER 2

SUPPLY CHAIN MANAGEMENT

Strategic Issues

This chapter covers eight papers on supply chain strategic management issues. Supply chain management is a complex management area both internal and external to the firm, and therefore strategy must precede action.

The first study outlines what is involved in supply chain management strategy. It defines the supply chain design, including what areas the firm should invest in to develop internal supply chain expertise and capabilities. It also specifies which activities of the supply chain design to allocate to the suppliers, and to make it clear to suppliers what is expected of them.

The second study is somewhat similar to the first study except it focuses on fast-moving supply chains. The results are based on a survey of retailers and manufacturers in the United Kingdom. The study therefore adds an international flavor to the strategic development of supply chains. The study identifies 12 operating strategies that the survey respondents utilized.

The third study focuses on how strategic outsourcing can provide a competitive edge to the firm. The key result of the study is the fact that 80 percent of managers surveyed stated that a flexible organizational structure, which includes increasing outsourcing activities, is a key success factor in the coming years.

Proven Solutions for Improving Supply Chain Performance, pages 15–27

The fourth study covers a case study that describes how Hewlett-Packard transformed itself from a vertically-integrated firm to a supply chain–integrated firm. To accomplish this feat the firm used supply chain integrators extensively. In other words, the transformation described above needs planning, training, expertise, and flawless execution.

The fifth study describes the changing trends in supply chain management in the worldwide automobile industry. The study is based on a survey sent to both automobile manufacturers and suppliers in Europe, North America, and Asia. The questions posed focused on trends in the worldwide automobile industry. The results indicate that there have been substantial changes in the period from 1988 to 2003.

The sixth study addresses a more specific topic. It poses the question: What are the optimal number of vendors that should be employed? The study was done in a hypothetical environment. The three objectives the researchers studied were price, quality, and delivery delay. The constraints consisted of minimum volume for each vendor, maximum capacity for each vendor, and maximum requirements for the firm. The study is illustrative of how the question of optimal vendors to employ can be explored.

The seventh study is an exploratory study on how purchasing teams are employed in the supply chain management area. A survey of over 200 North American service and manufacturing firms was used to obtain the information for the analysis. The results indicate that cross-functional purchasing teams are fairly widely used but interfirm teams are somewhat problematic and are not as extensively used.

The eighth and final study in this chapter addresses the issue of supplier involvement in new product development. The study is based on analysis of 38 new product development projects in five electronic companies. The important result is the fact that involving suppliers in product development leads to improvements in product quality. Supplier involvement also has a positive impact on product reliability, performance, and aesthetics.

Although the topics in this chapter are somewhat eclectic, they all relate to the importance of strategy development and planning to ensure a smoothly functioning supply chain.

STRATEGIES FOR SUPPLY CHAIN DESIGN

This paper posits that supply chain design is the ultimate core competency of an organization. Supply chain design is defined as: (1) choosing what capabilities along the value chain to invest in and develop internally, and (2) which activities or components to allocate for design and development by suppliers.

Professor Fine of Massachusetts Institute of Technology does a brilliant job of outlining where the focus of an organization should be in relation to the various components of a supply chain and why.

The basis of the paper's thesis is the experience IBM had in launching its IBM personal computer (PC). IBM depended extensively on two main suppliers, Intel and Microsoft. The two suppliers provided the two key core components of the PC, the chip and the operating system. Although IBM initially had the marketing power and expertise to sell its PCs, eventually Intel and Microsoft, because of their expertise, were able to develop their core PC products, sell them to other PC manufacturers, and the output of these manufacturers outgrew IBM in the PC market. The above scenario was the beginning of a horizontally integrated market from a previously vertically integrated market in the computer industry. And IBM only later discovered the dangers of making the switch from internal suppliers to external suppliers.

The author recommends a three-dimensional concurrent engineering model in the design of the supply chain. Three-dimensional concurrent engineering consists of the traditional product and process dimensions, to which is added the supply chain dimension. The concept focuses on the development aspects of the three dimensions.

Product development consists of two choices: architectural choices such as integrality versus modularity decisions, and detailed design choices such as performance and functional specifications.

Process development is divided into development of unit processes and manufacturing systems. Unit processes consist of process technologies and equipment. Manufacturing systems development consists of decisions about plant and operations systems design such as process/job focus versus product/cellular manufacturing focus.

Supply chain development is divided into supply chain architecture decisions and logistics/coordination system design decisions. Supply chain architecture decisions include sourcing decisions such as make or buy and in the case of buy, the decision of which suppliers to select. Logistics and coordination decisions include the inventory, delivery, and information systems to support the supply chain in operation.

OPERATIONS STRATEGIES AND FAST-MOVING SUPPLY SYSTEMS

To what extent are defined operations strategies used in supply systems where fast movement of goods and information is critical to the success of the operation?

Researcher Robert Lowson of the University of East Anglia posed that supply chain question and developed a study to find answers. The researcher contacted 170 retail and manufacturing firms in the United Kingdom to participate in the study. Over 40 percent decided to participate, consisting of 40 retailers and 31 suppliers. He developed an extensive questionnaire to elicit information and followed that up with extensive interviews to fill in gaps in the information provided.

The results of his data and information gathering produced descriptions of six operations strategies used by subsections of the total sample of 71 firms. The major operating strategies were: (1) supply or demand management, supply chain management, or value stream management; (2) quick response; (3) just-in-time and vendor-managed inventory; (4) agility in the supply system, agile manufacturing, strategically flexible production; (5) strategic purchasing, strategic procurement, network sourcing, materials management; and (6) continuous improvement. The above six strategies were each identified by at least 10 percent and more typically 20 percent of respondents.

It will be noted that the above six operations strategies tend not to be concisely descriptive except for two of them. In order to develop a more concise description the researcher broke down the operations strategies into operations strategy components. He developed 24 of them and then mapped them onto the 71 respondent firms, and identified the percentage of firms in each industry sector that utilized that particular operations strategy component. He also segmented the sample into the industry sectors: (1) grocery, (2) clothing, (3) electronics, (4) electrical, (5) toys, (6) stationery, and (7) consumer goods.

The most common operations strategy components consisted of: (1) joint product and merchandise planning with customer and supplier, (2) bar-coded merchandise, (3) product data and information sharing with trading partners, (4) use of electronic data interchange, (5) continual and automatic replenishment systems, (6) universal product codes and article numbering in the supply system, (7) electronic reorder, (8) container shipping codes, (9) Internet connectivity and electronic operations, (10) new logistics systems, (11) interface management and supply system visibility, and (12) sales captured at item level.

This paper provides an excellent and comprehensive overview of operations strategies currently in use in the retailer–supplier sector, and also provides good descriptions of each one of them.

STRATEGIC OUTSOURCING—A COMPETITIVE EDGE

Strategic outsourcing has become an increasingly familiar practice in today's business world. In fact, outsourcing will become even more prevalent in the near future. The worldwide market for outsourcing services is expected to double in the next 5 years. In addition, a recent survey conducted by the Economist Intelligence Unit and Andersen Consulting has indicated that a majority of managers/executives will consider outsourcing practically every noncore business process within their organization by the year 2010. According to Joellin Comerford, strategic outsourcing will become a key source of competitive advantage for firms. Managers/executives who take advantage of this opportunity will most likely lead a successful firm, but require new management skills, from a disciplined selection process to an understanding of the critical intangibles of culture and chemistry that can make or break a sourcing relationship.

The key result of the research was that 80 percent of the managers/executives stated that a flexible organizational structure was a key success factor in the coming years. Managers/executives see strategic outsourcing as a way to reshape their organization from one that is vertically integrated toward a more focused and flexible organization that relies on sourcing relationships to enhance its core abilities.

More than 40 percent of the managers/executives believe that their organization will be a substantially or fully virtual organization by the year 2010, and they categorize outsourcing as having the same level of importance as acquisitions and mergers in creating the world-class competitive organizations of tomorrow. Comerford states that this research study indicates that managers/executives are forging relationships with their suppliers that are increasingly close and cooperative.

The research also points out another recently released study conducted by The Warren Company, a Rhode Island–based consulting firm, which describes an emerging spectrum of outsourcing relationships, the current trend being a networked enterprise that is able to combine and recombine its core strengths with those of multiple partners such that they can move swiftly into new emerging markets.

The researcher goes on to point out that no two strategic sourcing relationships are alike. Each depends on the unique nature of the partners who are in the relationship. She states that her experience has repeatedly shown that strategic sourcing arrangements share a number of key traits that distinguish them from traditional outsourcing relationships. They tend to suppress legalistic, autocratic command and control approaches, and instead promote joint problem solving. Thus, they involve shared goals, risks, and rewards. Finally, they are set up for the long term such that each party will have the time needed to produce strategic results.

Managers/executives must possess/acquire the ability to create and sustain strategic outsourcing relationships that will be vital to competitive success. However, this is quite a challenge for the managers/executives of today's organizations. Developing and acquiring such skills is a huge transition for managers/executives and requires a change of mindset, which is one of the most difficult kinds of changes for them to make. The rewards for those who do will consist of the powerful means of strategic outsourcing and the mindset to keep continually pushing the boundaries of the organization further and further to create distinct competitive advantages.

FROM VERTICAL INTEGRATION TO SUPPLY CHAIN INTEGRATION

This paper describes a case study, verified by other case studies, on how a firm reorganized itself from a vertically integrated firm to a supply chain integrated firm. In doing so, the firm depended heavily on using specialists called supply chain integrators.

Professors Parker and Anderson, respectively, of Tulane University and the University of Texas made an extensive study of how Hewlett-Packard (HP) converted its design, manufacture, and marketing of such products as laptop computers and printers from a vertically integrated model to a collaborative supply chain model. Under the vertically integrated model HP did most of the product design, process design, manufacturing, and marketing in-house. Under the collaborative supply chain model, nearly all the product design, process design, manufacturing, and marketing was outsourced to collaborative suppliers.

In order to make the above system work, HP had to ensure that the flow of technical and other information flowed freely between the collaborative suppliers and HP. To accomplish this task, HP developed and trained technically and managerially qualified people to do all the coordination and integration to ensure a smooth and timely flow of information and products. The term coined by the authors for these experts is *supply chain integrators.*

The supply chain integrator, alone or with assistance of others, employs a mix of technical and managerial skills to coordinate, translate, and negotiate across the supply chain interfaces to maintain the integrity of the product from initial concept, design, and manufacture to product delivery. Successful supply chain integrator skills also include project management skills, soft people management skills, negotiation skills, and a modicum of technical skills related to the product and its components.

One successful example of supply chain integration application cites the case of a notebook computer that was brought on line in record time. Following the switch from vertical integration to supply chain integration, revenue of the notebook computer division increased approximately by a factor of 10, reduced cost of sales, and improved return on assets.

In general, HP manages the supply chain integration model as a collaborative model of product development, design, and manufacture. The HP division generates design requirements while contract manufacturers do the detailed design work and manufacturing. This approach requires an effective method to mold together the suppliers' design and development capabilities. To accomplish this requires that the supply chain integrator is well trained, experienced, and responsible and has the authority to control the integrity of the entire program.

The above approach may appear to be straightforward and relatively simple. But in fact, it requires flawless and experienced execution by the supply chain integrator and his team.

CHANGING TRENDS IN THE AUTOMOBILE INDUSTRY

What have been the sourcing trends in the worldwide automobile industry during the past 15 years? Researchers Fredrik von Corswant and Peter Fredriksson of Chalmers University of Technology in Goteburg, Sweden, posed this question and developed a survey method to find answers to the question.

The researchers posed eight questions on trends in the worldwide automobile industry. They consisted of: (1) increasing importance of three key performance criteria: delivery, quality, and cost; (2) length of product life cycles; (3) globalization in production and product development activities; (4) increase in outsourcing; (5) reduction of supply base by automobile firms; (6) changes in product development time; (7) increase in product development by suppliers; and (8) increase in just-in-time deliveries.

To find answers to the above trends the researchers developed a survey questionnaire that they sent out to both automobile manufacturers and suppliers in Europe, North America, and Asia. They sent out 124 questionnaires and their effort resulted in 27 usable responses, consisting of 11 automobile manufacturers and 16 suppliers.

The researchers collected information from the respondents for three points in time, 1988, 1998, and 2003. Since the paper was published in 2002, the 2003 data was clearly a projection. They then measured whether the changes between the three time points were statistically significant. For each of the eight trends from two to three questions were posed except for trend one, which required eight questions.

The summarized results will be listed below. In order to keep it concise, only the overall difference between 1988 and 2003 will be presented here.

Trend 1 asked about the importance of three performance criteria consisting of delivery, cost, and quality. Delivery and quality increased in importance but cost did not during the 15-year interval.

Trend 2 asked if the product life cycle became shorter. The answer was a not-so-surprising yes. The product life cycle shortened by a little less than 2 years as reported by the manufacturers and by a little more than 2 years as reported by the suppliers.

Trend 3 asked if production and product development were becoming more globalized. According to the manufacturers there was little change, but according to the suppliers there was significant change.

Trend 4 asked if outsourcing is increasing. The manufacturers responded that there was no change. However, the suppliers felt that there was a statistically significant increase during the 15-year period.

Trend 5 asked if the companies had reduced their supply bases. Both the automobile manufacturers and suppliers felt that a change had occurred.

Trend 6 asked if product development time is increasing. Both manufacturers and suppliers felt that there had been a reduction in product development time of about 2 years.

Trend 7 asked if suppliers had become more involved with product development. Automobile manufacturers felt that their share of product development had decreased from about 75 percent to 50 percent. Suppliers felt that their share of product development had more than doubled.

Trend 8 asked if just-in-time deliveries are increasing. Both manufacturers and suppliers agreed that just-in-time deliveries had tripled over the 15-year period.

In conclusion, the study indicates that there had been substantial changes in the automobile manufacturer–supplier relationship over the 15-year period from 1988 to 2003.

OPTIMAL NUMBER OF VENDORS TO EMPLOY

Although it is generally accepted that there are benefits to employ only a single vendor to supply a firm's needs for a particular raw material item, a component, a subassembly, or a complete product, this approach is frequently not feasible because of the capacity limitations of a single vendor.

Researchers Charles A. Weber, John Current, and Anand Desai describe an approach to determine the optimal number of vendors when the capacity of any one, two, or three firms is insufficient to supply all of the needs of the firm. The researchers show how for a given set of objectives and constraints in an illustrative case study, their proposed model is able to select the optimal number of vendors to employ. The objectives used in their illustrations consist of price, quality, and delivery delay. The constraints for each planning period consist of minimum delivery amount per vendor, maximum capacity of each vendor, and maximum requirements for the firm. For the illustrative case study, from four to six vendors were to be used. Less than four vendors would not be able to supply total requirements. And as a policy the firm did not want to use more than six firms.

The researchers used two mathematical solution methods to solve the problem. The first was multiple objective programming and the second was data envelopment analysis. Both methods have been widely used for problem-solving applications.

The results of the study indicate that for the illustrative example the five-vendor solution is the best solution because the three objectives of average price, average quality, and average late delivery are optimal. Each one of the objectives is measurably better than those for the four-vendor solution, but only marginally better than those for the six-vendor solution. So on the basis of these results management can select either five or six vendors and be confident that a good decision has been made.

In summary, the method proposed is mathematically elegant and would not be that difficult to implement for a firm. But it has limitations. In the example there were only three feasible choices, either four, five, or six vendors. In other words, management could not be far from the optimum solution by any one of the three choices. The model, however, provides confidence or verification, or a challenge to a managerial decision.

PURCHASING TEAM USAGE IN SUPPLY CHAIN MANAGEMENT

There are many flowcharts that show how companies should control the complete flow of goods, information, and capital from the supplier to the final customer. Unfortunately, most of these are not very useful. This leads to increasing interest in looking for approaches that will enable companies to use supply chain management to improve their competitive position. One of these approaches has been to manage supply chain activities through the use of purchasing teams. The purpose of this research is to provide a better understanding of the influence of industry content, purchasing organization structure, and purchasing strategic role on the use of team-based purchasing activities. Also, the research has the objective of developing insights with respect to the influence of industry sector and purchasing organizational structure on purchasing's strategic role.

Professors Johnson, Klassen, Leenders, and Fearon did a survey of chief purchasing officers (CPOs) in 236 large North American service and manufacturing firms. Seven types of purchasing teams were identified as generally accepted. They include: purchasing councils, supplier councils, commodity teams, cross-functional teams, teams involving suppliers, teams involving customers, and teams involving both suppliers and customers. A sample mean score was provided for the relative usage of the seven forms of purchasing teams. All of the firms appeared to have one or more of the forms of purchasing teams. The cross-functional teams were the most extensively used form of purchasing team. Firms use the different forms of purchasing teams for different purposes. For example, many firms use purchasing councils as a means of sharing information among decentralized units.

The researchers were also interested in finding out the degree to which purchasing played a strategic role. In order to do this they asked chief purchasing officers to rate their purchasing department's level of involvement in 13 different major corporate activities using a five-point scale. The results were translated into sample means and standard deviations. Outsourcing was the most involved major corporate activity.

Past research has indicated that the use of purchasing teams will enhance both external and internal integration. They were able to point out more advantages than disadvantages of using purchasing teams to control supply chain activities. They found that purchasing teams combine skills and resources of many stakeholders, which will span across subunits to facilitate the timely completion of supply chain activities. This approach was said to have advantages such as lower prices, reduced total cost of ownership, and improved supplier quality.

Factors related to industry structure and involvement in strategic activities played a strong role regarding team use. Also, internal teams and councils were more extensively used by firms that manufacture discrete goods. After controlling for firm size, purchasing's strategic role was positively related to greater use of internal teams and councils but not of customer teams.

There were five propositions that were made as a result of this research. They are:

1. Firms with a decentralized organizational structure for purchasing utilize purchasing teams to a lesser extent than the firms with either a centralized or hybrid structure.
2. The purchasing function has less of a strategic role in firms with a decentralized organizational structure than in firms with either a centralized or hybrid structure.
3. As purchasing's strategic role increases, the use of purchasing teams increases.
4. The purchasing function has a greater strategic role in the firms that manufacture discrete goods than in firms from process industries, which in turn is greater than in firms from service industries.

5. Purchasing team usage is greater in firms that manufacture discrete goods than in firms from process industries, which in turn is greater than in firms from service industries.

The research shows that there are many potential benefits to customer involvement on purchase teams, such as speed to markets, and co-coordinating product design and manufacturing. However, there are also situations where the use of supply teams is discouraged. Some organizations may not want their suppliers developing relationships with end-customers for the fear of disclosing proprietary information. It is the role of organizations to weigh the advantages against the disadvantages to make decisions regarding using certain forms of purchase teams.

EFFECTS OF SUPPLIER RELATIONSHIPS ON NEW PRODUCT DEVELOPMENT OUTCOMES

It is generally understood that new product development is of great importance for a company in order to expand and flourish. Therefore, one might wonder what external influences affect this process of product development. More specifically, when developing a new product, do suppliers affect the process by slowing the development stage? This is the question the two researchers asked.

As new product development (NPD) is vital to any company, it is important to evaluate past research on effects of supplier relationships. According to past research, companies that involve suppliers in their new product development achieve fast project times, better product quality, and lower project costs. However, other evidence exists, showing that suppliers have little practical influence on overall project technical success, and have negative impact on project development time. Additionally, it is unclear exactly when or how to involve suppliers in the NPD process.

With this conflicting evidence, Professor Primo, from Arizona State University, and Professor Amundson, of the University of Minnesota, decided to investigate further. They had three objectives embedded in their study. One was to analyze previous research on supplier involvement on NPD outcomes. Second was to create a model explaining how supplier relationship variables are related to each other and how they affect NPD outcomes. And lastly, after creation, they wanted to test their model.

Before beginning actual testing the researchers decided to concentrate specifically on the influence of suppliers on NPD, focusing on supplier relationships and the concept of supplier involvement. This focus resulted in the creation of a two-stage model, which was created on the basis of past research and was thoroughly tested. This model explained previous supplier relationships and their impacts on product quality, development, time, and cost.

Before testing their model the researchers devised various hypotheses based on each stage. The first stage of the model entailed three variables—supplier quality control, supplier obstructionism, and supplier involvement—and resulted in four buyer–supplier relationship hypotheses. The second stage, which had a list of three NPD outcomes, including project development time, project cost, and project quality, resulted in four more hypotheses based on NPD project outcome.

The researchers applied various measurements to research their variables. By using existing scales in conjunction with past literature, case studies, interviews, and focus groups, the researchers strived to produce accurate results. More specifically, they utilized 38 new product development projects from five electronic companies. Integrated into the study was survey information taken from a variety of managers including project, quality, and procurement managers of the 38 projects. Also, multiple members of each NPD project development team, including the leader and sponsor, responded to the survey as well. Survey questions were meant to incorporate information from different levels of management as well as from suppliers. This was done by asking a set of specific questions based on each one of the variables. The surveyed would then rate the truthfulness of each statement.

All calculated results included interrater reliability measures for complete accuracy. With all of their collected data the researchers put their hypotheses to the test. The results of the statistical test confirmed hypothesis one, the strong positive effect of supplier quality control on the level of supplier involvement. Meanwhile, supplier quality control has a negative effect on supplier obstructionism, supporting hypothesis two. This implies that suppliers who provide quality information and control systems are unlikely to hinder NPD projects. In reference to the second state of the model, they found that supplier involvement does not significantly affect any measure of project costs, therefore it could not support hypotheses five or seven. However, they did prove that the measure of project development time has a strong negative effect on supplier obstructionism.

The important result of this study is the fact that involving suppliers generates improvements in product quality. This is because all the product quality components have shown a strong correlation with supplier involvement. Also, the results indicate the decisive influence of suppliers on design aspects of the NPD project such as reliability, performance characteristics, and aesthetics. The main implication for business is to remain actively involved in careful supplier selection. This is especially true as outsourcing continues to be a popular trend, and sometimes the only option for many companies.

REFERENCES

Comerford, J. (1997). The changing shape of outsourcing. *InfoServer: The Journal for Strategic Information Services Providers, 1*(1), 1–3.

Fine, C. H. (2000). Clockspeed-based strategies for supply chain design. *Production and Operations Management, 9*(3), 213–221.

Johnson, P. F., Klassen, R.D., Leenders, M. L., & Fearon, H. E. (2002). Determinants of purchasing team usage in the supply chain. *Journal of Operations Management, 20*(1), 77–89.

Lowson, R. (2002). The implementation and impact of operations strategies in fast-moving supply systems. *Supply Chain Management: An International Journal, 7*(3), 146–163.

Parker, G. G., & Anderson, E.G. (2003). From buyer to integrator: The transformation of the supply chain manager in the vertically disintegrating firm. *Production and Operations Management, 11*(1), 75–91.

Primo, M. A. M., & Amundson, S. D. (2001). An exploratory study of the effects of supplier relationships on new product development outcomes. *Journal of Operations Management, 20*(1), 33–55.

Von Corswant, F., & Fredriksson, P. (2002). Sourcing trends in the car industry. *International Journal of Operations and Production Management, 22*(7), 741–758.

Weber, C. A., Current, G., & Desai, A. (2000). An optimization approach to determining the number of vendors to employ. *Supply Chain Management—An International Journal, 5*(2), 90–98.

CHAPTER 3

SUPPLY CHAIN MANAGEMENT

Operational Issues

This chapter is oriented around the operational issues in supply chain management. It addresses issues both from a technical as well as operational area.

The first paper focuses on the need to consider the interorganizational aspects of supply chains. Both buyer and supplier must be on the same wavelength in order to have smooth functioning of the supply chain. The main driver of smooth functioning is information flow. For smooth and complete information flow a climate of trust must prevail between buyers and suppliers.

The second paper provides a study of the relationships between the buyer–supplier dyads in supply chains. The researcher's study aimed to find out what attributes makes buyer–supplier alliances successful. The study was based on a field survey of 286 alliances. The variables that provided positive alliance outcomes were reputation, shared decision making, and strategic similarities.

The third study investigated the impact of interorganizational information systems on the functioning of supply chains. The function of the information systems is to facilitate the flow of information between the supply

Proven Solutions for Improving Supply Chain Performance, pages 29–41

chain members. Information for the study was obtained from 1349 firms in 20 industries. The main results revealed that the more extensive the supply chain and the information system was developed, the higher are the supply chain performance measures.

The fourth study describes a case study of one buyer–supplier link in Ireland. Although a study of one case does not provide generalization, it does give one an interesting snapshot of the problems the two partners encountered in developing, adjusting, and maintaining their relationship.

The fifth study focuses on the purchasing function of the firm. Data was collected from about 300 purchasing managers in the United States. The researchers identified five measures of purchasing competence that could be defined by 15 purchasing practices. They then identified three firm performance variables. Their final results indicated that purchasing competence positively influenced total quality management and customer satisfaction.

The sixth study addressed the vendor selection issue. The researcher developed a decision support system for selecting vendors on the basis of quality and delivery performance. Variations of his original vendor selection model were also developed and evaluated. The environment in which the model functioned was one in which numerous vendors were available but only a limited number were needed.

The seventh paper addressed the issue on how production schedules could be integrated with the supply chain. The research revealed that schedule integration was most likely to succeed if the buyer and the supplier belong to the same firm. The issue they addressed was especially critical in the case where large holding costs are involved in the supply chain, as exemplified in the automobile industry.

The eighth and final paper focuses on upstream volatility in the machine tool industry. Machine tool demand is heavily influenced by the strength of demand for the products produced by the machine tool industry's customers. If demand of the customers is strong, there will be strong demand for machine tools. Similarly, if demand of the customers is weak, demand for machine tools is weak. The problem is the delay in the demand of the two industry sectors. The solution pointed out by the researchers is for the machine tool industry to build and stock more standardized machines and also by closer engineering cooperation between buyers and sellers.

This chapter has focused on more specific operational issues in the supply chain. Many of the issues cannot always be resolved, but amelioration of problems is the objective in those cases.

SUPPLY CHAIN MANAGEMENT AND INTERORGANIZATION SYSTEMS

The focus in supply chain management is on the efficient, effective, and timely movement of goods from raw materials and supplies through manufacturing to the ultimate customer, the user. What makes this happen is the flow of information in both forward and rearward directions in the supply chain. Without effective information flow, supply chains cannot be efficient, effective, or timely.

The author, G. Pren Premkumar, makes the above point and then introduces the reader to the concept of interorganization systems and the contribution they make to the effective functioning of the supply chain.

Interorganizational systems have not created information flow between different organizational units. Information flow has existed ever since man began trading with others. Organizational systems, especially the computer-based variety, make the information flow more efficient, effective, and timely. In other words, interorganizational systems do to information what the supply chain has done to goods.

The author points out that since both the supply chain and the interorganizational system is external to the focal organization, they therefore involve many unique management issues that are outside of the control of senior management. The successful implementation of an effective supply chain and of an effective interorganizational system requires the cooperation of a large number of external partners. It is also a complex technical endeavor, as it is necessary to link widely diverse and technically incompatible systems.

Among the many technical and management issues are commonality of objectives, data security, alignment with business strategies, internal systems and performance measures, and technical compatibility issues. The most troublesome issue of the above is probably the first. For instance, if the information flow from a retailer to the manufacturer is direct, the distributor may feel threatened and sabotage the system. There also has to be agreement between the participants what policies are followed in terms of inventory, location, inventory ownership, timeliness in shipping, type of shipping, and numerous other agreements. In other words, the concept of the supply chain and the interorganizational system is a lot simpler than the implementation.

In conclusion, a climate of trust must be established between the partners for the supply chain and the interorganizational system to be successful.

ALLIANCE OUTCOMES: THE PARTNERS AND THE RELATIONSHIP

This paper attempts to empirically show that certain attributes of a company will affect any type of alliance (or joint-venture) that the firm engages in. Professor Todd Saxton of the University of Wisconsin points out that there is a lack of previous empirical research performed on the topic of what makes alliances successful. He feels that since alliances are becoming increasingly important in the business world, attempts must be made to quantify why alliances are successful or unsuccessful.

Saxton proposes a series of hypotheses that involve various characteristics of companies:

1. *Partner reputation will be positively related to alliance outcomes.* Reputation is a very valuable asset to a firm. It can significantly reduce the search costs of finding a partner for alliance. A positive reputation presents itself as an indicator of what a partnering firm can expect from a firm. In addition, it acts as a factor that breaks down the distrust sometimes formed from firm relationships.
2. *A prior relationship will be positively related to alliance outcomes.* A prior affiliation with a firm should positively affect the outcome of a joint venture or an alliance. With familiarity comes synergy and economies of scale, which may not be created in a new relationship. A prior relationship speeds up the alliance process because there is little or no honeymoon period in which the partners get accustomed to each other.
3. *Shared decision making will be positively related to alliance outcomes.* Shared decision making reduces the perception of the other company as being opportunistic or attempting to take advantage of the situation. The transfer of knowledge in an alliance generally seems to be correlated with the amount of decision making that each company is involved with.
4. *Similarities between partners will be positively related to alliance outcomes.* Similarities in areas such as products, technologies, processes, culture, administrative structure, or management styles seem to produce cohesion between two companies entering into a strategic alliance. Unrelated diversification seems to not be very successful in the long run. This provides further evidence that similarities can help to produce positive outcomes.

A two-stage, longitudinal field survey was distributed to a total of 286 alliances during 1994 and 1995. Of these, 98 alliance partners returned relevant data for analysis on their perceptions of success for the first year of the alliance. Other data on reputation, prior relationships, shared decision making, and company similarities were also collected. Firms from eight different countries participated, including Canada, the United States, the United Kingdom, France, Malaysia, Germany, India, and Japan.

The dependent variable in the analysis was the outcome of the alliance. The independent variables included reputation, prior relationships, shared decision making, and company similarities.

Using means, standard deviations, correlations, and regression analysis, Saxton was able to determine that there was a positive relationship between the independent and dependent variables for three of the hypotheses: reputation, shared decision making, and strategic similarities. It is unclear how much of an effect a prior relationship statistically has on an alliance outcome. However, a combination of partner and relationship characteristics provides a much stronger explanation for continuing alliance success.

RELATIONSHIP OF SUPPLY CHAIN MANAGEMENT CHARACTERISTICS AND INTERORGANIZATIONAL INFORMATION SYSTEM TYPES

Supply chain management (SCM) is very dependent on interorganizational information systems (IOIS) because the latter provide an efficient and effective communication system between customers and suppliers, and also between suppliers and customers.

Researchers Rachna Shah, Susan Meyer Goldstein, and Peter T. Ward empirically investigated the above relationship with a sample of over 1,300 responding firms. They utilized a matrix where the one axis was a measure of the supply chain sophistication and the other axis was a measure of the degree of implementation and use of the IOIS.

The supply chain measures were divided into a firm's SCM relationship with its suppliers, and the SCM relationship a firm had with its customers. It turned out that the two sets of supplier and customer constructs (overall measures) were highly correlated. For it to be useful the SCM relationship measures were categorized into four stages or quartiles measuring the degree of involvement in SCM.

The information system measures were also categorized into four levels. However, each level had a specific definition. The lowest level, level 0, had no measurable IOIS usage. Level 1, the next level, had either supplier IOIS use for procurement and payment for suppliers, or customer order entry and payment for customers. Level 2 had both the supplier and the customer connections described for level 1 above. Finally, level 3 had collaborative business forecasting and new product development activities with both suppliers and customers.

The data for the study was obtained from firms in 20 industries ranging from apparel and textiles to transportation equipment. The usable sample size numbered 1,349 firms with the machinery sector producing the largest number.

The main results are presented in three matrices based on the matrix described above. The three matrices represent three SCM performance measures. They are: (1) mean on-time delivery rate; (2) mean percent incoming materials not inspected; and (3) mean productivity measured as shipment value per employee. The goals for all three performance measures are the higher the better.

The results indicate that the higher the SCM degree of implementation level and the higher the IOIS degree of complexity level, the higher will be the three SCM performance measures.

The SCM performance measures also increased as the SCM degree of implementation level increased with the IOIS degree of complexity level held constant, except for the degree of complexity level 0. As a matter of fact, the SCM performance measure was quite sensitive to the SCM degree of implementation level, but much less sensitive to the IOIS degree of complexity level.

A CASE STUDY OF SUPPLY CHAIN RELATIONS

To achieve improvement in the function of a supply chain it is vitally important that good relations and communications exist between each partner link in the supply chain.

Researchers Beverly A. Wagner, Douglas K. Macbeth, and David Boddy undertook a case study of a partner link in a supply chain over a 3-year period while changes were occurring in the supply chain partner link. The outcome of the study makes a convincing case for the importance of partner link improvements in a supply chain. The case study covers a partner link between a major buyer, IDV Operations Ireland Limited, and a supplier, Killeen Corrugated, a packaging foods supplier to IDV.

The researchers developed and used a partnering change model to perform the study. The model is concerned with: (1) content—the substantive issues being developed; (2) process—the way in which change is implemented; (3) control—monitoring events in both the content and process agendas; (4) learning—in which project lessons are captured and spread; and (5) integrating—incorporating the other agendas.

The initial substantive issue between the two partners was the high price of Killeen's supplies to IDV. The buyer, IDV, considered this to be the main problem issue between the two partners. There were, however, three others. They were board quality of the corrugated boxes Killeen supplied, print quality on the boxes, and logistics. The latter problem was especially important because of the large amount of physical space corrugated boxes take.

To start solving the problems, the two firms agreed to organize cross-functional teams with members of both firms. One of the problems identified at this point is the need to provide specific and focused instructions to the teams on what they are to focus on.

One of the main process benefits achieved between the two firms during the study was the much improved and more extensive relationship between employees of each of the two firms. In both firms attitudes toward employees of the other firm improved and a cooperative culture was developed and became an established fact.

The main nonprocess benefit achieved was the lower cost that the buyer eventually was able to attain from the supplier. Although the supplier was not able to achieve all the price reductions it was asked to achieve, it was able to identify that internal overhead allocations needed updating, and this updating process allowed Killeen to achieve the cost/price goals IDV had demanded.

The researchers concluded their study with the statement that establishing the partnering process between buyer and supplier had been successful, but also had been a difficult journey during the 3 years of the study. The initial objectives, the cost reduction, had been achieved, and this initial objective provided the main motivation for the two partners to establish the partnering process.

The case study demonstrates the systemic and dynamic nature of change. The change was difficult to manage because it operated across functional, organizational, and interorganizational boundaries.

DIMENSIONS OF PURCHASING COMPETENCE AND PERFORMANCE

The dimensions of purchasing competence are developed and tested for reliability and several measures of validity and then evaluated as a prediction of firm performance.

The researchers, Narasimhan, Jayaram, and Carter, respectively of Michigan State University, the University of Oregon, and Arizona State University, collected data from about 300 purchasing managers to test their propositions. The authors proposed that purchasing competence can be defined in terms of: (1) empowerment, (2) employee competence, (3) interaction frequency, (4) interaction effectiveness, and (5) buyer–seller relationship management. They also proposed that the five purchasing competence dimensions can be defined in 15 purchasing practices.

The three firm performance variables used in the study are: (1) market share, (2) degree of achievement of TQM goals, and (3) degree of achievement of customer satisfaction goals.

The construct of purchasing competence was shown to be a reliable indicator of the actual purchasing competence of a firm. This was shown through a variety of statistical testing procedures. Reliability analysis demonstrated a high degree of internal consistency among the scale items.

The results of the study indicated that purchasing competence influenced total quality management goals and achievement of customer satisfaction goals. However, purchasing competence did not affect market share. The results were consistent with earlier findings in the literature.

The study confirms that empowerment of employees, a key aspect of total quality management, and buyer–seller relationship management, a key aspect of customer satisfaction goals, are the key dimensions that management should monitor to ensure the improvement of firm-level strategic performance. Examples of empowerment are such practices as autonomy in jobs, involvement in decision making, and job security.

The study also found that the effective management of buyer–seller relationships includes cost-saving sharing with suppliers, providing technical assistance, and risk sharing in relation to capital investments. Also found in the study was the effectiveness of a strong commitment toward the practice of joint partnering with suppliers, especially in the joint planning for production.

In conclusion, this study on the construct of purchasing competence and its relationship to performance argues for close management scrutiny and concrete and considerable support for the function of purchasing.

SELECTING VENDORS IN A MANUFACTURING ENVIRONMENT

In the past, Western management has been reluctant to accept the Japanese just-in-time (JIT) concepts. Presently there is no doubt that excellence in manufacturing, which is the core of JIT manufacturing, is a major factor to global competitiveness and business survival. JIT achieves this excellence through practical common sense activities directed toward eliminating all types of waste, which includes anything that adds no value to the product or service. In order to implement JIT, businesses must alter many aspects of the way they conduct business. A key component that must be altered is vendor relations, which includes which vendors to select and how to deal with these respective vendors. When a somewhat smaller number of parts are required, single sourcing on a part-by-part basis can be very effective in accomplishing the required small vendor foundation. When the number of parts is large, however, decisions as to which vendors to keep, what to buy, and which to drop is not as simple as finding the best single source for each part. This difficulty originates from the need to centralize numerous parts to the same supplier and to come to a compromise with the tradeoffs among important qualitative data.

Professor Akinc, of Wake Forest University, proposes a decision support approach to selecting vendors. This decision support approach is a tool to help the decision-maker utilize data and models to analyze this problem. Decision support systems are computer-based systems that help the decision-makers analyze ill-structured problems through the utilization of data analysis and models. They usually consist of three components: a model base for analysis of the structured aspects of the problem, a database containing relevant data needed by the model, and a user-friendly interface to simplify the use of the previous two components.

The researcher used the number of suppliers and annual material costs for the structured part of the problem. He used quality and delivery performance of the vendors as the unstructured elements. In order to provide the user with the tradeoff information between the two structured elements, annual material costs and number of suppliers, he used three models. The first model finds the set of vendors that minimize the total invoice cost, regardless of their numbers. This may result in an unacceptably large number of vendors.

The second model finds the smallest set of vendors who can supply all the needed materials within the minimal quality and delivery standards. This may result in unacceptably high invoice costs. The previous two models are used as benchmarks for the third model. The third model is used to investigate the quantitative tradeoff between these two extreme solutions. The solution of the first model is unimportant. The second and third models are solved to give the very good, quality solutions with a reasonable amount of computational effort.

The paper presented a decision support tool that could be utilized to take better advantage of JIT manufacturing by achieving one of its primary objectives: choosing a few reliable and high-quality vendors or suppliers without sacrificing too much of the other important factor, namely, the material costs. It supports the decision-maker by way of easy access to data and several models whose results are presented in the form of tables and graphic information. This system is not to be utilized to make the decision itself, despite the information available, but rather to be used as a tool to aid the decision-maker. There are many subjective, relevant aspects of this problem that are best solved with human intuition.

In view of growing global competition and the demands that it places upon the management of resources, companies are forced to take advantage of any opportunity to improve their resource utilization. JIT is an advantage that many companies can utilize to improve their resource usage. JIT adopts the objective of total material costs, expanding the invoice cost with avoidable wastes such as inspection, large lot sizes, and losses due to poor quality and delivery. Through the use of the system proposed by this paper, along with other tools, an optimal solution can be found to the vendor selection problem associated with JIT.

PRODUCTION SCHEDULE INTEGRATION IN SUPPLY CHAINS

Recent research suggests that many benefits can be derived through intercompany collaboration. The integration of production schedules may be one such form of intercompany collaboration that can reward the final product assembler and its suppliers. Factors such as inventory holding costs, supplier lead times, forecasting and the supplier's flexibility of accommodating schedule changes are factors, which must be considered in determining those situations in which it is advantageous to integrate production scheduling.

Researchers Lee J. Krajewski and Jerry C. Wei of the University of Notre Dame considered a supply chain situation, which consisted of a customer, an assembler, and tier 1 suppliers to the assembler. The assembler, in this scenario, acts as the point of interaction between customer demands for the product and the suppliers of the components required to assemble that product. The model seeks to minimize the total cost of adjusting production rates, maintaining safety stocks, and costs of scheduling changes for all of the supply chain members, while adjusting schedules using a rolling production horizon. The model also makes the assumption that transportation and material costs are fixed.

The researchers first considered the effects of assembly rate adjustment costs, safety stock costs, and schedule change costs as they pertain to both the assembler and the supplier. Assembly rate adjustment costs were found by considering those costs borne by the assembler, as well as those taken on by the suppliers.

Safety stock costs of the assembler were determined by considering the lead times required by the suppliers of the components required by the assembler to make its product, as well as the lead time required by the assembler. The required safety stock for the suppliers was determined by considering the lead time of the supplier and the advanced warning of a scheduled change by the assembler.

In this model, the researchers determined that schedule change costs consist of the costs incurred because the assembler has made schedule changes with little advanced warning. The costs of schedule changes depend on whether those changes occur within the lead time of the supplier. The researchers cite the possible need for overtime, expediting, rework, and rejects as costs that may be incurred by the supplier as a result of short advance warnings.

The research determined that the total cost of the supply chain can be minimized, however, it is likely to be minimized at the expense of the assembler. This result arises because the assembler will have the burden of maintaining a large safety stock, while allowing the suppliers to maintain a small safety stock, if any. The researchers suggest that schedule integration will be most likely to succeed if the assembler and suppliers belong to the same corporation or if the assembler can place a cost on the benefits it allows its suppliers by holding a large safety stock, and use those figures to negotiate a discount in its pricing in the purchasing contracts with the suppliers.

The research has several implications for business. The study finds that situations where holding costs are high and lead times are long are not conducive to schedule integration. This suggests that industries, which produce items that have a high value, may not benefit from schedule integration. The research also suggests that it may be necessary for one component of the supply chain to absorb costs that are greater than they would be if they were able to maintain an independent scheduling routine.

The benefits of integrated scheduling may not be realized by all of the participating firms involved in the production of an item. These considerations become of less concern when the same corporation owns the participating firms. This suggests that the benefit of integrated scheduling is of greatest benefit to those who have interest in several of the participating firms involved in the supply chain.

UPSTREAM VOLATILITY IN THE MACHINE TOOL INDUSTRY

Upstream volatility in the supply chain, also known as the "bullwhip" effect, is a persuasive problem in most industries, but is especially nefarious in the machine tool industry or similar industries. Orders for the machine tool industry are generated typically by finished retail goods manufacturers. As increases occur in the demand of finished retail goods manufacturers, they will place machine tool orders. Similarly, as decreases in demand occur for the retail finished goods manufacturers, they will either cancel or not place orders to the machine tool industry. These phenomena tend to create wide variations in demand for the machine tool industry.

Researchers Anderson, Fine, and Parker of the University of Texas, MIT, and Tulane University, respectively, developed a simulation model to study the extreme variations of demand for machine tool suppliers and how they could possibly deal with it to smooth production.

The researchers' results show that machine tool builders can do little to reduce order volatility; they can relieve the effects of the order volatility through choice of a proper forecast rule and a longer view of the market, which will lead them to retain more of their skilled work force.

The simulation results show that use of a longer past horizon over which to forecast orders tends to impose less of their own volatility upon their supply base. The above rule assumes that cyclicality in orders is the case of demand volatility.

Retention of skilled workers is not as easy to implement as the change in forecast rule. However, the authors point out that if machine tool builders provide more applications engineering and systems integration services to their customers, the machine tool builders would be able to build and stock more standardized machines, which the customers can then customize to their own requirements. This latter task would, of course, be aided by the machine tool builders support engineering staff.

To attain the above, the researchers also suggest that machine tool builders should take the lead in creating new relationships with their customers. This approach benefits both parties. It provides the machine tool user with the ability to gain more from their machines. It also provides the machine tool builder with more visibility of what the future demand for machine tools will be from that customer.

An important future task, the researchers point out, is the development of a taxonomy of how such collaborative relationships as described above can fruitfully develop.

REFERENCES

Akinc, U. (1993). Selecting a set of vendors in a manufacturing environment. *Journal of Operations Management, 11*(1), 107–122.

Anderson Jr., E. G., Fine, C. H., & Parker, G. G. (2000). Upstream volatility in the supply chain: The machine tool industry as a case study. *Production and Operations Management, 9*(3), 239–261.

Krajewski, L., & Wei, J. C. (2001). The value of production schedule integration in supply chains. *Decision Sciences, 32*(4), 601–634.

Narasimhan, R., Jayaram, J., & Carter, J. R. (2001). An empirical examination of the underlying dimensions of purchasing competence. *Production and Inventory Management, 10*(1), 1–15.

Premkumar, G. P. (2000, Summer). Inter-organization systems and supply chain Management: An information processing perspective. *Information Systems Management,* pp. 56–68.

Saxton, T. (1997). The effects of partner and relationship characteristics on alliance outcomes. *Academy of Management Journal, 40*(2), 443–461.

Shah, R., Goldstein, S. M., & Ward, P. T. (2002). Aligning supply chain management characteristics and inter-organizational information system types: An exploratory study. *IEEE Transactions on Engineering Management, 49*(3), 282–292.

Wagner, B. A., Macbeth, D. K., & Boddy, D. (2002). Improving supply chain relations: An empirical case study. *Supply Chain Management: An International Journal, 7*(4), 253–264.

CHAPTER 4

SUPPLY CHAIN MANAGEMENT

International Cases

This chapter describes a number of papers on how supply chain management issues are addressed in other countries or across countries. Countries and regions involved include Australia, Canada, Mexico, the United Kingdom, Spain, South East Asia, and others.

The first chapter compares the competitive position of Canadian, Mexican, and U.S. suppliers. Surveys were sent to 3,600 purchasing professionals to elicit information. The performance of the firms' supply chains were measured in terms of cooperative behavior, quality, costs, and delivery, among others. The results showed some national bias. Both U.S. and Canadian respondents rated their own country firms relatively higher than the foreign suppliers. The result also showed a lower level of acceptance for Mexican suppliers.

The second study focuses on supply chain management practices in the United Kingdom. A survey questionnaire was utilized and 288 useable responses were obtained. The results showed that the priorities of buyers were quality, pricing, reliability, protection from liability, and support capability. The priorities of suppliers were pricing, quality, support capability, and reliability. The areas of innovation and technology were given low scores on the survey.

Proven Solutions for Improving Supply Chain Performance, pages 43–56

The third study addressed practices in Spain's automobile industry with a focus on just-in-time purchasing practices. There was a focus on operational and on complementary practices. Complementary practices consisted of supplier involvement in product design and development, supplier development, training courses, and engineering visits. A survey was sent to purchasing and logistics managers of 40 automotive suppliers. A total of 150 usable returns were obtained.

The fourth study focused on environmental progress made by South East Asia's global suppliers. A survey was sent to ISO 14001–certified companies in the Philippines, Indonesia, Malaysia, Thailand, and Singapore. A total of 42 usable surveys were obtained. The results revealed that environmental initiatives by the surveyed firms had ultimate positive effects on competitiveness and economic performance.

The fifth paper reported on a study of how firms learn to operate international joint ventures in developing countries. The empirical focus of the study was on 25 large Dutch companies that operated 244 international joint ventures. The results showed that firms with successful joint ventures had benefited most from experience with wholly owned subsidiaries in developed countries. They, however, did not benefit from experience with previous joint ventures in developing countries.

The sixth paper addressed ethical issues in international buyer–supplier relationships. The focus of the study was on the relationships of U.S. purchasing managers and their non-U.S. suppliers. A survey was sent to members of the National Association of Purchasing Management. The results of the survey suggest that perceptions of supplier behavior by a buyer do not impact the relationship between buyer and supplier. However, a large credibility gap between a buyer and supplier will negatively impact a buyer's perception, which in turn impacts the buyer's satisfaction with the relationship.

The seventh study focuses on the acquisition of a foreign firm by a local firm. A survey was sent out and usable responses were received from 52 companies. The results showed that the larger the cultural difference, the better the companies performed in terms of sales. Also, acquiring smaller firms produced relatively more rapid sales growth than the acquisition of larger firms.

The eighth and final paper studied whether information technology management practices can be applied successfully across borders. The national focus of the study was Nigeria. The research found that organizational support is a key component to enhance computer usage in other countries and especially in developing countries.

This chapter has reviewed a number of international supply chain issues that are important because of the prevalence of international sourcing.

The results indicate that practices in developed countries can relatively easily be transferred to developing countries.

COMPARISONS OF THE COMPETITIVE POSITIONS OF CANADIAN, MEXICAN, AND U.S. SUPPLIERS

Companies always want to provide products, which have the highest quality and lowest prices in order to capture the customers. Under the North American Free Trade Agreement, Mexican, U.S., and Canadian companies have more competitive advantages in North America than any other country wanting to do business in North America. Although these three countries are competitive in North America, suppliers in these countries still have to compete with each other. How do purchasing professionals look at the products from these three countries? Is the quality of the products considered the same for each of the three countries?

Researcher Thomas J. Callahan is a professor at the University of Michigan in Dearborn. A grant from the Canadian Embassy in Washington, D.C., provided partial support for this research. The researcher surveyed 203 Canadian purchasing professionals and 311 U.S. purchasing professionals. He sent surveys to 1,800 companies in Canada, and 1,800 companies in the United States. The response rate was about 18 percent. The purpose of this research is to assess customers' perceptions of the competitiveness of specific suppliers from these three nations and to identify areas in which the performance of Canadian, Mexican, and U.S. suppliers might be improved. Prior research on the competitive performance of suppliers in bilateral relationships is reviewed below.

The performance of Canadian, Mexican, and U.S. suppliers is examined in the following dimensions: cooperative behaviors, quality, costs, delivery, manufacturing, and products and country-of-origin effects. For example, in cooperative behaviors, achieving good relationships with foreign suppliers is more difficult than with domestic suppliers. Not only does the greater physical distance separating buyer and seller affect the relationship, but also language and cultural differences may preclude the close, frequent, and informal contacts associated with successful relationships. In each dimension, the researcher talked about the performance of these three countries, which one is the best or the worst. For instance, the United States has the best performance in terms of quality, but it also has the worst performance in terms of costs because of its high labor costs.

Studies of Canada and the United States have reported that purchasing professionals and their organizations try to act in a rational manner, but sometimes they still are not rational buyers. Both prior experiences with and stereotypes about products from a particular country interfere with the rational process of selection based on price, quality, manufacturing capability, and other criteria. In these instances, stereotypes about a country's product on any of these competitive dimensions might result in decisions not to search for supply sources in that country or to remove its potential suppliers from consideration.

This study has produced some important results based on data from purchasing professionals about their suppliers in Canada, Mexico, and the United States. U.S. respondents rated Canadian suppliers high in the competitive areas of cost and quality. However, on the cooperation dimension, U.S. purchasing professionals disagree with Canadians about the level of cooperation that Canadian suppliers provide. Likewise, Canadian purchasing professionals disagree with their U.S. counterparts about the level of cooperation they receive from U.S. suppliers. Generally, purchasing professionals still prefer U.S. suppliers over Canadian suppliers. The Mexican suppliers are usually the last choice for these purchasing professionals. The sample did not include a Mexican subsample of purchasing professionals. The overall results might have been less negative if such a sample had been included.

This study has value implications. Both American purchasing professionals and Canadian purchasing professionals think that the foreign suppliers in cooperative behavior dimensions are lower than their native suppliers. Geographically and culturally, the United States and Canada are very similar and therefore should have a close relationship. What causes American and Canadian purchasing professionals to have problems with their suppliers? It appears that suppliers from the United States and Canada should consider this problem. In Mexico, suppliers still have a long way to go in order to achieve the American and Canadian acceptance level in all dimensions.

SUPPLY CHAIN MANAGEMENT PRACTICES IN THE UNITED KINGDOM

What are the most important and least important management practices in supply chain management in the United Kingdom? Researcher Michael Quayle of the University of Glamorgan in the United Kingdom designed and developed a survey questionnaire to discover answers to this question.

The researcher focused his study on small and medium-size enterprises in the United Kingdom. He sent out 480 questionnaires and received usable responses from 288 firms. Ninety percent of the respondents were from five industry sectors, consisting of: (1) manufacturing; (2) high technology; (3) electrical and engineering; (4) packaging and distribution; and (5) finance-related firms. A total of 18 areas in supply chain management were identified and the respondents were asked to rank each area from 1 (low) to 5 (high) in terms of their respective firms.

The overall results were tabulated and sorted by customer firms and supplier firms. For each group the top five high priorities and the five low priorities were identified. For the customer firms the top five high priorities were: (1) quality, (2) pricing, (3) product reliability, (4) protection from service liability, and (5) capability to support. The five bottom low priorities were: (1) time-to-market, (2) e-commerce, (3) research and development, (4) procurement expertise, and (5) value analysis.

For the supplier firms the top five high priorities were: (1) pricing, (2) quality, (3) capability to support, (4) product reliability, and (5) service reliability. The five bottom low priorities were: (1) time-to-market, (2) research and development, (3) procurement expertise, (4) e-commerce, and (5) value engineering.

From the above it is clear that there virtually is no difference in the opinion on the importance of supply chain management practices except for a slight difference in the order of importance. What is surprising is that the areas of innovation and technology are given such low scores. Both customers and suppliers list as bottom five issues such management practices as research and development, e-commerce, value analysis, and value engineering.

Based on the overall results, the respondents are all focused on product issues such as pricing, quality, reliability, and support capability. This is not surprising since the focus is on what is closest at hand. The long-term issues such as e-procurement, research and development, and value engineering are strategic issues but are not considered to be the focus on what the respondents consider to be the current important issues in supply chain management.

OPERATIONAL AND COMPLEMENTARY JIT PRACTICES IN SPAIN'S AUTOMOBILE INDUSTRY

Just-in-time purchasing practices cover a gamut of activities in the relationship between manufacturers and suppliers. Much has been written about the just-in-time process and about its success or nonsuccess. Also, the process has been criticized as a cost-shifting arrangement from manufacturers to suppliers, thus showing that cost savings by manufacturers are really cost transfers to suppliers.

Researchers Javier Gonzalez-Benito of the University of Salamanca in Spain and Martin Spring of the Manchester School of Management in the United Kingdom decided to analyze just-in-time purchasing practices in the Spanish auto components industry. The researchers decided to focus on implementation patterns of just-in-time purchasing. They distinguished between operational practices in just-in-time environments and complementary practices characteristic of partnership sourcing arrangements.

Some examples of operational just-in-time practices are: (1) frequent delivery, (2) reduced inventory, (3) kanban use with suppliers, (4) tight time windows for delivery, (5) use of electronic data interchange, (6) geographical concentration of plants or warehouses, and (7) use of standardized containers. Some examples of complementary practices are: (1) supplier involvement in product design and development, (2) supplier development programs, (3) training courses, and (4) engineering visits.

A survey questionnaire was designed and developed and mailed to purchasing and logistics managers of about 40 automotive suppliers. A total of 150 usable returns were obtained and on these the statistical analysis was performed.

The questionnaire identified nine operational practices and 16 complementary practices. The top three operational practices as reported by the respondents were: (1) exact delivery time, (2) use of standardized containers, and (3) frequency of delivery. The top six complementary practices were: (1) supplier selection, (2) performance control, (3) certification, (4) lasting relationships, (5) relational programs, and (6) mutual assistance.

Cluster analysis was performed on the entire sample. It was based on the implementation of just-in-time purchasing as measured by operational practices and complementary practices. The analysis produced three groups of suppliers. They were: (1) pioneering companies (32) that reached high implementation levels in all the practices; (2) intermediate companies (66); and (3) laggard companies (52) with low levels of implementation in all the practices. In general, large, first-tier suppliers with international presence tend to reach higher implementation levels.

ENVIRONMENTAL PROGRESS IN SOUTH EAST ASIA'S GLOBAL SUPPLIERS

What is the status of greening the supply chain in South East Asia, where South East Asia is represented by the countries of the Philippines, Indonesia, Malaysia, Thailand, and Singapore? Researcher Purba Rao of the Asian Institute of Management in the Philippines designed and developed a survey questionnaire to find an answer to this question. He identified five constructs, which he incorporated into the model and then tested the model using statistical methods.

The five constructs consist of: (1) environmental initiative, (2) greening of suppliers, (3) environmental performance, (4) competitiveness, and (5) economic performance. The construct environmental initiative consists of the items: (1) environmentally friendly raw materials, (2) substitution of environmentally questionable materials, (3) taking environment criteria into consideration, (4) optimization of process to reduce solid waste, (5) optimization of process to reduce air emissions, (6) optimization of process to reduce noise, and (7) use of cleaner technology process to reduce costs. The greening of suppliers construct consists of: (1) holding awareness seminars for suppliers and contractors; (2) guiding suppliers to establish their own environmental programs; (3) informing suppliers about the benefits of cleaner production and technologies; (4) urging suppliers to take environmental action; and (5) choice of suppliers by environmental criteria. The environmental construct consists of: (1) reduction of solid/liquid waste, (2) reduction of emissions, and (3) improvement of compliance. The competitiveness construct consists of: (1) product quality improvement, (2) increased efficiency, (3) productivity, and (4) cost saving. And finally the economic performance construct consists of: (1) new market opportunities, (2) product price increase, (3) profit margin, (4) market share, and (5) sales revenues.

The survey questionnaire was sent to ISO 14001–certified companies in the five South East Asian countries. A total of 42 usable questionnaires were received consisting of 14 Filipino, 6 Indonesian, 17 Malaysian, 5 Thai, and 10 Singapore companies.

The statistical analysis of the data revealed that the five constructs had statistically significant relationships to each other. Also, environmental initiatives had ultimate positive effects on competitiveness and economic performance. Specifically, the construct environment initiative had statistically significant impacts on both environmental performance and greening of suppliers. Greening of suppliers had a statistically significant impact on environmental performance. Environmental performance, in turn, had a statistically significant impact on competitiveness. And finally, competitiveness had a statistically significant impact on economic performance.

The above results indicate that in South East Asia the greening of suppliers had taken root and was proven beneficial to society but also to the initiators. To be sure, the firms in the sample are the leading global supplier firms in the region. But their successful results bode well for the future greening of second- and third-tier suppliers.

HOW FIRMS LEARN TO OPERATE INTERNATIONAL JOINT VENTURES

International joint ventures have become a prevalent mode of entry into global markets. To successfully cross national boundaries, a firm must develop information-processing and control capabilities so as to coordinate activities across diverse environments, and it must develop the skills of tuning into and interpreting strategic signals specific to foreign countries. Publications on the topic mostly focus on the motivations behind international joint venture formation and the conditions encouraging it. Little has been done, however, to identify the factors that underlie success and failure in such ventures; this is a remarkable omission, given their high failure rate.

Researchers Oded Shekar of the University of Hawaii, and Harry Barkema, Freek Vermeulen, and John Bell of Tilburg University examined the two sets of skills within an evolutionary perspective to explain how firms learn to handle international joint ventures. Hypotheses were derived from organizational learning theory to indicate learning stemming from experience with international wholly owned subsidiaries, with domestic joint ventures, and with previous international joint ventures. The sample consisted of 25 large Dutch companies but excluded the four largest, which are a distinctive group in terms of their breadth of activities, international experience, scope, and size. The total of national and international expansions during the period were 596 and 897, respectively. Of the international expansions, 244 were joint ventures.

An event-history analysis method was used. The analysis entailed the exploration of whether the hazard rate of ventures varies with the amount and type of a firm's experience. The researchers performed sensitivity analysis by using models with interactions between learning effects and dummy variables for firm. This procedure captured firm-specific learning gained from previous types of affiliations and applied to new international joint ventures.

The researchers tested Hofstede's dimensions, which suggested culture is a complex phenomenon and difficult to measure. Also, an uncertainty avoidance gap is detrimental to international joint venture operation because uncertainty is an inherent characteristic of operating in a foreign environment. In addition, experience with international wholly owned subsidiaries in developed countries may be less useful when applied to joint ventures in developing countries, and vice versa. Hence, experience with international wholly owned subsidiaries was separated into experience in developed countries and in developing countries by using a dummy variable.

Two hypotheses predicted that international joint venture longevity increases with the experience of the firm that is investing abroad with international wholly owned subsidiaries and with domestic joint ventures. The result shows that both effects are in the expected direction. The effects of both international wholly owned subsidiary experience and joint venture experience are significant. Another hypothesis predicts that international joint venture longevity decreases with the cultural distance between foreign investors and host country. The results show that the effect of cultural distance is significant and in the expected direction.

The result also shows that international joint ventures in developed countries benefit significantly from the experience of the firm investing abroad with international wholly owned subsidiaries in developed countries, but not from such firms' previous ventures in developing countries. The study also indicates that the effect of cultural distance is significant for international joint ventures in developing countries, but not for international joint ventures in developed countries.

Firm-specific effects confirm that the firms did not learn from previous international joint ventures unless the experience was preceded by experience with either domestic joint ventures or with international wholly owned subsidiaries. The results of research based on Hofstede's dimensions show a significant effect for uncertainty avoidance, which proves the fact that uncertainty is an inherent characteristic of operating in a foreign environment and because such a gap implies contrasting expectations regarding the predictability of partner behavior.

A key notion underlying this research is that firms can only absorb experience as it relates to what they already know in a related line of business and if the experience is related to the firm's knowledge base. In contrast, expansion into an unrelated line of business may trigger information overload and make it difficult for a firm's managers to interpret the experience and benefit from it when entering international joint ventures later. This study identifies both experience with domestic joint ventures and experience with internationally wholly owned subsidiaries as stepping stones from which operation of international joint ventures can be successfully launched. The significant role played by domestic joint ventures' experience is especially noteworthy and represents a unique contribution of this research.

ETHICAL ISSUES IN INTERNATIONAL BUYER–SUPPLIER RELATIONSHIPS

The presence of unethical behavior appears to be a perennial topic in the business world. When dealing with suppliers, the issue of unethical behavior can be a big problem. Purchasing managers sit at the firm's boundary and interact frequently with suppliers and other upstream channel members. Their behavior can and does influence how the firm is viewed by suppliers and other outside organizations. The purchasing function of a company controls over 60 percent of a firm's cost in some industries, considerable temptations can exist when such large amounts of money are involved. Also because it interacts with other members of the supply chain and is thus exposed to a firm's external environment, it may under considerable pressure depart from accepted norms of behavior and ethics set by the firm.

Craig R. Carter combines extant literature with findings from focus group interviews and a set of surveys to identify the ethical issues involved in relationships of U.S. purchasing managers and their non-U.S. suppliers. Survey data from matched sets of buyers and suppliers is then used to examine the influence of unethical behavior on the satisfaction with the relationship and on suppliers' performance.

The research consisted of two primary segments: (1) a series of focus group interviews and (2) a set of survey questionnaires sent to U.S. purchasing managers and to their non-U.S. suppliers. Two survey questionnaires were created after careful examination to see if the questions were appropriate and clearly worded. Then they were both sent to the purchasing organizations of 1,300 domestic firms in the spring of 1997. The sample consisted of members of the National Association of Purchasing Management (NAPM), participants in previous purchasing performance benchmarking studies, and participants in the 1997 Executive Purchasing Roundtable. Respondents in the buying firms were asked to focus most of their responses to the survey questions on their relationship with a particular international supplier, and were also asked to forward the second questionnaire to the international supplier.

The results of the focus group interviews unanimously agree that lying and breaking the law to a supplier is explicitly unethical. The focus group discussions also complemented the literature review, which suggests that there are a number of less tangible ways in which deception can occur: using ambiguous contract terms or other forms of communication to gain an advantage over a party, exaggerating the seriousness of a problem to gain concessions, overestimating demand to gain volume discounts, or in any other way misleading the other party.

The result of the surveys suggests that differences between buyer and supplier perceptions of a supplier's behavior do not directly impact a buyer's satisfaction with the relationship. Instead, the results show that such a gap negatively impacts a buyer's perception, which in turn impacts the buyer's satisfaction with the relationship. The findings further suggest that in order to enhance supplier performance and the buyer's satisfaction with the relationship, it may be necessary to develop convergence between buyer and supplier perceptions of the supplier's actions.

The implication of this study has a lot to do with business. It shows that the buyer/supplier relationship has to be examined thoroughly by the purchasing department and checked by top management of the company to make sure that no unethical practices occur which can potentially jeopardize the company as a whole. Also, the study shows that when dealing with international suppliers, the buyer must be aware of their actions, whether ethical or not, in order to achieve satisfaction from that supplier.

CROSS-BORDER MERGER PERFORMANCE

When a company is deciding on whether or not to purchase another company by acquiring them, or involving another company in a joint venture, should they choose a company that is more related culturally to them or should they choose a company that is very different from their culture? The idea of the article is to figure out which option will affect the performance of the newly acquired company in the best possible way.

Researchers Piero Morosini of the Wharton School of the University of Pennsylvania, Scott Shane of the Sloan School of Management at the Massachusetts of Technology, and Harbir Singh of the Wharton School of the University of Pennsylvania sent out questionnaires to over 400 companies, with 73 companies responding. Of these 73 companies, 52 were used for the test, because their replies to the questionnaire could be verified from archived data. The researchers wanted to make sure that the data presented to them was accurate. Their research tested ideas that acquisitions of other companies could improve firm performance by giving the parent company new resources and repertoires that they previously did not have. They thought that performance would be improved because the parent company can learn from the acquired company involving new "ways of doing things" and that specialization can now occur if the new company does something better than the parent.

The study involved analyzing the data the researchers gathered from the questionnaires that they received from the companies. Performance was calculated as a percentage rate in the growth of sales over a 2-year period following the acquisition of the company. Two years was used because after a 2-year period, the two companies are usually working well together and can basically be called one company. This was the dependent variable of the study. The independent variable was the natural cultural distance, or in other words, how closely related the two companies are based on their national cultural norms. The difference in culture was determined by studying the uncertainty avoidance, masculinity/femininity, individual scores, and by using Hofstede's (1980) power distance.

There were also control variables put into the calculation. Some of the control variables were the relatedness of the industries that the acquiring company was involved with and the industry that the acquired company was in. Size was also another determinant. The size was determined based on the target's net sales in the year of the purchase. The target firm's business strategy was analyzed as well. The researchers in the questionnaire asked what the target's strategy was from a list of different types of strategies that the target could be following. The year was a final control variable, because there were some hard-pressed economic issues happening around Italy at the time of the test, so the researchers had to stratify the data in this way. The researchers used ordinary least squares regression analysis to evaluate their model.

The results showed that there was a high correlation between the difference of culture and the performance of the companies after acquisition. The more different the two cultures were, the better the companies performed in their sales. However, there was no relationship with the target firm's strategy and sales growth. Acquiring smaller firms also made the sales growth increase more rapidly than when larger firms were acquired.

This study has a profound impact on the way companies should look into making their acquisitions. If a company wants to acquire another firm, then they should look at targets that are relatively small and have national cultures that are very different from their own. This allows the parent company to learn new ways of doing business and other vital information. It also allows the parent to be able to do business in a culture that they know nothing about, seeing the target is already situated in that new market and knows how business is done in that area. Providing new resources to an already established company can have an enormous impact on sales if the parent chooses the correct company to purchase.

CAN CERTAIN INFORMATION TECHNOLOGY MANAGEMENT PRACTICES BE APPLIED ACROSS BORDERS?

When going internationally, what strategies can be applied across borders (global integration) and what strategies have to be modified regarding the culture in the target country (local responsiveness)? Does company support for technology lead to more technology usage, and if so, what are the patterns?

Researchers Uzoamaka P. Anakwe of Pace University, Magrid Igbaria of Claremont Graduate University/Tel Aviv University, and Murugan Anandarajan of Drexel University surveyed 143 employees from nine Nigerian organizations. Their research tested whether management support practices to increase computer usage are transferable, and whether different computer skill levels influence the relationship between organizational support and computer usage.

The researchers asked employees of six banks, two oil companies, and a computer learning center to respond to a survey that was composed of three main categories: Organizational Support, Computer Training, and

Microcomputer Usage. The first category contained eight statements, assessing organizational support on a five-point scale. In the second category, the employees were asked about their computer skills. These involved the source (university coursework, self-training, etc.), as well as the level (none to extremely extensive) of the knowledge. The last one employed four indicators for the use of computers: actual daily use, frequency of use, total applications used, and total tasks performed. The actual daily use and the frequency of use were measured on a six-point scale. To get a good measurement for the total applications used, the survey showed a list of nine generic packages. The respondent was asked to indicate what kind of packages he or she uses to perform work. The same scheme was used to determine the number of total tasks performed with a computer. In this case, the person had to indicate, on a list of tasks, what tasks are done by using a computer.

Recent research as well as literature indicates a strong relationship between organizational support and information system usage, whereby a lack of support proves counterproductive. This means that an organization that does not adequately support technology has a less effective utilization of information technology. This leads the researchers to the hypothesis that organizational support will be positively related to technology usage. Other research noted computer training as another key factor for effective system utilization. In Nigeria, this is of particular interest, since the information technology is just evolving. Since only a small number of people can afford a home computer, computer training is mainly gained by attending classes or getting organizational training. Hence, there is a huge gap between the number of people that are trained in the information technology field and the number of people who lack any experience. Therefore, the study also analyzes the relationship between computer skills and organizational support. It leads to the second hypothesis, which focuses on this and states that the skill level will influence the relationship between organizational support and technology usage.

The research confirmed that organizational support is a key component to enhance computer usage in organizations. These findings are consistent with previous studies in the United States and in Taiwan. However, the support did not influence the number of tasks that were performed by using a computer. This pattern is in contrast to prior research that showed a relationship between the two patterns. An explanation for this result might be found either in the sample characteristics or the sample population. Since the sample population was mainly associated with the banking and oil industry, as well as a computer learning center, it is possible that the tasks performed under the use of a computer are static in the particular fields within the companies. This means that employees use the computer to do certain tasks on a day-by-day basis.

The second finding shows a relationship between the organizational support and the computer skill level of the respondents. While lowly skilled respondents enhanced their computer usage due to organizational support, it had no influence on highly skilled respondents. This finding is in contrast to other studies, which found that computer training promotes the usage of information technology. One explanation might be that employees with a high level of computer skills do not attribute their usage of the technology to others. On the other hand, due to the fact that computer systems are just emerging in the business world in Nigeria, the organizational support might be more focused on employees with a low skill level, rather than on ones with a high skill level.

This research has important implications, particularly for companies that are engaged or plan to engage in international operations with developing countries. It suggests that standardized practices can be applied across cultures to a certain extent. However, it stresses also that country-specific factors must be taken into account when this approach is used. In conclusion, the findings go along with the global integration–local responsiveness framework, where global integration stands for standardization and local responsiveness for customization or adoption. So a mix of both is the right strategy.

REFERENCES

Anakwe, U. P., Igbaria, M., & Anandarajan, M. (2000). Management practices across cultures: Role of support in technology usage. *Journal of International Business Studies, 31*(4), 653–666.

Barkema, H. G., Shenkar, O., Vermeulen, F., & Bell, J. H. J. (1997). Working abroad, working with others: How firms learn to operate international joint ventures. *Academy of Management Journal, 40*(2), 426–442.

Callahan, T. J. (2000). Comparisons of competitive position of Canadian, Mexican, and U.S. suppliers. *Journal of Supply Chain Management, 36*(4), 43–54.

Carter, C. R. (2000). Ethical issues in buyer-supplier relationships: A dyadic examination. *Journal of Operations Management, 18*(2), 191–208.

Gonzalez-Benito, J., & Spring, M. (2000). JIT Purchasing in the Spanish auto components industry. *International Journal of Operations and Production Management, 20*(9), 1038–1061.

Morosini, P., Shane, S., & Singh, H. (1998). National cultural distance and cross-border acquisition performance. *Journal of International Business Studies, 29*(1), 137–158.

Quayle, M. (2003). A study of supply chain management practice in UK industrial SMEs. *Supply Chain Management—An International Journal, 8*(1), 79–86.

Rao, P. (2002). Greening the supply chain: A new initiative in South East Asia. *International Journal of Operations and Production Management, 22*(6), 632–665.

CHAPTER 5

JUST-IN-TIME MANAGEMENT

This chapter covers eight studies on just-in-time (JIT) issues in the management of the supply chain. JIT management principles have been applied to a number of areas such as supply chain management, inventory management, customer service, operations scheduling, and others.

The first study describes how just-in-time methods were first introduced around the middle of the 19th century. JIT methods were then already evident in repetitive manufacturing, quality philosophy, equipment layout, mechanization, machine specialization, and multiskill application. Even then the application of JIT-enabled manufacturers to produce greater output from a limited and somewhat unskilled workforce. In recent years JIT applications have been significantly refined from the first JIT efforts a century and a half ago.

The second study addresses critical issues in JIT manufacturing. The study approach involved a case study of six Canadian manufacturing plants. The six JIT activities covered include (1) promotion of employee responsibility, (2) training, (3) teamwork, (4) demonstration of commitment, (5) workforce security, and (6) group performance measures. Four of the six activities proved to be essential for JIT implementation. They were employee responsibility, training, teamwork, and demonstration of visible commitment.

Proven Solutions for Improving Supply Chain Performance, pages 57–68

The third paper looked at the relationship of JIT impact and economic theory. Again the study's location was Canada. Forty firms participated in the study and they were about equally divided into JIT and non-JIT firms. The conclusion was that JIT firms performed significantly better than non-JIT firms.

The fourth study focused on the impact of work system practices on competitive capabilities of manufacturers in the following industries: furniture and fixtures, fabricated metals, industrial machinery and equipment, electronics, and instruments. The results show that standardized and integrated work system practices have a significant impact on competitive capabilities.

The fifth study is a case study of JIT practices in the automotive industry. The focus was on Rover Manufacturing, a division of BMW, in the United Kingdom. The study's focus was on the supply system of the firm. The supply system was redesigned by the formation of multifunctional teams and improved computer technology. The new system provided considerable improvements in the firm's supply system.

The sixth study focused on the use of JIT in machine shops. The study utilized a survey questionnaire that produced 130 usable responses. The results of the study showed some significant differences between JIT and non-JIT machine shops. The benefits of JIT included better operating results, better customer service, reduction of shop congestion, and others.

The seventh study looked at the impact of organizational design of JIT task scope and work flow integration. The researchers sent out a questionnaire and received responses from knowledgeable individuals. The results of their study showed that JIT task scope affects JIT work flow integration and organizational design, but JIT work flow integration has no impact on organizational design.

The eighth study is a simulation study that focused on the effect of the number of products in a manufacturing operation and its JIT performance. The results showed that as the number of products increases and the resultant time required to change over manufacturing processes, the system becomes more congested and the effectiveness of JIT decreases.

The eight studies above show how just-in-time issues affect the smooth functioning of the supply chain, albeit implicitly. Supply chains consist of many links. The functioning of each link can be improved through the effective application of just-in-time principles.

AMERICAN SYSTEM OF MANUFACTURERS CIRCA 1850 AND JUST-IN-TIME METHODS

The introduction of JIT methods in American business often raises issues of cultural change. Many may not realize that JIT shares many characteristics with the methods used by the United States during the 1800s. This study compares the 19th-century American System of Manufacturers (ASM) with JIT systems showing that the development of the ASM was affected by factors similar to those that influenced JIT. There are a number of parallels as well as some differences.

Professor Meredith has used references from different researchers such as Porter, Ames, and Rosenberg, using a comparative analysis of the American System of Manufacturers in 1850 with JIT systems to show significant similarities in their development and characteristics. Similar characteristics such as repetitive manufacturing, quality philosophy, equipment layout, mechanization, machine specialization, and multiskilling describes both ASM and JIT.

The ASM was the foundation for American industrial management systems. It was an application that was essential for understanding current manufacturing systems. Management techniques and methodologies evolve and improve, and broader issues of strategy and purpose prevail. Since there was no analysis of ASM in the past, this shows that management lacked the details that were critical and showed that knowledge of past practice in industrial management was not widespread.

ASM in 19th-century America, and JIT in postwar Japan, both allowed better utilization of scarce resources. ASM allowed greater output from a limited and unskilled workforce with inferior plants and equipment. In Japan, JIT allowed better utilization of costly imported materials. This reaffirms the economic rationale to substitute machines for scarce labor, a practice ASM also aimed to do.

This study indicates that knowledge of work organizations, material scheduling, logistics, production techniques, facility layout, and location have advanced since the 1800s. We now know how to use methods to increase productivity but focusing on what needs to be done has remained consistent. Other researchers have suggested that we could learn from ASM; the most important lessons being that the prerequisites for success in manufacturing are enduring and fundamental. By increasing the sophistication of this system, thoroughness in analysis and implementation are necessary for progress. But these cannot change the consistency of purpose and practice in current successful systems and in those from the mid-1800s.

CRITICAL ISSUES IN JUST-IN-TIME MANUFACTURING

Since its inception, firms that have implemented just-in-time manufacturing claim it has provided countless benefits to their operation. However, while the majority of firms (specifically Western firms) using the just-in-time approach to manufacturing have met with success, other firms that could potentially benefit from the system have adopted only part of the JIT philosophy. McLachlin's research considers whether each of a number of varying management initiatives is necessary for the successful implementation of just-in-time manufacturing.

Researchers Ron McLachlin, of the University of Manitoba, conducted a case study involving six plants located in central Canada, which claimed to be employing just-in-time manufacturing. The plants involved were comprised mainly of assembly-to-order fabricated metal manufacturers, employing between 350–900 people, with annual sales of $20–30 million Canadian. The chosen sites were a cross-section of plants operating in different industries, ranging from those that had attempted JIT for a number of years to those just beginning efforts at JIT implementation.

McLachlin obtained data via interviews, questionnaires, direct observation, and a collection of documents. His research focused on testing six management initiatives to determine which if any would be necessary for JIT flow and JIT quality. The initiatives tested include: (1) promotion of employee responsibility, (2) provision of training, (3) promotion of teamwork, (4) demonstration of visible commitment, (5) provision of workforce security, and (6) use of group performance measures.

Each of the six plants was visited for a period of at least 4 days. At each site, an average of 16 interviews were conducted. A typical assortment of informants might include the plant supervisor, immediate subordinates, line workers, engineers, or the human resources manager. In addition to informant interviews, plant tours, company documents, and post-interview questionnaires served as valuable data for the researcher. To maintain a degree of uniformity in the qualitative data gathered, McLachlin developed representative responses for each construct. Quantitative data was compiled using multi-item scales.

The research yielded the following findings. Four of the six initiatives were shown to be essential conditions for the successful implementation of just-in-time manufacturing. These initiatives include: (1) promotion of employee responsibility, (2) provision of training, (3) promotion of teamwork, and (4) visible demonstration of management commitment. Therefore, the researcher believes managers should include the above-stated initiatives in the framework for JIT implementation. The study did not present any substantial evidence to support the management initiatives of either provision of workforce security or use of group performance measures. A possible rationale for the rejection of the initiative dealing with job security lies with the notion that it is provided directly by management, rather than from a firm's ability to be competitive.

The study of management initiatives' role in just-in-time implementation demonstrated important implications for firms in both beginning and mature phases of JIT implementation. After analysis, McLachlin concluded that employee involvement was the key component of successful just-in-time implementation at any stage of implementation. None of the four accepted management activities led to a high level of JIT flow of JIT quality without also leading to a high level of employee involvement. Despite the lack of temporal sequences between the employee involvement, JIT flow, and JIT quality, their association to each other is strong. These findings suggest that managers would be well advised to include shop floor employees in the JIT implementation process. As previously mentioned, neither a provision for workforce security nor use of group performance measures are necessary. However, McLachlin does see the elimination of piece rates as a minimum condition for moving toward JIT even if group performance measures are not adopted by management.

THE IMPACT OF JIT BASED ON ECONOMIC THEORY

This study by James A. Brox and Christine Fader puts to the test whether the Japanese management concept of just-in-time will work in North America. The study focuses on the electronic industry throughout Southern Ontario, Canada. This industry was targeted because the concept of JIT has been welcomed openly by some companies, and turned down by others. The study tries to provide economic proof that there is a difference in performance between JIT companies and non-JIT companies.

The methodology used in this study provides proof that JIT has an effect on the total cost function of the manufacturing process. The authors explain the four crucial inputs of manufacturing. They are labor, capital, energy, and materials. They also stress the importance of these inputs and the cost associated with these inputs.

To determine differences between JIT and non-JIT companies, the authors decided to use a number of elasticities to determine the basic relationships between the four inputs and how they relate to the cost function. The elasticities used were own-price elasticity, substitution of elasticity, average cost, and total cost elasticity.

Forty firms agreed to the study. The study, through telephone and oral surveys, asked several questions to determine if companies were JIT or non-JIT. Twenty-one firms were classified as JIT and 18 were non-JIT; one firm was disqualified. The researchers collected other information consisting of firm size, manufacturing costs, and other key accounting costs.

At the end of the study, it was concluded that there was a significant performance difference between JIT firms and non-JIT firms. The evidence was derived from the cost savings of the output observed over a 1-year period.

The study also suggests that labor in the JIT environment is more flexible, therefore adapting to change more proactively. This interpretation suggests that the profitability margins of JIT firms are also higher. The authors give evidence that JIT firms generate 6 percent more output than non-JIT firms based on the same inputs.

Clearly, JIT firms prospered over non-JIT firms. The study has also proven that the JIT concept can be adopted by North American companies. JIT has become a tool for manufacturers to produce quality products, while also achieving greater economic profits.

WORK SYSTEM PRACTICES AND THEIR IMPACT ON COMPETITIVE CAPABILITIES

This large-scale study was conducted by interviewing senior manufacturing executives from the following manufacturing categories: furniture and fixtures, fabricated metals, industrial machinery and equipment, electronic and other equipment, and instruments and related products. The firms from which the executives came all had at least 250 employees. The external consistency of work system practices were evaluated by submitting simultaneously the items for all four factors to exploratory factor analysis. No constraint was put on the number of factors that could emerge. If an item did not fit properly, it was not counted and eliminated.

Results of this study show that organizations with work system practices that are standardized and integrated also have advanced competitive capabilities. Their workforce should be able to be involved in development and applications so employees can be creative and have flexibility in their workplace. In the models developed it shows that firms with high levels of time-based manufacturing have high levels of standardization, formalization, and integration. There does not seem to be a relationship between time-based manufacturing and routinization.

The implications for managers from this study reveal that organizations that employ time-based manufacturing should have work-based systems that are standardized, formalized, and integrated. As a result, one can measure the productiveness of employees and supervisors. Manufacturers should be focusing on setting goals and giving feedback rather than on trying to control employees.

AUTOMATED JUST-IN-TIME MANUFACTURING SYSTEM FOR THE AUTOMOTIVE INDUSTRY

The auto industry was once known for having huge warehouses of inventory on hand. Materials are costly to house and the huge volume is often not needed. Manufacturers in the past have relied on sales forecasts that are presented to the manufacturing operations to smooth the pipeline of supplies. Excess raw materials often needed to be carried. A customer order was usually satisfied from in-warehouse stock.

The Rover Group, now a part of BMW, conducted the study. They studied the operations of the automated just-in-time system using a pull control philosophy. This philosophy is a system of logistics processes based on lot manufactures and combines plans and supplier schedules with the JIT model. They also looked at the design of the system that had been configured for the need for multiple versions of the process and flexibility in mind, with little modification; it could be applied to other JIT applications.

The study involved several aspects: forming multifunctional teams to handle the new processes, ensuring system efficiency, and maintaining an accurate database and information technology (IT) system.

The old system involved a group of material controllers to monitor the production line continuously and using their best judgment and knowledge of the current plan for the period and decide when and what parts to order. The build pipeline was designed to provide a monthly forecast, stretching 3 months ahead.

This old system has been replaced by the auto issue request (AIR) system, which is a system to reengineer the conventional business processes and support any newly launched product. The AIR system automatically triggers any lot-based material to be ordered. Specific parts are ordered when required, and in only the quantity that is necessary. This leads to minimal stock on the trackside (production line) and a reduction in such activities as material storage and movement from buffer storage to trackside operations. A trigger from the order track system calls the materials needed to build one lot of vehicles as per customers' configuration orders. This is done using lasers, which read a barcode on the vehicle.

The material database used in JIT has to be up-to-date and accurate, any errors will result in disaster. Since the database is a crucial part of the system, a qualified IT technician is required to input data and keep suppliers and supply chains current. The AIR and JIT system are designed to quickly respond to any changes in the production line, such as new models or new subassemblies to be constructed. The conventional JIT process for material management relies on a build pipeline that is regularly refurbished to reflect actual customer orders and refined forecasts.

In summary, Rover was very pleased with the JIT system. Rover Group reduced their core supplies base from 2,000 to fewer than 600 today. All of the parts required to build a customer-configured vehicle are now triggered by as few as five automatic triggers. Automating the material call has resulted in reducing material stock, both within Rover and its supply chain. A more effective utilization of resources and storage space is now realized. Utilizing the JIT has enabled emphasis away from the time-consuming activity of requesting pallets one at a time. This leaves more time for reducing order-to-delivery times, targeting future reduction in pipeline stock, and supplier development.

The implications for other businesses are to provide the capability to manage materials requests for the manufacturing of products in variable lot sizes. These variable lot sizes will enable greater customer configuration capabilities by reducing warehouse inventory, thereby reducing costs and saving money.

JUST-IN-TIME–ORIENTED U.S. MACHINE SHOPS

The problem addressed in this research study was the gap in empirical literature dealing with JIT machine shops. The model for JIT operations was also further defined based on previous research studies. The study also provided researchers with more realistic descriptions of machine shop operations. It compared machine shops with low and high levels of sales to JIT customers to assist in identifying areas of change.

The researcher for this study was Joel D. Wisner, of the University of Nevada, Las Vegas. The research for this study was funded by a grant from the First Interstate Bank Institute for Business Leadership in Las Vegas, Nevada. The research was used to define the JIT machine shop model. The study specifically describes the changes taking place in the operating characteristics of today's machine shops.

Wisner developed a survey that was mailed to machine shop managers. The survey was pretested by using a pilot sample of 15 machine shop owners. The survey was based on four topics of manufacturing operations. These consisted of basic facility operating characteristics, machine operator characteristics, shopfloor control policies, and shop performance measures. The questionnaire also included definitions of machine shop terms to minimize confusion on the part of the respondents.

The surveys were sent out to 902 machine shops. There were two mailings of the survey and a reminder mailing was sent in between the two survey mailings. A total of 130 usable responses were received. The response rate was 14.4 percent, which was considered to be reasonable considering the length and nature of the survey. The survey maintained the machine shops' confidentiality by not requiring company information and included postage-paid envelopes. The survey questions required yes/no or five-point Likert-scale responses. The respondents were classified as either JIT-oriented or non-JIT-oriented machine shops, based on their ratio of JIT jobs to total jobs. The two groups were then compared based on a number of operating characteristics.

The results of the survey showed some significant differences between the operating characteristics of machine shops with JIT customers and those with few or without any JIT customers. Some of the JIT machine shops completed orders before their delivery dates and were forced to hold these jobs as finished goods inventory. The JIT machine shops had significantly shorter queue lengths per machine and significantly larger batch sizes in comparison to non-JIT-oriented shops. There were no differences found in job release policies or due date determinations between the two groups. However, there were significant differences found between JIT-oriented and non-JIT-oriented machine shops in regards to job sequencing policies. Both types of machine shops used similar types of operator transfer policies. There were also significant differences in strategies used to reduce operator relearning times. The JIT machine shops relied more on operator retraining and process redesign for easier operation. Overall, the JIT machine shops were able to generate significantly higher levels of sales and net income in comparison to the non-JIT-oriented machine shops.

This study has shown that the operating characteristics of JIT machine shops provide greater levels of customer service and result in greater financial benefits. The JIT-oriented machine shops made efforts to reduce shop congestion, seek out customer partnership arrangements, and increase customer service. This could be the predominant factor that resulted in better sales and profit performance from JIT machine shops. This study also suggests that further research is necessary to better understand the relationships between the production processes, the shopfloor control systems, the customer base, the operators, and shop profitability between JIT-oriented and non-JIT-oriented machine shops.

THE IMPACT ON ORGANIZATIONAL DESIGN OF JIT TASK SCOPE AND WORKFLOW INTEGRATION

Firms adopting the just-in-time approach are attempting to create a competitive advantage on both cost and value. By eliminating waste and non-added-value activities, JIT firms have been able to lower their costs and improve their product quality. Besides those twin effects, what are the other reasons and goals for firms to adopt JIT? Should the firm adopt JIT to look more or less decentralized? Should firms become less specialized through cross-training or more specialized by hiring inventory control specialists?

Researchers Richard Germain, of Oklahoma State University, and Cornelia Droge, of Michigan State University, investigated organizational design flows: (1) from both JIT task scope and JIT workflow integration directly, (2) from only one of them directly, or (3) from JIT workflow integration directly but from JIT task scope indirectly. The second important question addressed is whether JIT task scope and JIT workflow integration have conflicting effects on organizational design.

The researchers selected the Council of Logistics Management manufacturers membership list because its members would be knowledgeable about JIT. From all of the 3,069 members, they only used 199 manufacturers for their sample. They sent the questionnaire to the manufacturers and included 14 items on the questionnaire. Eight of the items represent a firm's JIT task scope and include the use of analytic tools to detect defects and the involvement of suppliers in product design. The remaining six items are indicative of JIT workflow integration and include small lot production and purchasing, supplier proximity, and daily deliveries from suppliers.

The researchers relied on past research as a guide for measuring the organizational design variables. Specialization was measured by asking whether each of 11 indirect labor tasks were dealt with exclusively by at least one full-time individual. Decentralization was measured to capture the vertical level of responsibility.

The results show that JIT task scope affects JIT workflow integration and organizational design as predicted, but JIT workflow integration has no impact on organizational design. Overall, JIT workflow integration is not a mediator of the relationship between JIT task scope and organizational design because there was no impact of JIT workflow integration on any of the organizational design variables. Thus the effect of JIT task scope on organizational design is direct only; there is no indirect effect of JIT task scope on organizational design through JIT workflow integration.

The direct effects of JIT task scope in their model are pervasive. First, as JIT task scope increases, so does JIT workflow integration. Second, as JIT task scope increases, so do specialization, decentralization, formal control, and integration. Increased JIT task scope is associated with specialization because the firm manages new knowledge infusion by compartmentalizing it. New JIT knowledge increases the complexity of decision issues, resulting in decentralization to reduce senior manager decision-making burdens. Formal performance control increases with JIT task scope because performance information forms the basis for managing throughput. Finally, integration increases with JIT task scope to ensure coordination and synergy among decentralized specialized units.

This research has several managerial implications; it offers managers a new conceptualization of the central essence of JIT. Managers must understand that fit cannot be effectively and efficiently implemented by management fit concerning lot size or flow and JIT as knowledge versus JIT as process concept provides a cogent explanation for the sustainable competitive advantage accruing to those firms that have been translated into a lower cost structure along with superior product quality. Managers should understand that JIT knowledge is the ultimate source of effective JIT implementation in becoming more continuous, and the organizational design, in becoming more organic, will undergo significant change.

JIT PERFORMANCE AND PRODUCT ADDITIONS

Today's economy requires businesses to perform a variety of services and features while maintaining a high level of quality in order to remain competitive. Companies need to be able to customize products, provide broad distribution, make volume and mix changes, and introduce products rapidly. The current environment in which businesses compete is constantly changing. Therefore, companies need to be flexible in order to meet the changing customer demands. While the JIT inventory approach is widely used in order to increase flexibility, it is often the case that producing more than one product may require a longer processing time or more setup time as production shifts between models.

Professor Lummus used a simulation of a JIT process to investigate the effects of sequencing production given various product mix combinations and various setup or processing time additions. The simulation approach was designed to represent an approximation of JIT manufacturing under varying conditions.

This simulated system consisted of three-station assembly lines, which drew subassemblies from three supporting lines and raw materials and parts from stores. The system was a two-card kanban system. At each work center, workers processed work-in-process inventory on a first-come-first-serve basis. A kanban inventory control system was used, therefore producing a pull-based system. The simulation evaluated process performance by measuring the total time required to meet the daily production schedule.

The study evaluated various product mix combinations including the addition of one or two products. In addition, eight different setup/processing time variations were tested for all sequence and mix combinations.

The simulation generated 72 test cases in total. Thirty days was designated as the starting point for the collected data because that was the point at which inventory reached a stable level. In order to allow enough time for each simulation run, a length of 30 days was chosen.

The results produced through this study indicated that large increases in setup/processing time at one work center could disrupt a sequencing pattern when a two-card kanban system is used to control production. As the size of processing time of the standard product increased to above 5 percent of processing time performance decreased. The simulation result supported the theory of constraints, which indicates that the output of a process is constrained by the work center with the longest processing time.

This study reinforced the fact that scheduling, product increases, and production times all impact the effectiveness of JIT systems. Added setup time should be a prime consideration when designing and incorporating a new product into the JIT process, otherwise it is possible for the JIT system to fail. However, the study did indicate that a firm schedule does not always improve performance. This simulation showed that it would improve performance more by allowing demand to trigger production.

REFERENCES

Brox, J. A., & Fader, C. (1997). Assessing the impact of JIT using economic theory. *Journal of Operations Management, 15*(3), 371–383.

Germain, R., & Droge, C. (1997). An empirical study of the impact of just-in-time task scope versus just-in-time workflow integration on organizational design. *Decision Sciences, 28*(3), 615–635.

Jina, J. (1996). Automated JIT based materials management for lot manufacture. *International Journal of Operations and Production Management, 16*(3), 62–76.

Lummus, R. R. (1995). A simulation analysis of sequencing alternatives for JIT lines using kanbans. *Journal of Operations Management, 13*(2), 183–190.

McLachlin, R. (1997). Management initiatives and just-in-time manufacturing. *Journal of Operations Management, 15*(2), 271–292.

Meredith, J. R. (1998). A comparison of the American system of manufactures' circa 1850 with just-in-time methods. *Journal of Operations Management, 16*(1), 77–90.

Rondeau, P. J., Vonderembse, M. A., & Ragu-Nathan, T.S. (2000). Exploring work system practices for time-based manufacturers: Their impact on competitive capabilities. *Journal of Operations Management, 18*(5), 509–529.

Wisner, J. D. (1996). The study of U.S. machine shops with just-in-time customers. *International Journal of Operations and Production Management, 16*(7), 62–76.

CHAPTER 6

DEMAND FORECASTING

This chapter consists of eight papers on forecasting with a focus on demand forecasting. The forecasting literature is heavily dominated by time series forecasting because the time series data invites statistical analysis, an area favored by many researchers.

The first paper looks at the effects of feedback on judgmental forecast accuracy. The study used an experimental method using 54 university students as subjects. In the experiment feedback was provided to the subjects and the impact of that feedback was evaluated. The results showed that feedback to the forecasters on how well they were doing substantially improved the accuracy of forecasts.

The second paper addressed the impact of forecast errors on the firm. If the error cost is known firms can decide how much they should pay for forecast models. The results convincingly show that improved forecasts can substantially lower operating costs for firms.

The third paper is similar to the previous paper in the sense that it measures the cost of making poor forecasts. The researcher convincingly shows that firms can improve profits by improving their demand forecasts. The three areas where savings can be realized are: (1) by lowering stock shortages and resultant lost sales; (2) by buying components on a long-term basis through improved forecasts; and (3) by improved localized forecasts covering certain regions of a geographic market area.

The fourth paper shows how the technique of neural networks can improve forecasting accuracy. The researchers used simulation to prove

Proven Solutions for Improving Supply Chain Performance, pages 69–79

their point. They showed that neural networks not only are more accurate but also are easier to apply.

The fifth paper presents a comparison of three forecasting methods for time series data produced by supermarket scanner data. The researchers compared the neural networks forecasting approach with two other statistical approaches. They proved that the neural network approach proved to be a reliable forecasting tool for the type of data produced by supermarket scanners. The conclusions in this paper are similar as the previous paper on the robustness and accuracy of neural networks forecasting approaches.

The sixth paper addresses the problem of supplying retailers with high demand items on time. The researchers looked at the effects of forecast errors, early ordering, and supplier–retailer cooperation on the costs of both supplier and retailer. The researchers found that early order commitment from the retailer will lower total supply chain cost. The overall conclusion of the study is that both parties but especially the retailers will benefit from accurate demand forecasting models, which allow them to place their orders in a timely manner.

The seventh paper asks the question whether different forecasting models should be used for high-technology versus low-technology products. The results indicate that the two types of products need significantly different forecasting approaches. High-technology products need internal forecasting techniques including judgmental methods with inputs by internal staff. The opposite is true for low-technology products where external input is most valuable.

The eighth and last paper evaluates an inventory management policy with a focus on demand forecasting of time series data. The paper is highly technical and statistically oriented. Its premise is that the time series can be evaluated and on the basis of the statistical analysis the proper method can be selected. The researchers showed that by selecting the correct method, cost savings can be achieved.

The eight papers in this chapter show the importance of accurate forecasting in controlling costs and reducing shortages or overordering. Accurate forecasting is an important means of controlling cost in the supply chain.

EFFECTS OF FEEDBACK ON JUDGMENTAL FORECAST ACCURACY

Although it has been established in repeated scientific testing that quantitative forecasting is more accurate than judgmental forecasting in recurrent forecasts such as those found in time series, judgmental forecasting is still the overwhelming choice by forecast practitioners.

Researchers William Remus, Marcus O'Connor, and Kenneth Griggs decided to test whether feedback on the judgmental forecasting process could possibly improve the accuracy of the judgmental forecasts. They designed a research model where individuals would make repeated time series forecasts and as they made each forecast they would either receive feedback on how they were doing in terms of forecast accuracy or alternatively they would be informed on how they could improve their next forecast.

The individuals used to make the forecasts consisted of 54 university students. The students had been exposed to time series forecasting in a course they were taking and as such knew what forecasting was all about. To motivate the students to do well they were awarded with modest cash prizes depending on how well they did in terms of forecast accuracy.

The feedback in terms of forecast accuracy consisted of a report on a common statistical measure of forecast accuracy shown in graphical form as well as in terms of qualitative form (i.e., you are doing poorly or you are doing well, etc.). This feedback was termed *performance feedback*. The feedback in terms of how they could improve their forecasts was given to them in such statements as, "Your forecast is low/high on the basis of the trend that is in evidence." This feedback was termed *task feedback*.

All the testing was done on computers and the feedback was given to the participants by statements shown following each forecast they made.

After the data was collected it was analyzed by analysis of variance. The results showed that task feedback was substantially more beneficial in terms of forecast accuracy than performance feedback. Also, task feedback showed substantially better results in terms of forecast accuracy than the outcome without any feedback whatsoever. Both results shown above were statistically significant.

The implications of the study are that if one decides to use judgmental forecasting then one might want to consider an approach where task feedback is provided following each forecast made. The results of such an approach will improve the accuracy of the forecasts.

IMPACT OF FORECAST ERROR ON THE FIRM

What benefits can be obtained from improving the forecasting accuracy of the firm? This question is important to management because the cost of improving forecasts can be substantial in terms of acquisition costs of new forecast systems and the cost of operating these systems.

Researcher Kenneth B. Kahn posed this question and made a thorough investigation of this dilemma. He decided to focus on the cost of forecast errors and not on the cost of forecasting, which can vary considerably depending on which forecasting model is selected and implemented.

The researchers broke the cost of forecast errors into two components: the cost of overforecasting and the cost of underforecasting. Overforecasting errors can produce excess inventory costs, excess inventory holding costs, excess transshipment costs, excess obsolescence costs, and reduced profits. Underforecasting errors can produce added order expediting costs, higher product costs, lost sales costs, lost companion product sales, and reduced customer satisfaction.

The magnitude of costs related to over- and underforecasting is much higher than one would suspect because of the need for having accurate forecasts by each product line and also by each distribution location. For instance, if a company has 20 products and five geographically distributed locations, it will need to make 100 accurate forecasts for each planning period in order to minimize its over- and underforecasting error costs. The aggregate forecast for this type of firm could be quite accurate and helpful in operating levels of its manufacturing sources. But to avoid costs associated with over- and underforecasting, this firm must make 100 accurate product-location forecasts. And these 100 forecasts will determine how much money the firm can save.

The author of this paper also produced a monograph that enables management to quickly determine the sum of the under- and overforecast errors made on the basis of total sales volume and a forecast error of 1 percent.

This paper convincingly shows how costly it is for a multiproduct firm to not have an accurate forecasting system to make forecasts for all of its products by item and geographic location.

BENEFITS OF DEMAND FORECASTING

What are the benefits to be gained from improved forecasting methods? This is a question that will or should be posed each time a suggestion or recommendation is made to invest in better forecasting methods. Researcher John T. Mentzer of the University of Tennessee investigated this problem and started with the valid premise that before management invests in a new or improved forecasting method, it should be informed of how improved forecasting accuracy can be translated into lower operating costs and possibly also lower capital investment.

The researcher illustrated how improved forecasting accuracy in overall demand and also in localized demand for a product could generate substantial savings to the firm. For instance, improved forecasting accuracy can result in lower stock shortages, provided management takes appropriate action in response to the improved forecasts. Lower stock shortages nearly always result in higher revenues and resultant profits. The profits can also originate from several sources, such as, with better forecasts, inventory levels can be lowered, resulting in lower levels of required working capital. Although lower inventories will also take less space, the savings for this item will probably be negligible.

Another saving of more accurate forecasts allows the company to buy more of their raw materials or purchased parts on a long-term contract basis. This generally enables the firm to lower material acquisition costs.

The final source of savings results from more accurate forecasts for localized demand. This will avoid shortages in one location and possible surpluses in other locations. Better localized forecasts have the potential to lower the overall company-wide inventory levels, and thus lower overall operating costs.

The researcher showed that the above three areas of improvement for a hypothetical firm could produce improvements in overall profitability for the firm in excess of 10 percent.

NEURAL NETWORKS FORECASTING METHODS FOR ACCOUNTING DATA

This paper provides a comparison of the forecasting accuracy of univariate and multivariate linear models with neural network models. In both cases, fundamental accounting variables such as inventory, accounts receivable, and accounts payable will be included in the models.

Researchers Wei Zhang of Clarkson University, Qing Cao of the University of Missouri in Kansas City, and Marc J. Schniederjans of the University of Nebraska in Lincoln utilized a sample of 283 firms in 41 industries to perform their study. The main focus of the forecast was the critical value of earnings per share (EPS).

Prior studies have shown that neural networks give the best overall result in many forecasting applications. The neural network approach has been used in a wide range of forecasting applications. However, there is still a suspicion that neural network applications to forecasting may be business-context sensitive and therefore may not be superior in all applications.

The researchers were able to show that the neural networking approach to forecasting proved to be superior for estimating earnings per share. More frequent accuracy was attained with the neural network approach than with the classical univariate and multivariate models. Also they found that the improved accuracy was more pronounced with the inclusion of fundamental accounting variables such as accounts receivable and inventory.

The researchers also point out that the study utilized data over a rather short horizon and the neural network performed better under this scenario. Since in many cases the horizon of past data may be limited, the use of neural networks forecasting systems will still be able to make good forecasts under this limitation.

Since neural networks are easier to apply than the more complex univariate and multivariate models, the benefits of neural networks are even more pronounced.

COMPARISON OF THREE FORECASTING METHODS

This paper presents a study in which three time series forecasting methods are compared. The intent of the paper is to investigate if an artificial neural network (ANN) forecasting method will provide the same forecasting accuracy as the more complex and econometric forecasting methods named Baysian vector autoregression (BVAR) and generalized autoregressive conditional heteroscedasticity (GARCH) models.

Researchers James J. Jiang of Louisiana Tech University, Maosen Zhong of the University of Texas at Brownsville, and Gary Klein of the University of Colorado at Colorado Springs utilized scanner data from supermarkets to test the three forecasting methods.

The ANN forecasting method utilized the past time series and attached self-adaptive weights to the past data in order to arrive at a forecast. It is a relatively straightforward approach to time series forecasting. The BVAR forecasting method is a complex forecasting approach using normal prior distributions. In other words, BVAR assumes homoscedasticity, normality, and linearity, assumptions not required for the ANN approach.

The GARCH forecasting method also assumes homoscedasticity, which is inappropriate for the scanner data used in the study. The GARCH method is a complex econometric approach that has proved useful in various macroeconomic and financial phenomena such as the volatility of inflation.

The results of the comparative study showed that for scanner data the ANN forecasting method is superior to both the BVAR and GARCH forecasting approaches. Although the BVAR model provided similar results as the ANN model, the ease of application of the ANN model proved it to be superior. The ANN model also performed better in terms of forecast accuracy than the GARCH forecasting model.

The ANN model proved to be a reliable forecasting tool for a category of data characterized by frequent new entries and dropouts. The model proved to be robust and relatively easy to use, a quality not part of the other two econometric techniques.

RETAILER–SUPPLIER COOPERATION IN SUPPLY CHAIN

One of the vexing problems for retailers is to get replenishments of high-demand products from their suppliers in time. This is especially a problem when the demand for the products is stronger than anticipated.

In the above case, the supplier does not want to overproduce and the retailer does not want to make early commitments for orders. The problem is that the lead time in most supply chains is lengthy because of production lead time, transportation lead time, and supplier capacity limitations, at least in the short run.

Researchers Xiande Zhao of the Chinese University of Hong Kong, Jinning Xie of Tsinghao University of Beijing, and Jerry C. Wei of Notre Dame University studied the above problem in a simulated environment. They looked at the effects of forecast errors, early ordering, and supplier–retailer cooperation on the real and opportunity costs of both supplier and retailer, as well as the sum of the costs of both retailer and supplier, which represents the costs in the supply chain connecting the two parties.

The researchers' objective was to find actions both retailers and suppliers could take to reduce cost in the supply chain. The results of the study had some interesting implications for both retailer and supplier and, of course, for the supply chain connecting the two parties.

The researchers found that early order commitment from the retailers to the supplier will reduce total supply chain cost, but only for shorter time commitments. The larger the demand uncertainty, the shorter should be the early order lead time by the retailers.

The researchers measured two forecast errors: the absolute deviation and the bias. The latter measures either high or low demand, while the former only looks at the forecast error in either direction. A lower or negative bias causes underestimation of the demand, which translates into backorders for retailers and resultant opportunity losses. However, the suppliers' costs are not affected.

The supplier gains by early order commitments by the retailer because it enables him to plan his level of output. However, the retailer suffers from both early or large orders if demand is lower than forecast. If demand turns out to be high, the retailer, of course, benefits from having the merchandise to sell and the resultant profits. So the key for both partners in the supply chain, but especially for the retailer, is to forecast as accurately as possible. And the bias forecast errors will be more costly than the deviation forecast errors.

The researchers also found that the existence of a trend in the demand increases total supply chain cost, and a negative trend causes a higher cost than a positive trend. With a negative trend the retailer ends up with more unsold merchandise and with a positive trend shortages occur and opportunity losses are incurred.

Another result that was found was the fact that the more retailers share one supplier, the more important it is for the retailers to place early order commitments.

The overall conclusion that can be drawn from the study is that retailers will benefit from accurate demand forecasting models. Accurate forecasting models allow the retailers to place orders in time for the supplier to plan his level of operations up to the capacity of his operations.

DEMAND FORECASTING FOR HIGH-TECH VERSUS LOW-TECH PRODUCTS

The question this paper addresses is whether the forecasting methods used differ for new high-technology and new low-technology products. Researchers Gary S. Lynn and C. Joy Green developed a research approach to find an answer to this question. They identified two low-technology industries with relatively stable competitive environments and two high-technology industries with dynamic and unstable environments. The low-technology industries selected were office furniture and building materials, and the high-technology industries were computer equipment and communication equipment.

The selection procedure produced a sample of 56 qualified companies. Of these companies, about two-thirds agreed to participate, yielding a sample of 38 firms. Some firms agreed to provide information on two products. The result was that information could be collected on 14 computer equipment firms, on 23 telecommunications firms, on 14 office furniture firms, and on 24 building materials firms.

Each firm was asked to supply one new product success and one new product failure. This procedure resulted in 75 products comprising 39 successes and 36 failures. Thirty-five new products came from high-technology firms and 40 from low-technology firms.

Following the sample completion stage, respondents from each company were asked to indicate on a four-point scale the extent to which a group of 25 market forecasting techniques were used. The market forecasting techniques ranged from such qualitative techniques as management opinion, past experience, internal and external surveys, and brainstorming to such quantitative techniques as statistical regression, conjoint analysis, and time series analysis.

In comparing the results it became evident that high-technology companies use external techniques such as outside expert opinion, customer interviews, external market research less extensively than low-technology companies.

A specific comparison of successful high-technology products versus successful low-technology products shows that the differences were more distinct. For high-technology products internal techniques such as internal expert opinion and brainstorming are more extensively used than for low-technology successful products. Likewise, for low-technology successful products, external techniques such as buyer surveys are more extensively used.

The implications of the study are that from a market forecasting perspective, high-technology products are very different from low-technology products. Internal forecasting techniques seem to be more applicable than external forecasting techniques for high-technology products. In a similar vein, external forecasting techniques appear to be better suited for low-technology products.

INVENTORY MANAGEMENT POLICY

When managing inventories one should have a full understanding of the demand for the product being managed. In the real world, suppliers and customers do not bargain directly with each other; they simply carry out their transactions with the market as mediator. As markets attempt to clear when price and quantity are not in equilibrium and there is either excess supply or excess demand, then feedbacks and time lags due to market mediation can lead to nonlinear complexities. Experiments indicate that nonlinear complexities in demand have significant implications for inventory management; therefore, managers should consider these properties when choosing inventory management methods. The paper by Pinder introduces appropriate inventory models to reduce inventory holding and backorder/stockout costs when demand data contain nonlinear complexities.

Nonlinear dynamical systems generate time series that appear to be random. The nonlinear complexities in demand prevent the system from reaching an equilibrium capacity. Demand that has nonlinear characteristics causes the estimate of demand during lead time and safety stock to be inaccurate. As a result, this leads to incorrect reorder points, causing increased inventory costs. The paper shows appropriate tools to detect nonlinear demand and also suggests statistical models to forecast demand for nonlinear cases.

Several nonlinear dynamical demand and inventory models have been postulated and examined by researchers in economics and marketing. These models present experimental and theoretical evidence of demand with nonlinear complexities and provide motivating factors for such demand. In a simulation of price and capacity choices for an airline, researchers have shown that dynamical complexities occur in price and quantity settings due to feedback and time lag mechanisms. Furthermore, these dynamical complexities often lead to extremes of either very rapid growth or bankruptcy.

The key to detect the presence of nonlinear complexities is the dimension of the attractor. To obtain a measure of the attractor, researchers have developed a correlation statistic, which approximates the attractor dimension.

Since there is no statistical inference for the correlation statistic, Brock developed a test statistic, based on the correlation integral. The Brock statistic can be applied to the residuals of a forecasting model to determine if there is only white noise remaining in the residuals. If there is some structure remaining in the residuals, then additional structure is required in the model. The additional structure can take a wide variety of forms, including nonlinear model structure, additional variables, autoregressive conditional heteroscedasticity, or simultaneous equations.

Using the Brock test provides three important pieces of information regarding the reliability of a demand forecast. First, a large Brock statistic indicates that the time series may rapidly diverge from slightly different estimates of the initial conditions. Second, a large Brock statistic limits the time horizon for forecasting accuracy, and indicates that estimates must have tight confidence intervals.

To determine the actual effectiveness of an inventory policy for demand, two inventory models were calculated based on 139 periods of information on demand. The first policy was calculated by the simultaneous determination method, which assumes stationarity, independence, and normality. The second policy was calculated by the order-statistic method. The latter method does not assume normality, but does assume stationarity and independence. These two policies were applied to forecast 50 periods of actual demand. The first policy yielded an average cost per period of $781.19 and the second policy yielded an average cost per period of $667.01.

The correlation dimension and Brock test help to identify structure in forecasting models. In addition, the Brock test can identify departures from stochastic inventory model assumptions of independence and stationarity. Nonlinear dynamical theory does not suggest that stochastic, econometric, and statistical methods are inappropriate. Instead, it suggests that stochastic, econometric, and statistical methods should be augmented by the analytic methods described in the paper.

REFERENCES

Jiang, J. J., Zhong, M., & Klein, G. (2002). Marketing category forecasting: An alternative of BVAR–artificial neural networks. *Decision Sciences, 31*(4), 789–812.

Kahn, K. B. (2003, Spring). How to measure the impact of a forecast error on an enterprise. *The Journal of Business Forecasting,* pp. 21–25.

Lynn, G. S., & Green, C. J. (1998), Market forecasting for high-tech vs. low-tech industrial products. *Engineering Management Journal, 10*(1), 15–18.

Mentzer, J. T. (1999, Fall). The impact of forecasting on return on shareholder value. *The Journal of Business Forecasting,* pp. 8–11.

Pinder, J. P. (1996). Nonlinear dynamical system and inventory management. *Managerial and Decision Economics, 17*(1), 27–43.

Remus, W., O'Connor, M., & Griggs, K. (1996). Does feedback improve the accuracy of recurrent judgmental forecasts? *Organizational Behavior and Human Decision Processes, 66*(1), 22–30.

Zhang, W., Cao, Q., & Schniederjans, M. J. (2004). Neural network earnings per share forecasting models: A comparative analysis of alternative methods. *Decision Sciences, 35*(2), 205–237.

Zhao, X., Xie, J., & Wei, J.C. (2002). The impact of forecast errors on early order commitment in a supply chain. *Decision Sciences, 33*(2), 251–280.

CHAPTER 7

INVENTORY MANAGEMENT AND SCHEDULING

This chapter covers nine studies on inventory-related areas. The focus is on the manufacturing sector covering material requirements planning (MRP), work in process inventory, and other manufacturing-related inventory management problems.

The first study looks at the critical factors of MRP implementation. The researcher used a survey sent out to manufacturers in Italy. The results indicate that the most important factor for successful implementation of MRP systems is top management support. The researcher also found out that the accuracy of inventory records, market forecasts, and capacity planning are positively associated with implementation success. A final factor was involvement of affected individuals in the implementation process.

The second study is an analysis of the benefits that are derived from an MRP installation. A survey was sent out to 750 companies in Singapore resulting in 128 usable responses. The results showed that data accuracy, participant support, degree of integration, and company size positively affect several dimensions of operational performance.

The third study reports on an investigation of the kanban system developed in Japan. Simulation is used to evaluate a number of policy variations. The hypothetical problem studied was a five-station operation manufacturing six products. The two policies evaluated were first-come-first-serve

Proven Solutions for Improving Supply Chain Performance, pages 81–96

(FCFS) and shortest-processing-time (SPT). The results showed that the FCFS policies outperformed the SPT policies.

The fourth study evaluates just-in-time (JIT) manufacturing in small firms. A survey was mailed to 280 large and 174 small U.S. manufacturers. The results indicated that large manufacturers are more advanced with JIT implementation. Also, large manufacturers are more likely to implement quality circles, total quality control, focused factory, total productive maintenance, kanban, and JIT purchasing. Smaller firms, on the other hand, are more likely to utilize multifunction employees. In general, JIT is more widely used by the larger firms.

The fifth study compares JIT assembly lines with traditionally balanced assembly lines. The comparison was made in hypothetical situations using simulation. The results indicate that the cycle time is minimized with the JIT line if adequate inventory is available. With low inventory the balanced line's cycle time is minimized.

The sixth study looks at short-life-cycle and product-to-stock goods under variable demand conditions. The means of investigation for this paper was mathematical modeling. The results of the study show that inventory levels will increase in the early stages of its lifecycle. Inventory then levels off as the midpoint on the lifecycle is reached. Near the end of its lifecycle the inventory decreases to the point where the produce-to-stock approach presents the best results.

The seventh study evaluates the impact of parts commonality. The means of investigation is a simulation model based on three furniture manufacturers in North Carolina and Virginia. The study reveals strategies on which parts to make common, which parts to eliminate, as well as which work centers should be eliminated.

The eighth study proposes new formulations for production lot sizing. Traditional models only focus on holding cost and setup or changeover costs. The researchers propose a model that also includes periodic fixed costs, regular time production capacity constraints, and the availability of overtime production capacity. They tested their new model on both hypothetical and real-life situations. All applications validated the usefulness of their proposed model.

The ninth paper departs from the factory models discussed above and focuses on inventory policies in the retail store. The study essentially investigates whether larger stores are more or less profitable than more numerous smaller stores. Their model is a heuristic formula applied to 77 products. The implications of the study show that excessive inventory levels impede profitability. Also, it is more important to have a large category of products so that customers have more choice.

The nine papers in this chapter provide a sampling of the variety of inventory problems that arise in the manufacturing plant and also in the retail sector.

CRITICAL FACTORS OF MRP IMPLEMENTATION

Material requirements planning (MRP) systems are ideal for managing a business's inventory. But, are businesses fully taking advantage of what MRP systems really do? There are many parameters associated with implementation of a software program, yet few businesses put up the investment to executing those parameters. They do not know how to effectively use this system to build a stronger, better business. Therefore, to effectively use the MRP system, all parameters need to be implemented.

The researcher, Professor Petroni of the University of Parma, Italy, surveyed the MRP literature to research the factors associated with implementing MRP systems. The research only showed the generalized aspects of implementation and very little observed evidence to support the arguments of the respective researchers. However, there were elements identified by authors who directly wrote about the MRP implementation process as an issue, but not as the key issue to success.

A confirmatory factor analysis was used by the researchers to accurately group the elements together. This resulted in 36 elements that were grouped into 8 key factors. Some of the elements consisted of:

- clear specification of individual roles and responsibilities
- appointment of a steering committee
- technical training on software use
- selection of the appropriate hardware
- formal procedures for forecasting, master scheduling and capacity planning

A survey was handed out to measure the benefits of the performance of MRP systems of the past and present indices of various dimensions, which include both physical indicators (throughput), cost information (inventory), time performance (lead times), and organizational achievements (coordination).

The research method consisted of a mail survey. Small and medium-sized manufacturing firms were surveyed throughout Northern Italy, and data was collected. The questionnaire was designed and developed by having "roundtable" meetings with six managers who are directly responsible for implementing MRP systems in their companies. The managers took out all the irrelevant questions and added questions that needed to be in the questionnaire. The result was a final survey that incorporated over 60 items divided into four different sections.

The first section helps to find out the basic characteristics of the surveyed firm in terms of manufacturing process (assembly, fabrication), type of product (assemble-to-stock, assemble-to-order and make-to-stock, assemble-to-order and make-to-order, engineer-to-order), process-layout (job-shop vs. manufacturing cells), and production volumes (one-of-a-kind, batch, or continuous production). The second part consists of questions that will help understand the scope and relevance of the operation of the MRP system implemented. This brings out information such as the number of levels in the bill of materials (BOM), the number and range of product changeovers, the level of experience and knowledge with other software tools prior to MRP implementation, the length of MRP use within the organization, the level of customization of the MRP package, and, finally, the type of utilization of the MRP system according to the taxonomy proposed by another researcher. The third section asked about the benefits of implementation of the MRP system, and the fourth section involved the investigation of implementation factors and other elements.

The result from the surveys, which were carefully analyzed by statisticians and researchers with factor score and regression analysis, confirms that top management support is very important for achieving some of the specific benefits associated with operating a MRP system. The accuracy of inventory records, market forecasts, and capacity planning is positively associated to a company's success. The support from colleagues were also found to be an important factor to implementing MRP systems, where the company should involve as many of the affected personnel as possible in the beginning of the implementation. Therefore, involvement is a huge determinant for implementations.

In conclusion, improved customer service, better production scheduling, and reduced manufacturing costs are significant benefits accrued from a successful implementation of a MRP system. For the small and medium-sized firms to be successful, they should increase management support, level of integration, and data accuracy, which all strongly affect the benefits of the MRP system.

AN ANALYSIS OF MATERIAL REQUIREMENTS PLANNING (MRP) BENEFITS

Evaluation of the effects of organizational, implementational, and technological variables on an MRP system is the focus of this study. Possessing a clear understanding of these determinants will enable MRP managers and users to concentrate efforts on key areas to reach the goals of their organizations. This is the first study to use the statistical technique, alternating conditional expectation (ACE), to identify the relationships between these determinants and MRP benefits. It specifically revealed the nonlinear relationships that exist between the determinants and MRP benefits. This study shows that specific factors can have a drastic effect on the benefits of the MRP system.

The findings showed that determinant variables such as data accuracy, participant support, degree of integration, and company size affect benefits in a nonlinear fashion or on many different dimensions. Data accuracy was found to be crucial in influencing operational efficiency, customer service, and interdepartmental coordination benefits. The study also found that users can bypass the negative effects of depressed levels of people support and data accuracy through the use of secondary sources to get their work done and receive increased benefits. There were other findings along these lines.

The study consisted of a survey circulated to about 750 companies in Singapore with a total of 128 responses, or about 17 percent. A total of 59 of the respondents had implemented MRP. This sample size of 128 represents the largest sample size for this type of study to date. The determinant variables were selected from previous studies where they were reported to affect MRP benefits. ACE, an advanced statistical technique, was used for estimations. In most cases, the relationship appeared to be nonlinear.

In summary, this study tells MRP managers and users that there are many variables affecting the successful implementation of their MRP systems and that these variables determine the benefits. To that end, understanding these variables and the relationships they hold with MRP benefits will give them a better chance for successful implementation. One of the determinants of this study was degree of integration. This study states that a high degree of integration promotes the achievement of the full benefits of operational efficiency and interdepartmental coordination.

FIRST-COME-FIRST-SERVE AND SHORTEST-PROCESSING-TIME RULES IN A DUAL-KANBAN FLOW SHOP

This research article analyzes and determines the reason why managers are adopting a first-come, first-serve (FCFS) policy in just-in-time production, even though the shortest processing time (SPT) policy has been so historically promising. The study provides insights to managers and demonstrates how the FCFS policy results in higher performance.

The researcher of this study, Alireza Ardalan, simulated the operation of a dual-kanban controlled flow shop in an attempt to extend past research. She introduced two policies considering the status of withdrawal kanbans and the number of kanbans utilized, hoping to provide insights into improving the performance of a pure flow shop.

The study entailed a simulation of a five-station operation, manufacturing six products, and under the control of a dual-kanban policy. The products each went through the five stations in the same sequence. The benchmark interarrival times and processing times of the products were 15 and 10 periods, respectively. In addition, both FCFS and SPT policies were used.

The operations policies were compared with respect to average wait time of the end products' withdrawal kanbans and the total number of full containers in the system. The total number of full containers was the measure of the total work-in-process and the policies in comparison with the wait time was a measure of customer service within the system.

At each level of the withdrawal cycle, processes with FCFS policies that used the information about withdrawal kanbans performed better than those that used the SPT policy. This was mainly due to the fact that the SPT rule ignores the process time of any activity and therefore higher priority can be assigned to jobs that should be processed immediately and that take a long time as well. The level of inventory increased directly with the number of kanbans used in the system, due to the decreasing control it has on the upper limit of allowable inventory. Also, having long withdrawal cycles caused a reduction in the ability of stations to replenish their raw material inventory frequently, which led to low levels of inventory. The FCFS priority rule also resulted in lower levels of inventory because it can assign a higher priority to jobs that take longer to process and can replenish inventory at a slower rate.

This study has numerous implications dealing with the manufacturing aspect of business. A proper use of information about the status of withdrawal kanbans in decision making has proven to increase the service level and at the same time reduce the level of inventory. Processes that use this information result in shorter customer wait times, especially when a smaller number of kanbans is used. The combination of the use of this information on withdrawal kanbans and the use of the FCFS priority rule will improve the service level and reduce total inventory simultaneously.

JIT MANUFACTURING IN LARGE AND SMALL FIRMS

The movement on the part of American companies to close the competitive gap by employing the lean practices adopted by such Japanese firms as Toyota over 40 years ago is still very much in the early stages. One of the questions to be asked concerning this movement is whether or not some firms are more likely to benefit from the implementation of JIT manufacturing practices than others. Indeed, research indicates that not only are the rates of implementation different, but also the benefits realized may vary between large and small firms.

Richard White of the University of North Texas, John Pearson of Arizona State University, and Jeffrey Wilson of Arizona State University compared the results of JIT implementation between 280 large and 174 small U.S. manufacturers. With the support of the Association for Manufacturing Excellence (AME), two null hypotheses were tested. First, manufacturer size has no effect on JIT practices implemented. Second, changes in performance attributed to implementation status of JIT practices are the same whether the manufacturer is small or large. Ultimately, both hypotheses were disproved.

This study was conducted by surveying a large sample of the organizational members of the AME, representing a cross-section of industries and geographic locations in the United States. Questionnaires were mailed to all members, and yielded an overall response rate of about 44 percent. These responses were then sorted to eliminate those that provided incomplete information or that had not implemented any JIT practices. Finally, those manufacturers with fewer than 250 employees were classified as small, and those with over 1,000 were classified as large. (Those ranging between 250 and 1,000 were not included in the study to avoid ambiguity.)

The questionnaire was developed according to the Dillman Total Design Method. To avoid confusion, a complete listing of definitions of the 10 JIT practices (including quality circles, total quality control, focused factory, total productive maintenance, reduced setup times, group technology, uniform workload, multifunction employees, kanban, and just-in-time purchasing) was included with the questionnaire package. To assess the first hypothesis, respondents were asked to provide a measure of implementation status, based on the length of time since implementation began, of each of these practices. This data was then evaluated using simple odds ratios (implemented vs. not implemented). To assess the second hypothesis, changes in performance attributed to the implementation of these practices were determined using a nominal scale. Changes such as throughput time, internal quality levels, external quality levels, labor productivity, and employee behavior were scored as better or not better. Other changes, such as inventory levels, unit cost, cost of equipment, cost of employee training, and administrative costs were scored as lower or not lower. This data was then analyzed using regression models to determine the measure of correlation between JIT practices implemented and organizational improvements.

Results indicated that there were some appreciable differences in implementation between large and small firms. Overall, large manufacturers are more advanced in their implementation. Both the percentage of firms adopting a practice and the average time since adoption for almost all JIT practices is larger for large firms than for small ones. Additionally, it was found that some JIT practices are more likely to be implemented by a large firm than a small one, and vice versa. According to statistically significant statistical ratios, small manufacturers are less likely than large ones to implement the following practices: quality circles, total quality control, focused factory, total productive maintenance, reduced setup times, kanban, and JIT purchasing. In contrast, small firms were more likely to implement the practice of multifunction employees. (Small and large firms seemed equally likely to implement the group technology and uniform workload practices.) So, eight of the 10 practices examined showed that company size does have an effect, and the first hypothesis was not supported.

The results of the regression models to assess impact on performance then suggested that changes in performance were affected differently by implementation status of the 10 practices between large and small firms. For example, in small firms it was found that a negative relationship existed between implementation status for JIT purchasing and internal quality (unlike that for large firms, which had a positive relationship). Only three of the 10 practices were shown to yield similar, significantly positive relationships (reduced setup time and better throughput, multifunction employees and better productivity, and kanban and lower training costs) for both large and small manufacturers. These results did not support the second hypothesis. It should still be mentioned, however, that implementation of JIT practices does appear to significantly improve the overall performance of the firms, both large and small.

This research should be of significant interest to all manufacturing companies that are either considering or are in the process of implementing lean/JIT manufacturing principles. It is especially important for the small firms that make up the vast majority of U.S. manufacturers, because most of the JIT experience has until now been utilized by large firms. The research strongly suggests that certain JIT practices might be more appropriate for implementation than others, depending on the size of the company. In the example given above concerning the negative relationship between implementation of JIT purchasing and internal quality improvements, this might have to do with the amount of clout the company has with the supplier. In cases involving a small company, the supplier may have too little incentive to provide the effort to maintain or improve quality when its delivery requirements are increased. An awareness and understanding of the relationships evident in this research can allow for more effective implementation, whether the company is large or small.

JIT LINES VERSUS TRADITIONALLY BALANCED LINES

Many authors believe that the primary focus of competition for the next decade will be the ability to develop and deliver products faster than the competition. Numerous companies in the past few years have applied the JIT plan. The traditional Western approach for developing a production line is called line balancing, and under this plan a desired cycle time is determined. Companies have tried to figure out which plan or scheme is best for their production line and customers.

Satya S. Chakravorty and J. Brian Atwater, the authors of this article, did extensive research through reading of other authors' beliefs and findings. No research has been conducted to specifically compare the relative performance of these two design approaches. Their article reports the findings of a simulation-based experiment, which compares the cycle time performance of these two approaches for designing and operating a production line under a variety of operating conditions. Their research was used to determine which production line design, either the just-in-time or traditional line balancing approach, performs most efficiently.

The performance of two production line design approaches, just-in-time and traditional line balancing, is compared under various operating conditions using simulation methodology. A simulation model was developed for both forms of line design. In addition to the two line design approaches, two other independent variables were introduced to observe their impact on the cycle time of each line. The two independent variables are system variability, which will be tested at two levels, and total inventory in the system, which will be tested at eight levels. Cycle time was used as the dependent variable for this study.

Each line was modeled as a closed system so that inventory would be held constant across all models. After a unit was pulled through the last station, it was counted as one unit of output and then sent back to the queue at the time of operation. In both the simulation models dummy subsystems were used to generate random down time for each station on the line. The subsystem for each station was composed of two queues. The first queue represented the mean time between failures (MTBF) for the station; the second queue was the mean time to repair (MTR) for the station. At the start of the simulation a single entity was introduced into each station's MTBF queue, which fed into the station's MTR queue. Once it arrived at the MTR station, it seized the shared resource from its corresponding processing station on the line and that station was down. After the entity at the MTR station finished processing, the shared resource was released and the station was operative again. The entity was sent back to the MTBF queue and the process repeated itself.

The balanced line was designed with four 10-minute operations. Each station was assigned a queue size adequate to hold all inventory in the system. This was done to prevent blocking between stations and to allow inventory to flow freely anywhere in the system. The free flow of inventory is consistent with the traditional method of operating a balanced line. The JIT line was designed with five 8-minute operations and a dummy station at the end of the line, which pulled material, if any available, out of the finished goods queue every 10 minutes. In this way, the line is balanced with each station having 20 percent capacity slack. In the simulation model, the dummy station at the end of the line, which attempts to draw a unit from finished goods every 10 minutes, triggers production. If a unit is available, it is withdrawn and sent back to the queue in front of station one. If a unit is not available, then it is withdrawn at the next available time. If no material is available in a station's queue, then that station is starved and cannot work even if material is pulled out of the preceding queue signaling demand.

Significant differences are noted where they exist. The comparisons reveal that the JIT line achieves a lower cycle time than the balanced line when inventory is greater than 10 units. Clearly, this comparison reveals that when system variability is low, the JIT line achieves a lower cycle time than the traditionally balanced line except when the level of inventory in the system is very low. The results indicate that when inventory in the system is low, the balanced line performs better than the JIT line and when the inventory in the system is high, the JIT line performs better than the balanced line. Specifically, balanced lines achieve lower cycle times than JIT lines when total inventory in the system is at 10, 20, and 30 units. At 40 units of total inventory in the system, there is no significant difference in the cycle time of each line. With 50 or more units of total inventory in the system, the JIT line maintains a lower cycle time than the balanced line.

This study provides a very important finding relevant for practicing managers. The primary finding from this research that is useful to managers is that regardless of the amount of system variability, balanced lines achieved a lower cycle time than JIT lines when system inventory was low. However, the JIT line does attain a lower cycle time and comes closer to the optimal cycle time than the balanced line when system inventory was increased. In short, ironically, balanced lines achieve a lower cycle time than JIT lines when system inventory is low, but with sufficient inventory the JIT line performs best. Managers should take this finding into consideration when deciding on what type of production line to use. If they have high demand and high inventory they should use the JIT production line, otherwise for smaller orders they should use the balanced line.

SHORT-LIFECYCLE AND PRODUCE-TO-STOCK GOODS UNDER STOCHASTIC DEMAND

In the case of capacity and production planning, the following questions arise: What methods should be used in order to manage the levels of output a firm produces? How should capacity and production be set? This particular case focuses on goods that are produce-to-stock, short-lifecycle, and under stochastic demand. It takes into account unsold goods that a firm can either carry over or sell on a secondary market. Both cases produce similar graphical results. In the end we discover that through a series of formulas we can find optimal service rates for a firm and that these rates do not remain constant over time. This is a policy called target interval policy.

Alexander Angelus and Evan L. Portues of Strategic Decisions Group, in conjunction with the Graduate School of Business at Stanford University, developed and tested a hypothesis on simultaneous capacity and production management. It was their goal to develop a method that firms could use to plan production and capacity levels. The data that they used in this study have proven their initial hypothesis.

In production management situations, there are many different ways in which to handle output and inventory. This study takes into account two types of inventory management methods. This first method tested was the no-carry-over method. This case assumes that at the end of a period all excess goods are sold off in a secondary market, at a reduced price. These units are recorded as lost sales and then become a shortage. The other inventory method that was tested was the carry-over method. Instead of units becoming lost sales at the end of a period, they become backlogged and incur holding costs. The units do not become a shortage until the product is unsellable at the end of its product lifecycle.

Each case study contains assumptions that are standard when using that particular inventory method. From these assumptions the researchers drew up theorems for each case, which were represented algebraically. These theorems show how to control inventory and capacity through formulas. A main idea that the theorems keep in mind is that the producer should know approximately where in the product lifecycle the good is, as this has a direct effect on the capacity for the firm. Since this study focuses on short-run products, one example that they use is computer chips and they conclude that the lifecycle is about 17 months. The other industry example they use is the rental car industry, where new vehicles are purchased every year or as needed.

Through the researchers' hypotheses, we find a pattern for optimal production and capacity planning. For the inventory carry-over method, the results show that inventory levels will increase as the product is in the development and expansion stages of the product life cycle. This is then followed by a short period of leveling off as the demand for the product also levels off. Final inventory will decrease as demand for the product decreases near the end of its cycle. If a firm does not carry over inventory, it was found that the best method of operation is to follow a produce-to-order method to limit losses from selling goods on the secondary market.

Since inventory control is an issue in almost any business, including service firms, this study has a wide range of practical applications. From computer chip manufacturers to car rental firms, this study's inclusion of a wide range of firms makes it a valuable study and a practical business application. Since it focuses on short-run production, it also works for firms that operate with high seasonal variability. Instead of those firms having a product lifecycle, they have a seasonal cycle that mirrors the product lifecycle of a good that would only be in demand for a year. This study should be used by firms that want to cut inventory holding costs and losses due to lost sales.

IMPACT OF PARTS COMMONALITY

Parts commonality can lead to a significant decrease in average workload, setup time, work-in-process, and holding costs, according to Asoo J. Vakharia of the University of Florida at Gainesville, David A. Parmenter of Illinois Governor's State University, and Susan M. Sanchez of the University of Missouri at St. Louis. However, their results show that increasing commonality also leads to negative effects on the shop floor.

Consumers are demanding a wider variety of products than ever before. This has required that manufacturing firms fabricate or purchase increasing numbers of distinct parts in order to manufacture the variety of products that consumers are attracted to. This increase in the number of part types can lead to unnecessary design effort, as well as inefficiencies of the manufacturing process.

Although many studies have been done that describe the benefits of increased commonality for product design, there is little research that addresses commonality's impact on operations. The major implication of this study is the system disruption that parts commonality can lead to. The authors used a simulation model to study the impact of commonality on measures such as average shop load and shop load variability. The effects were observed under a variety of shop conditions, and the study focused on four operating/shop factors (variance of end item demand, correlation of end item demand, setup time/cost, and number of work centers) and two primary factors (within-product commonality and between-product commonality).

The authors focused on manufacturing firms that use a material requirements planning (MRP) system, in particular three furniture manufacturers in North Carolina and Virginia. All three companies were involved in implementing cellular manufacturing for the production of office, bedroom, and standardized furniture for restaurants and hotels. The companies were reducing the number of unique parts that comprise the different types of furniture. Although this aided the production planning process, serious load imbalances on the shop floor resulted. Certain machines were becoming overutilized while others that processed the eliminated parts were now underutilized.

The results suggest that care should be taken when a company implements parts commonality to select both the common and eliminated parts such that the expense involved in the required one-time resource allocation is reasonably low. The benefits of eliminating work centers were also clearly illustrated by the results. The strategic selection of which parts to make common, which parts to eliminate, and the elimination of expensive and hard-to-manage work centers should enable manufacturing firms to overcome the system disruptions inherent in parts commonality production systems.

PRODUCTION LOT SIZING WITH PERIODIC COSTS AND OVERTIME

While the traditional model displays the tradeoff between inventory holding costs and equipment setup costs, it fails to consider periodic fixed costs, regular-time production capacity constraints, and the availability of overtime production capacity. Professors Robinson and Sahin of the Lowry Mays College and Graduate School of Business propose two new mathematical problem formulations and optimization algorithms to investigate the conditions under which the proposed approaches are superior to traditional models, and to study the potential economic benefits of the new procedures. The problem objective is to determine the least cost production lot size that satisfies demand. This requires a tradeoff among equipment setup costs, periodic fixed costs, inventory holding costs, and overtime costs.

The researchers tested the procedures over a wide range of problem characteristics to assess the condition that favored one model over the other. These included three different demand levels, ratios of equipment setup to periodic setup costs, and hourly overtime costs, and two different production rates. In total, 54 unique test problems were solved. In all of the problems, they set regular time production at 8 hours per day and annual inventory carrying costs at 1.2 per unit. The firm was assumed to operate 250 days per year.

Traditional approaches for modeling economic production lot-sizing problems assume that a single, fixed equipment setup cost is incurred each time a product is run, regardless of the quantity manufactured. This permits multiple days of production from one production setup. In this paper, they extended the model to consider additional fixed charges, such as cleanup or inspection costs, that are associated with each time period's production and the availability of overtime production capacity. Experimental results indicated the conditions under which the algorithm's performance is superior to traditional approaches. They also tested the procedures on a set of lot-sizing problems facing a national food processor and documented their potential economic benefits.

A major contribution of the research is the definition of the economic production lot-sizing problem with periodic costs and overtime. They provided a general problem description accompanied by a specific industry example facing a leading manufacturer of governmental and commercial food products. As part of the problem definition, they identified the major cost drivers associated with the lot-sizing decision and incorporated them into two distinct decision models—one for regular-time production and the other considering overtime production.

INVENTORY POLICY FOR RETAIL STORES

This article deals with the question of whether it is more desirable for retail stores to design and open dense retail outlets, which will in the most part reduce inventory as well as increase profits, or is it just more desirable to open smaller stores? In a new and recent trend, retail managers have been trying to gain an edge in the market by opening high-density stores. The term *density* refers to the number of product or categories that a store provides per unit of selling space. For some stores, this change deals with the increase in number of product categories, also known as SKUs (stock keeping units).

The reason behind increasing SKUs is to attract more customers and to offer them an opportunity for one-stop shopping. The authors decided to conduct the study in the grocery industry. According to recent figures, the number of SKUs in the average grocery store has increased by 96 percent while at the same time increasing the store size by nearly 50 percent. This article takes a look at the advantages and disadvantages toward these types of stores, which have the potential to increase sales and reduce inventory turnover.

Professors Michael Ketzenberg of Kenan-Flager Business School, Richard Metters of Cox School of Business, and Vincente Vargas of Goizueta Business School took a combined total of 77 products and tested them by heuristic formulas. The first heuristic rule is the current practice heuristic (CP); they next tested the base stock heuristic (BAS) rule and finally the modified Veinott heuristic (MOD) rule. The reason for testing the three different heuristic rules is that each is beneficial in its own way. For each heuristic rule evaluated, the ROII (return on inventory investment) was calculated.

The CP rule seeks to replicate the managerial emphasis on filling with product all the available space provided by the allocation scheme. This is just what is normally done now. Managers order to reach shelf capacity.

The BAS heuristic calculates traditional base stock inventory position plus some extra inventory so that inventory after ordering is above the traditional base stock reorder point. What retailers are aiming for in this type of heuristic is an inventory, which is targeted to shelf capacity. The BAS rule is included in this study because it is simple and it takes into consideration the profitability of the items.

The MOD heuristic attempts to consider both case-pack size and substitutability in addition to differential product margins. It evaluates the optimal policy for ordering by case-packs. For this type of problem they have to identify two functions for each product; the first is the expected sales for a given stock level and the second is an approximation of the profitability of a given stocking level using the expected sales. This heuristic assumes a penalty cost when a consumer is forced to substitute an item, and premium items are normally substituted for another premium item.

The result showed that gross profits are nearly identical for all policies because each heuristic has a fill rate beyond 99 percent. The reason that the fill rate was so high was due to the large differences in holding versus lost sales costs and the effect of case-pack sizes.

In every experimental cell, researchers concluded that MOD was the superior heuristic. They were also surprised to see the lack of numerical change of ROII results for the BAS and CP heuristics as parameters change. The mean results of a typical experimental cell mirror those seen earlier. Gross and net profits are similar but ROII differs considerably between heuristics.

The implications of this study are that it does not necessarily matter which heuristic is used but it demonstrates that excessive inventory levels are impeding profitability. It is not necessary to have a large inventory but it is good to have a large category of products so that customers can choose a similar product if their first choice is not available.

REFERENCES

Angelus, A., & Porteus, E. L. (2002). Simultaneous capacity and production management of short-life cycle, produce-to-stock goods under stochastic demand. *Management Science, 48*(3), 399–413.

Ardalan, A. (1997). Analysis of local decision rules in a dual kanban flow shop. *Decision Sciences, 20*(1), 195–212.

Chakravorty, S. S., & Atwater, J. B. (1995). Do JIT lines perform better than traditionally balanced lines? *International Journal of Operations and Production Management, 15*(2), 77–89.

Ketzenberg, M., Metters, R., & Vargas, V. (2000). Inventory policy for dense retail outlets. *Journal of Operations Management, 18*(3), 303–316.

Petroni, A. (2002). Critical factors of MRP implementation in small and medium-sized firms. *International Journal of Operations and Production Management, 22*(3), 329–348.

Robinson, Jr., E. P., & Smith, F. (2001). Economic production lot sizing with periodic costs and overtime. *Decision Sciences, 32*(3), 423–452.

Sum, C. C., Yang, K. K., Ang, J. S. K., & Quek, S. A. (1995). An analysis of material requirements planning (MRP) benefits using alternating conditional expectation (ACE). *Journal of Operations Management, 13*(1), 35–58.

Vakharia, A. J., Parmenter, D. A., & Sanchez, S. M. (1996). The operating impact of parts commonality. *Journal of Operations Management, 14*(1), 3–18.

White, R. E., Pearson, J. N., & Wilson, J. R. (1999). JIT manufacturing: A survey of implementation in small and large U.S. manufacturers. *Management Science 45*(1), 1–15.

CHAPTER 8

OUTSOURCING AND PURCHASING

This chapter provides summaries on eight papers covering outsourcing and purchasing. Again the focus is on manufacturing in both the U.S. and foreign locations. Two of the papers focus on the automotive industry.

The first study looks at the impact of strategic sourcing and manufacturing technology on manufacturing flexibilities. A questionnaire was mailed out to members of the National Association of Purchasing Managers and 68 usable responses were obtained. The results of the study point out the benefits of integrated supply chain management when the focus is on strategic sourcing and advanced manufacturing technologies.

The second study focuses on modular outsourcing in the automobile industry. The study consists of an evaluation of three automobile plants in Brazil and Poland. They investigated the degree to which the three plants utilized modular outsourcing. They found the largest degree of modular outsourcing occurred at Volkswagen's Resende plant in Brazil. The suppliers at Resende provided capital to build the plant and of the 1,200 employees at the plant only 200 are Volkswagen employees.

The third paper evaluates just-in-time (JIT) purchasing and performance. The researchers used a survey questionnaire to both buyers and suppliers. A total of 321 usable responses were received. The research indicates that buyers can directly benefit from JIT purchasing while suppliers may need to adjust their manufacturing practices to also benefit.

Proven Solutions for Improving Supply Chain Performance, pages 97–110

The fourth paper evaluates the relationship between product characteristics and JIT purchasing dimensions. The research was done in Spain. A survey questionnaire was used producing 152 usable responses. A simple correlation analysis was performed between seven product characteristics and five JIT purchasing dimensions. The study confirmed the relevance of product characteristics on the implementation of JIT purchasing.

The fifth study looks at the effects of process management techniques on firm performance. The results indicated that greater use of process-focused improvement methods, greater involvement with suppliers and customers in planning and greater management involvement in team and project selection correlated positively with higher returns on assets.

The sixth study addressed the electronic procurement of maintenance, repair, and operating (RMO) items. The research method used was a field survey accompanied by field interviews. One particularly startling benefit was the lower procurement cost of electronic purchasing. It was only one-third of the manual cost. Other benefits were supply base reduction, wide and open visibility of the MRO supply base, and the potential to develop a more strategic approach to MRO procurement. The study was performed in the United Kingdom.

The seventh study looked at the status of product development in the Italian motorcycle industry. A survey questionnaire was utilized to acquire the data for analysis. The entire industry consists of five specialty producers and three volume producers. Each segment was unique because the specialty producers manufactured small, low-cost scooters and small motorcycles. The remaining focus of the study is on cooperation in product development and design between the suppliers and the manufacturers.

The eighth and final study addresses the success of information technology (IT) in the services and manufacturing industries. The researchers used a survey questionnaire and received 81 usable responses from Australian companies. The results of the study show that IT has been applied in all areas of services and manufacturing. The main benefit from IT application included productivity improvements and cost reduction. So far most firms had overlooked the potential strategic benefits of IT.

The eight studies evaluate issues surrounding the outsourcing, purchasing, and cooperative activities between suppliers and manufacturers. Although many benefits are still to be reaped from cooperation between the various parties, considerable progress has already been made.

STRATEGIC SOURCING AND MANUFACTURING TECHNOLOGY: IMPACT ON MANUFACTURING FLEXIBILITIES

What is the relationship between strategic sourcing and advanced manufacturing technology with the various forms of operations flexibility, and how does this flexibility affect manufacturing performance? Researchers Ram Narasimhan of Michigan State University and Ajay Das of Baruch College of the City University of New York decided to research this question.

They designed a survey questionnaire and mailed it out to 600 members of the National Association of Purchasing Managers. They received 68 usable responses back, and then used follow-up calls to fill gaps in the information and to get a better appreciation of the problem being studied.

To round out their research model, the researchers expanded it somewhat by investigating the impact of two variable constructs on the strategic sourcing construct and on the advanced manufacturing technologies construct.

For the strategic sourcing construct, they investigated the impact of supplier responsiveness and supplier assistance in product design, production process, and product introduction cycle time. They found that both of the latter constructs had a statistically significant impact on strategic sourcing.

For advanced manufacturing technologies, they investigated the impact of cellular manufacturing and just-in-time with integrated manufacturing systems. They found that each of the latter two constructs had a statistically significant impact on advanced manufacturing technologies.

They then tested the impact of strategic sourcing and advanced manufacturing technologies on the three measures of manufacturing flexibility consisting of: (1) modification flexibility, (2) volume flexibility, and (3) new product development flexibility. They found that strategic sourcing had a statistically significant impact on modification flexibility, but no impact on the other two manufacturing flexibilities. Advanced manufacturing technologies had a statistically significant impact on volume flexibility, but no impact on the other two manufacturing flexibilities.

The researchers next explored if modification flexibility and volume flexibility had any impact on new product development flexibility. The results show that each of the two flexibilities had a statistically significant impact on new product development flexibility.

The final part of the test was evaluating the impact of the three manufacturing flexibilities on the manufacturing cost reductions. No statistically significant results were found.

The results of this study point out the benefits of integrated supply chain management. Strategic sourcing and advanced manufacturing technologies and their impact on manufacturing flexibilities are an important part of the supply chain. Also, the impact of the volume and modification flexibilities on new product development flexibility are of high importance in supply chain design.

MODULAR OUTSOURCING IN THE AUTOMOTIVE INDUSTRY

Just-in-time was formally introduced as a manufacturing practice approximately 25 years ago to provide companies with a competitive advantage with respect to reduced costs, agile response, and better quality. Because JIT is effective at achieving these goals, it has experienced great popularity, especially among automotive manufacturers. But, due to this popularity, JIT no longer provides an original equipment manufacturer (OEM) or a supplier with any distinct competitive advantage. To reestablish means to achieve an advantage in the market, OEMs and suppliers are investigating progressive managerial systems to improve the efficiency of the supply chain. One such approach is based on higher levels of outsourcing.

The three researchers who conducted this research are Collins, Bechler, and Pires. They are a South American trio of professors who presented this information as part of the "Manufacturing 2000" project, a research project that examined future trends in supply chain management. The published results examined the supplier relationships at three assembly plants: the Skoda Felician plant in Poland, Skoda's Octavia plant in Poland, and VW's truck and bus plant in Resende, Brazil. Their analysis was from both the perspective of the OEM and the perspective of the supply base.

Two perspectives are driving higher levels of cooperation between automotive OEMs and suppliers: the supply side and OEM side. On the supplier side, they can increase revenues by stealing some of their competitors' business away, or by increasing products and services offered. On the OEM side, they are looking for progressive ways of decreasing engineering, development, and investment costs. With increased collaboration between the OEM and the supply base, the objectives of both parties are attainable.

Increased outsourcing in the automotive industry has manifested itself in two ways. The first is the outsourcing of complete modules. This is a strategy in which suppliers, called tier-one suppliers, are expected to take full responsibility for a subsystem of a vehicle. Examples of such modules are the seats, cockpits, and front-ends. When supplying a module, the tier-one supplier is responsible for coordinating and managing tier-two suppliers to the module, assembly of the module, and delivering the module to the assembly plant. The second form of increased collaboration is the outsourcing of services to module suppliers. The typical services may include design and development of the module, preproduction testing, and assembly services at the point of assembly into the vehicle.

The three assembly plants that the researchers examined each used outsourcing to a different extent. The Skoda Felicia plant arranged for six key suppliers to occupy floor space within the assembly plant in order to deliver small modules to the Felicia-managed assembly line with a 303-minute broadcast window. The level of outsourcing is increased at the Skoda Octavia plant. Here three suppliers built modules within the assembly plant and assemble the module onto the vehicle as it passes by. The level of outsourcing is increased more at the VW Resende plant. Here the assembly sequence is similar to the Octavia plant; however, the level of outsourcing has again increased. In Resende, the OEM has distributed the venture risk to the module suppliers. The suppliers provided capital to build the factory, get paid upon final assembly of the vehicle, and share vehicle repair costs, which are traced to the suppliers' module. There are 1,200 employees at the facility; 200 are VW employees while the remaining 1,000 are on the suppliers' payrolls. The Resende plant represents a revolutionary approach to supply chain management.

Increased collaboration between auto manufacturers and suppliers through outsourcing holds the opportunity for many benefits and risks for both partners. OEM resources (capital and professional) can be freed up to focus on brand management at the risk of losing technical control over the component technology and quality. A supplier has the opportunity to become a sole global supplier for a specific OEM and develop unique competencies to serve the OEM needs. This may establish new criteria that are themselves competitive advantages. Certainly, pairing the right OEM with the right supplier is crucial to the success of the relationship. Because this level of collaboration has only occurred within the last 3 years at very few assembly plants, the success or failure of it is yet to be seen. The researchers as well as the industry as a whole will be watching these innovative plants to determine if the benefits are in fact genuine.

JIT PURCHASING AND PERFORMANCE

It has been well known that a JIT purchasing system reduces levels of in-process inventories, purchased goods and finished goods, reduces space requirements, and shortens lead times. The problem arises when it is not as clear to what extent suppliers benefit from engaging in JIT purchasing with buyers. Some researchers have found that JIT purchasing results in inventory costs being transmitted from buyers to suppliers, although this may be due to bad implementation of the JIT purchasing system or poor implementation from a supply chain perspective. In this analysis, a model was developed and tested to determine if JIT purchasing reduces logistics costs for both suppliers and buyers.

Researchers Yan Dong, from the Carlson School of Management of the University of Minnesota, and Craig R. Carter and Martin E. Dresner, from the Robert H. Smith School of Business of the University of Maryland, College Park, developed and tested a model to determine whether JIT purchasing may result in suppliers adopting JIT manufacturing techniques, so they too can benefit, indirectly, from JIT purchasing. To obtain necessary data for this research, a survey method was adopted. The research sample was selected from the subscriber list of *Purchasing Magazine.*

The research was based on a study of buyers in three industries: industrial machinery and equipment, electronic and other electrical equipment, and transportation equipment and suppliers in electronic and other electrical equipment. The research was intended primarily to investigate the impact of JIT purchasing on both buyers' and sellers' logistics costs. A survey method was adopted to gather data for this research. Two very similar versions of the survey, one for buyers and one for suppliers, were created and pretested and the seven-point Likert scales were used to measure survey responses. In order to decrease measurement error, preliminary surveys were given to logistics managers working for major manufacturing companies and logistics professors. Comments were collected and changes were made to surveys before they were sent out. Each of the statements on the questionnaires were true, except for the items used to measure logistics costs.

The combined sample size (buyer sample plus supplier sample) was 5,000 (2,305 buyers and 2,695 suppliers). The buyer group consisted of purchasing managers from the three targeted industries while the supplier group consisted of sales, marketing, and traffic/distribution managers from the electronics industries. The response rate was 7 percent, amounting to 124 buyer surveys and 197 supplier surveys. Due to the low response, a t-test was employed to ensure that buyers and suppliers were not from the same firms in this way testing the presence of nonresponse bias.

Using structural equation modeling with latent variables and a full structural model, the study's hypotheses for buyers were tested. To test the hypothesis for the supplier firms, a structural equation analysis was also used. In summary, a total of four hypotheses were tested. The first hypothesis, that supply chain integration would directly increase the extent of JIT purchasing, was supported for both the buyers and suppliers. The second hypothesis, that supply chain integration would directly reduce logistics costs, was not supported in either the buyer model or the supplier model. The third hypothesis, that the extent of JIT purchasing directly increases supplier use of JIT manufacturing, was supported using both buyer and supplier samples. This result coincides with a previous study that stated that JIT manufacturing and JIT purchasing are often implemented together. The fourth hypothesis and the major hypothesis addressed on this research, that the extent of JIT purchasing directly reduces logistics costs, was supported only for the buyer sample. This result provides conditional support to previous research that found that logistics costs might be pushed upstream in the supply chain when JIT purchasing is implemented, resulting in gains for buyers but not suppliers. However, the research did show that JIT purchasing resulted in a reduction of logistics cost for suppliers as well, not directly but through the mediating variable, supplier JIT manufacturing.

An important finding was that the extent of JIT purchasing has a direct effect on reducing costs in buyer organizations but not in supplier organizations. Also, significant paths were found, using supplier data, between JIT purchasing and supplier JIT manufacturing and between supplier JIT manufacturing and supplier logistics costs. This result indicates that JIT purchasing can indirectly lead to low logistics cost for suppliers, if suppliers implement JIT manufacturing in conjunction with a JIT purchasing program. However, the researchers did not find a significant direct path between supply chain integration and cost reduction in either of the models.

In summary, this exploratory research suggests buyers can directly benefit from JIT purchasing while suppliers may need to adjust their manufacturing practices to benefit as well. Implications of the study for business, according to the researchers, are that: in order to built a long term supply chain relationship, it is likely that all members of the supply chain need to profit. This research shows that JIT purchasing only produces benefits for buyers. Therefore, to implement a successful JIT purchasing program from a supply chain perspective, managers in both the supplier and buyer organizations must act to produce the conditions favorable for JIT adoption. Implementing a JIT program that includes specific supplier JIT manufacturing activities appears to be a key in producing positive results for supplier organizations, and long-term success for the buyer–supplier relationship.

RELATIONSHIP BETWEEN PRODUCT CHARACTERISTICS AND JUST-IN-TIME PURCHASING DIMENSIONS

What are the most important product characteristics that determine whether just-in-time purchasing is utilized? Professor Javier Gonzalez-Benita of Spain's University of Salamanco designed a study to find answers to this difficult question. The researcher identified seven product characteristics that he posited to be important. They are: (1) volume, (2) specificity, (3) technological complexity, (4) essentiality, (5) fragility, (6) variability, and (7) economic value.

The researcher also identified five dimensions of just-in-time purchasing, including: (1) operational, (2) relational, (3) involvement, (4) quality, and (5) global practices.

Information to test the relationship between product characteristics and just-in-time purchasing dimensions was obtained by means of a survey questionnaire mailed out to nearly 400 Spanish auto component manufacturers. Fully completed questionnaires were returned for 152 firms, a relatively high return rate.

A simple correlation test was performed between the seven product characteristics and the five just-in-time purchasing dimensions, producing 35 correlation pairs.

Of the 35 correlation pairs, 18 were statistically significant in a positive direction. Two of the seven product characteristics were not statistically significant with any of the five just-in-time dimensions. The two product characteristics were volume and variability.

The product characteristic, specificity, was statistically significant in a positive direction with all of the just-in-time dimensions, except for the quality practices dimension. The product characteristic, technical complexity, was statistically significant in a positive direction with all of the just-in-time dimensions, except for the operational practices dimension. The product characteristic, fragility, was statistically significant in a positive direction with all of the just-in-time dimensions, except for the quality practices dimension. The product characteristic, economic value, was statistically significant in a positive direction with all of the just-in-time dimensions, except for the quality practices dimension. Finally, the product characteristic, essentiality, was statistically significant in a positive direction with all of the just-in-time dimensions, except for the operational and involvement practices dimensions.

In conclusion, the study has confirmed the relevance of product characteristics as determinants in whether or not just-in-time purchasing is implemented. The product characteristics—specificity, technological complexity, fragility, and economic value—stand out as the more important product characteristics.

THE EFFECTS OF PROCESS MANAGEMENT TECHNIQUES ON PERFORMANCE

The establishment of long-term partnerships with suppliers and customers improves performance in several industries such as in the automotive and computer industries, according to Christopher Ittner and David F. Larcker. Firms that employ such techniques enjoy higher returns on investment and returns on assets than those that do not.

The key result of the research was the following. The utilization of process management techniques and two profit measures, return on assets and return on investment, produce somewhat different results in separate industries. In the case of the establishment of long-term partnerships with suppliers and customers, both industries excelled. However, in other areas, such as team-based goals, the industries diverged on their results.

In the automotive industry, the greater use of process-focused improvement methods such as process value analysis and cycle time analysis, greater involvement with suppliers and customers in the strategic planning process, and management involvement in the approval of team formation and project selection are positively correlated with return on assets. However, team functions were inversely related with return on assets. This suggests that after controlling for the other process management techniques, greater use of teamwork may be counterproductive.

In the computer industry, as with the automotive industry, the greater use of process-focused improvement methods such as process value analysis and cycle time analysis, greater involvement with suppliers and customers in the strategic planning process, and management involvement in the approval of team formation and project selection are also positively correlated with return on assets. However, it is important to note that closer supplier relationships are associated with lower performance in the computer industry.

While the paper did lead to expected results in certain areas, such as the positive correlation between the greater use of process-focused improvement methods such as process value analysis and cycle time analysis, greater involvement of suppliers and customers in the strategic planning process, and management involvement in the approval of team formation and project selection, it did not fully explore in detail the disparity between the widely held belief of teamwork increasing productivity. The impact of further research in the area of teamwork in a manufacturing setting is necessary. The formation of a new company division, like Saturn, was built on the premise that team-oriented projects will produce higher returns than those not using teams. The paper suggests the contrary. It is interesting to note that the Saturn project has lost several million dollars. If the study results are correct, a reframing of manufacturing management theory and practice may be necessary.

ELECTRONIC PROCUREMENT FOR MAINTENANCE, REPAIR, AND OPERATING ITEMS

The question that this paper addresses is whether the use of electronic (Web-based) procurement of maintenance, repair, and operating (MRO) items leads to major changes in the firm's supply chain structure. Simon Croom of the University of Warwick in the United Kingdom decided to do an exploratory field survey of 32 private- and public-sector firms in order to find an answer to this question.

The method used to do the field survey consisted of semi-structured interviews with 37 individuals in the 32 firms.

The key questions posed to the interviewees consisted of: (1) current strategy relating to electronic procurement and supply chain control; (2) implications for the management and structure of the supply base; (3) impact or distribution channels; and (4) the emphasis on transactional vs. data sharing systems.

The individual process stages of a web-based procurement process were found to consist of: (1) requisition generation, (2) requisition distribution, (3) order generation, (4) order distribution, (5) expediting, (6) goods receipt, (7) invoice processing, and (8) material.

Based on the survey it was discovered that the adjusted electronic procurement costs were only one-third of the adjusted manual processing cost. Hence, apart from other benefits, the processing costs in electronic procurement are substantially lower than in manual process procurement. Another benefit, although not quantified, was that the electronic procurement process provides high visibility of the organization's many MRO transactions by individuals in the organizations, thus offering a considerable improvement in the audit trail.

A benefit of the greater visibility of total MRO procurement is the potential for supply base reduction, and the potential benefits associated with it. Benefits include consolidation economies, lower processing costs, and potential lowering of acquisition costs.

Still another benefit of electronic procurement is the wide and open visibility of the entire MRO supply base. This visibility may lead to increased outsourcing of MRO requirements now sourced from within the firm, thus leading to lower acquisition costs.

The final benefit is the potential to develop a more strategic approach to MRO procurement such as restructuring the supply chain, reducing the supply base, and eliminating existing links such as intermediaries used for travel and similar services procurement.

Finally, the above results may also affect the present configuration of the MRO supply base. Some consolidation is warranted and is bound to occur.

STATUS OF PRODUCT DEVELOPMENT IN THE ITALIAN MOTORCYCLE INDUSTRY

How can innovation and product development strategies in the Italian motorcycle industry be depicted and summarized? Researchers Moreno Muffatto and Roberto Panizzolo of Italy's Padua University developed a research model to find an answer to this problem.

The researchers developed an interview questionnaire and then contacted marketing and product development managers in the Italian motorcycle industry. Twenty-four managers representing eight firms agreed to be interviewed and subsequently were interviewed by the researchers. The eight firms represented in the study consisted of six Italians and two Japanese producers, all operating in Italy.

The study segmented the eight firms into three volume producers and five specialty producers. The five specialty producers were tightly clustered in terms of output volume and number of products offered. The three volume producers had higher output volumes than the specialty producers, as one would expect, but also generally had larger numbers of product offerings.

In terms of motorcycle size as measured by engine size, the three volume producers were all producing small motorcycles, usually referred to as scooters. Only one of the specialty producers was a scooter manufacturer. The other four specialty producers were builders of much larger motorcycles ranging in engine sizes from 600 cc to 1000 cc.

The number of product offerings by the eight manufacturers ranged from 4 to 20 products. Six of the firms had eight or fewer products. The other two firms, both volume producers, had 13 and 20 product offerings, respectively.

The researchers' major contribution was in reporting the degree of cooperation between the motorcycle manufacturers and their respective suppliers. They identified six main components or subassemblies of a motorcycle consisting of: (1) engine, (2) frame, (3) suspension, (4) dashboard, (5) transmission, and (6) aesthetics producers. For each of the six main components or subassemblies, the researchers identified which ones were either codesigned between manufacturer and supplier, how many were designed by the manufacturer (in house), and how many were designed by the supplier.

The results were then tabulated for the $6 \times 8 = 48$ components/subassemblies. Of the 48 components/subassemblies, 21 were designed in a codesign process, 22 were designed by the motorcycle manufacturers, and only five were designed by suppliers. These results indicate a considerable degree of cooperation between motorcycle manufacturers and suppliers.

The researchers also devote a considerable amount of their paper to product development and innovation strategies. They reported on: (1) product technology and product design, (2) product innovation, (3) product variety, and (4) time to market. They also looked at interfirm relationships such as partnership between firms in the industry and at the role of suppliers in the industry.

Within the firm, the researchers looked at organization roles and structures consisting of (1) large product leadership, (2) product leaders group, (3) project managers' matrix, and (4) business unit program managers.

INFORMATION TECHNOLOGY SUCCESS IN SERVICES AND MANUFACTURING

Information technology has been defined as the application of technology to business processes to gather data and create information that is valuable to managers. The importance and power of information technology (IT) as a tool for business is quite evident in its ability to transform the way business has been conducted over the past decade. IT has played a huge role in shaping the business community and the way in which the world operates. It is constantly evolving and this means that most businesses cannot compete on technology alone. The competitive advantage does not come from the latest technology a company uses, but instead from the skilled management of its information technology assets.

Researchers Amrik Sohal, Simon Moss, and Lionel Ng, of Monash University in Australia, conducted a study to compare manufacturing and services industries on a variety of practices and performance measures pertaining to information technology in an attempt to identify the differences between the two sectors. Data was collected through the use of a questionnaire survey that was conducted among Australia's top 500 businesses. A total of 81 responses were obtained, each falling into either the service or manufacturing category based on the company's profile.

Traditionally, IT has been used to reduce costs, but as new technology has become more prevalent in large corporations, there has been a move toward managing IT in a way that helps the organization achieve a competitive advantage. Many organizations miss the fact that technology alone cannot ensure a competitive advantage. It is the relationship between technology and the management of this technology that proves to be successful. Knowing this, the researchers set out to create a questionnaire survey for data gathering. They did this by interviewing the head of the IT department of a large manufacturing organization and the head of IT at a large retail organization. Based on these interviews, a draft questionnaire was developed and pilot tested with a number of IT professionals. A number of useful suggestions for improving the questionnaire were obtained from the pilot study, and these were then incorporated into the final questionnaire that was used for this study.

The subjects used for this survey were obtained from Dunn and Bradstreet's (1996) top 500 Australian companies. An additional 30 companies that represented divisions or subsidiaries of the top 500 companies were also used. The questionnaire was mailed out to the head of IT at each of these 530 companies along with a cover letter that explained the aims and goals of the survey. This resulted in a total of 81 responses or just over a 15.5 percent response rate.

The 81 respondents were then grouped into nine major industry sectors. The largest group came from the manufacturing sector (29 percent), followed by the wholesaling and retailing sectors (20 percent). For the purpose of comparing IT success within each company, the researchers combined the responses from each of the nine industries into two large sectors: service (62 percent) and manufacturing (38 percent).

After collecting all of this data, the researchers used logistic regression analyses to evaluate the practice of the manufacturing and service industries. Several sets of variables were investigated. They included the benefits provided by the implementation of IT, the extent to which IT is integrated within the organization, the impediments that detract from the success of the IT programs, and the factors that facilitate the implementation of IT. A separate logistic regression analysis was conducted for each set. In every case, the dependent variable was the primary activity being studied.

The benefits provided by the implementation of IT determined whether or not IT programs have been more or less successful in manufacturing industries and service industries. The extent to which IT is integrated within the organization focused on the company's global strategy and whether or not one sector had a larger advantage over another. Obstacles and constraints were examined and linked with factors that undermine the success of IT programs. The exact opposite was also researched and relates to those factors that are important to the success of the IT program. Participants of the survey rated the importance of 22 factors, and in each case, it was determined whether or not they varied between the two types of industries.

The results of the research show that information technology has been applied throughout all areas of both manufacturing and service industries. This sounds promising but in reality companies in both industries are only achieving a small benefit from their IT investments. The number one benefit achieved across both industries included improvements in productivity and a reduction in costs. IT is still being primarily used as a cost reduction tool rather than a strategic tool. This was much more apparent in the manufacturing sector than in the service sectors. Manufacturing organizations rely more on IT for reporting, whereas the service industries use IT as a major player in strategy development. Systems implementation and the quality of IT staff were both success factors shared by the service and manufacturing sectors.

One major point that came out through this study was the failure of organizations to recognize the possible strategic benefits of IT. Many companies did not bother to explore the possibilities of their IT department's potential. It became clear that no matter what industry you work in, the need to recognize the cooperation between the IT department and top management is key in developing a business strategy that will continue to bring profits and benefits to all members within the organization. Without such, the potential for IT success will exist but IT will never perform at an optimal level.

REFERENCES

Collins, R. S., Bechler, K. A., & Pires, S. R. I. (1997). Outsourcing in the automotive industry: From JIT to modular consortia. *Manufacturing 2000 Executive Report, 21*(1), 1–13.

Croom, S. (2001). Restructuring supply chain through information channel innovation. *International Journal of Operations and Production Management, 24*(4), 504–515.

Dong, Y., Carter, R., & Dresner, M. E. (2001). JIT purchasing and performance: An exploratory analysis of buyer and supplier perspectives. *Journal of Operations Management, 19*(4), 471–483.

Gonzalez-Benito, J. (2002). Effects of the characteristics of the purchased products in just-in-time purchasing implementation. *International Journal of Operations and Production Management, 22*(8), 868–888.

Ittner, C. D., & Larcker, D. F. (1997) The performance effects of process management techniques. *Management Science, 43*(4), 522–534.

Muffatto, M., & Pazizzolo, R. (1996). Innovation and product development strategies in the Italian motorcycle industry. *Journal of Product Innovation Management, 13*(3), 348–361.

Narasimhan, R., & Das, A. (1999). An empirical investigation of the contribution of strategic sourcing to manufacturing flexibilities and performance. *Decision Sciences, 30*(3), 683–718.

Sohal, A. S., Moss, S., & Ng, L. (2001). Comparing IT success in manufacturing and service industries. *International Journal of Operations and Production Management, 21*(1), 30–45.

CHAPTER 9

BUYER–SUPPLIER RELATIONS

This chapter presents eight papers on buyer–supplier relations. To a great extent it is an extension of the previous chapter, which focused on outsourcing and purchasing.

The first paper presents an evaluation of buying firms' strategies to improve supplier performance. Supplier improvement in terms of quality, cost, and on-time delivery is of great importance to the buyers because it affects the cost and quality of the components supplied by the suppliers as well as the timely delivery of those components. The results of the study suggest that supplier incentives clearly motivate suppliers to improve their performance in terms of the three variables described above.

The second study focuses on supply chain management and on firm performance. A survey questionnaire was utilized to solicit information on 36 supply chain practices from purchasing managers who are members of the National Association of Purchasing Management. The 36 supply chain practices were summarized into nine constructs. Statistical analysis revealed that eight of the nine constructs were statistically significant indicators of supply chain performance.

The third paper addresses the question of whether buyer/supplier involvement and purchasing strategy have an effect on strategic purchasing and firm performance. A survey questionnaire resulted in data on 175 firms. The results show that purchasing department involvement with the supplier has a statistically significant positive relationship on strategic pur-

Proven Solutions for Improving Supply Chain Performance, pages 111–122

chasing, and strategic purchasing has a positive effect on the firm's financial performance.

The fourth paper addresses the question of whether the way the supplier is selected and the degree of involvement of the buyer with the supplier have any effect on customer satisfaction and firm performance. A survey questionnaire resulted in 180 usable responses. The research confirmed that customer satisfaction in terms of price, quality, variety, and delivery as well as firm performance result from a sound evaluation of and relationship with the suppliers.

The fifth paper is a study of the effect of sunk costs on price negotiations. The subjects for this study were part-time MBA students. The experiment involved the negotiations involved in the buying and selling of a condominium. The results indicated that the agreed-on price was affected by the level of sunk costs of the seller in the property.

The sixth paper focused on the supplier evaluation process. The researchers developed a model that provided four sources or strategies of supplier evaluation. They then identified the key advantages of the four sources of supplier evaluation. They concluded that each of the four strategies has its advantages and limitations.

The seventh paper addressed supplier development through technology enhancement. The study used two case studies for its analysis. The researchers found that supplier development programs were found to be enhancing technological process capability on the part of the suppliers. These capabilities resulted in better supplier performance.

The eighth and final paper asked the question of whether information technology impacts the flow of information and the relationships between buyers and suppliers. The results showed that three of the four types of information technology are related to the frequency of communication between buyers and suppliers. Also, one of the three types of information technology improves trust between buyers and suppliers.

The eight papers covered in this chapter showed the importance of the quality and substance of the relationship between buyers and suppliers.

EVALUATION OF BUYERS' STRATEGIES TO IMPROVE SUPPLIER PERFORMANCE

Buying firms have been struggling and experimenting with ways to improve the performance of suppliers in terms of quality, cost, and on-time delivery. The Japanese model of reducing numbers of suppliers and more direct involvement with suppliers has been widely studied and emulated. Researchers Daniel R. Krause, Thomas V. Scannell, and Roer J. Calantone have studied and evaluated the above issues extensively in their *Decision Sciences* paper.

The researchers identified four supplier-related activities by the buying firm and then measured the impact of these activities on the performance of the supplier in terms of quality, cost, and on-time delivery.

The four supplier-related activities are: (1) supplier assessment, (2) direct involvement, (3) supplier incentives, and (4) competitive pressure. Supplier assessment represents in-depth evaluations of suppliers' quality, delivery cost, and technical and managerial capabilities. Direct involvement occurs when the buying firm directly involves itself in the supplier development effort and devotes resources to training and education of supplier personnel. Supplier incentives include increased volume of orders for future business if the supplier's performance exceeds that of other current suppliers. Finally, competitive pressure is applied by a buying firm to its supplier if the buying firm is able to either switch to a new supplier or is able to switch volume to an already existing supplier.

The researchers used two models to test their hypotheses about the effects of the supplier-related activities on supplier performance. In one model, they evaluated the direct effect of each of the four supplier-related activities on supplier performance. In the other model, they measured the effects of supplier assessment, supplier incentives, and competitive pressure on direct involvement. Then they measured the effect of direct involvement on supplier performance. The first model was called the direct impact (DI) model and the second model was called the mediated impact (MI) model.

They tested both models using several statistical techniques, and found that the DI model was not statistically significant and therefore had to be rejected. The MI model was found to be statistically significant after they removed the supplier-related activity, competitive pressure.

The results were based on a survey to 1,504 purchasing executives who were members of the National Association of Purchasing Management. After three mailings they received 527 usable responses consisting of 322 responses from manufacturing firms and 205 responses from service firms. Since the focus of the paper is on manufacturing, they only used the manufacturing-related responses. After discarding cases with missing data, they ended up with 279 usable cases.

The results of the study suggest that supplier assessment and supplier incentives are key enablers of supplier development for manufacturing firms. Supplier incentives clearly motivate suppliers to improve because it is rewarded with increased future business. Also, the mediating role of direct involvement through activities such as training supplier personnel play a direct and critical role in achieving supplier performance improvement.

SUPPLY CHAIN MANAGEMENT AND FIRM PERFORMANCE

Do supply chain management and supplier evaluation practices have any impact on firm performance measured in terms of product quality, overall competitive position, customer service levels, average selling price, return on assets, and market share?

The researchers, Keah Choon Tan, Steven B. Lyman, and Joel D. Wisner, addressed the above questions and arrived at some interesting but mixed results. The researchers used survey methodology to elicit information from purchasing managers who are members of the National Association of Purchasing Management. Their survey yielded 101 usable returned surveys.

The survey instrument used was a survey questionnaire that elicited information on 36 practices in a firm's supply chain. Each practice was scaled from low to high on a five-point Likert scale. Information was also elicited on six performance measures listed above. The 36 practices were segmented into 24 supply chain management practices and 12 supplier evaluation practices.

By applying factor analysis the researchers were able to reduce the 24 supply chain management practices into six practice constructs. They did the same for the 12 supplier evaluation practices and reduced them into three practice constructs. The six firm performance factors were not factor analyzed.

The six supply chain management practice constructs consisted of: (1) supply chain integration, (2) information sharing, (3) supply chain characteristics, (4) customer service management, (5) geographical proximity, and (6) just-in-time capability. The three supplier evaluation practice constructs consisted of: (1) product and delivery assessment, (2) capacity assessment, and (3) information assessment.

The researchers then did a simple correlation analysis of the nine practice constructs listed above with the six performance factors listed earlier. They found that there was no statistically significant correlation between the performance factors' overall competitive position and the nine practice constructs. The other five performance factors had statistically significant correlations with the practice constructs, although two were negative.

The performance factor, overall customer service level, had a statistically and positively significant correlation with the practice constructs, supply chain characteristics, and product and delivery assessment.

The performance factor, overall product quality, had a statistically and positively significant correlation with the practice constructs supply characteristics and just-in-time capability. The performance factor, return on assets, had a statistically significant and positive correlation with the practice construct, information assessment. The performance factor, market share, had a statistically significant and positive correlation with the practice construct, geographical proximity.

Two statistically significant negative correlations were observed between the performance factor, average selling price, and the practice construct, supply chain characteristics, and between the performance factor, market share, and the practice construct, capacity assessment.

In summary, of the eight statistically significant correlations, six were positive and two were negative. However, 46 of the correlations between the six performance factors and the nine practice constructs were not statistically significant.

PURCHASING/SUPPLIER INVOLVEMENT, PURCHASING STRATEGY, AND FIRM PERFORMANCE

This study addresses the question if the purchasing department/supplier involvement has an effect on strategic purchasing. It then poses the secondary question if strategic purchasing has any effect on the firm's financial performance.

The researchers, Amelia S. Carr of Ohio State University and John N. Pearson of Arizona State University, developed a survey questionnaire and surveyed U.S. firms whose purchasing managers held membership in the National Association of Purchasing Management. The researchers used objective data to measure the firm's financial performance so that they could compare the objective data with the subjective data supplied by the survey questionnaire.

The survey questionnaire provided data on 175 firms. Objective data was available for 41 firms surveyed by the questionnaire. The subjective data matched the objective data for 29 firms. Based on this degree of match, it was decided to use the entire survey questionnaire of 125 firms. However, 16 firms were not usable because of incomplete information. The remaining 159 firms were used in the statistical testing.

Subsequent analysis of the data on the 159 firms revealed that the sample could be split about evenly in large and small firms. The result produced 77 large firms and 82 smaller firms.

The statistical testing was done on the resulting two sets of data for large and small firms, respectively. The results confirmed that there is strong support for the posed research questions for both the small- and large-firm samples.

Purchasing department involvement with the supplier for both large and small firms has a statistically significant positive relationship with the strategic purchasing construct. This latter construct measures the degree to which the purchasing department is involved with new product design and development decisions, including concurrent engineering and strategic sourcing.

Also, strategic purchasing for both large and small firms has a statistically significant positive relationship with firm financial performance.

The above results indicate the importance of the purchasing department operating tactics and strategic involvement in new product decisions for improving firm financial performance.

IMPACT OF SUPPLIER SELECTION AND INVOLVEMENT ON CUSTOMER SATISFACTION AND FIRM PERFORMANCE

This paper addresses the question: Does the way a supplier is selected and the degree to which a supplier is involved with the buyer have any effect on customer satisfaction and firm performance?

The researchers, Michael Tracey and Chong Leng Tan of the University of Idaho, performed an empirical study to find an answer to the above question. They mailed out 2,000 questionnaires to subscribers of *Industry Week* from across the United States. They received 249 responses, of which 180 responses were usable for their statistical analysis.

The researchers used structural analysis, an accepted statistical analysis procedure, to test their model, which consisted of eight research constructs, or major components. Their general research question focused on whether supplier selection and supplier involvement had any effect on customer satisfaction. The secondary research question focused on the effect of customer satisfaction and supplier involvement on firm performance.

Customer satisfaction was measured by four separate research constructs consisting of product quality, product variety, delivery service, and competitive pricing.

For supplier selection, the researchers used two research constructs. The first was based on supplier quality, supplier reliability, and supplier performance. The second was based strictly on unit price.

The supplier involvement research construct consisted of two questions. First, are there supplier representatives on the buyer's product design teams? And second, are there joint continuous improvement programs between customers and suppliers?

Finally, the firm performance research construct consisted of four parts. First, is sales growth satisfactory? Second, is return on customer assets satisfactory? Third, is market share gain acceptable? And fourth, is the customer satisfied with his overall competitive position?

The results of the statistical analysis confirmed their general model. Specifically, general supplier selection had a positive and statistically significant effect on product quality, delivery service, and competitive pricing.

Supplier selection based on unit price had a positive statistically significant effect on delivery service. Supplier involvement had a positive and statistically significant effect on delivery service and firm performance. Product quality had a positive and statistically significant effect on delivery service and product variety. Delivery service had a positive and statistically significant effect on product variety and firm performance. Product variety had a positive and statistically significant effect on competitive pricing and firm performance. And finally, competitive pricing had a positive and statistically significant effect on firm performance.

A separate statistical analysis performed on the sample of 180 buyer firms revealed that 53 out of the 180 respondents reported that their firm performance was rated a 4.0 or higher out of 5.0. These 53 respondents agreed that their firm was performing satisfactorily in the areas of sales growth, return on assets, market share gain, and overall competitive position over the prior 3 years.

The research confirms that higher levels of customer satisfaction as measured by competitive pricing, product quality, product variety, delivery service, and firm performance result from selecting and evaluating suppliers based on their ability to provide quality products, reliability, and product performance.

THE EFFECT OF SUNK COSTS IN PRICE NEGOTIATIONS

Negotiated prices are a common way to come to agreement in many commercial exchange situations but also in such retail exchange situations as purchasing an automobile or a home. Researchers Kristina A. Diekmann, Ann Tenbrunsel, Pri Pradhan Shah, Holly A. Schroth, and Max H. Bazerman developed three scenarios of real estate exchange where previous purchase prices (sunk costs) were openly available.

Each of the scenarios was then tested with three separate groups of part-time MBA students who were motivated to participate through chances to win monetary awards.

In the first scenario, the subjects were told to simulate the purchase of a condominium. They had a choice of three condominiums and in each condominium the current owner had a different sunk cost. The subjects were asked to make an initial offer and the maximum offer they were willing to make. The resultant initial offers were significantly lower in the low sunk cost condition than in the high sunk cost condition, indicating that the subjects were influenced by the sellers' respective sunk costs.

In the second scenario the subjects were told that they were the sellers of a condominium with two seller conditions. In one case, the seller had a smaller amount invested (low sunk cost condition) than in the other case where the investment was substantially higher (the high sunk cost condition). Again the results showed that the sellers' lowest acceptable offers were significantly lower in the low sunk cost condition than in the high sunk cost condition. Keep in mind that the condominium was identical in each of the two conditions. The sellers, in this case, were influenced by their sunk costs, as the buyers were in the first scenario.

In the third scenario the subjects were told that they were to assume the role of a chief financial officer in a pharmaceutical company. Half of the subjects were to buy or build a plant to produce a new product, and the other half were to sell a plant that was no longer needed by the company. As in the first two scenarios, there was a large difference in sunk costs in the alternatives the subjects faced.

As predicted the sunk costs of the seller significantly affected the final outcome. The seller price was significantly lower in the low sunk cost condition than in the high sunk cost condition. Buyers predicted a significantly lower final price in the low sunk cost case than in the high sunk cost case. Buyers also settled for a lower price in the low sunk cost case than in the high sunk cost case.

The final results can be summarized with the statement that the negotiating parties agreed to a lower settlement for the property when the seller paid a lower price for that property in the past. In other words, the level of sunk costs by the seller affected the final settlement price.

The above results are quite rational. A buyer purchasing from a supplier, especially a regular supplier, is aware that the supplier must be able to keep his price above cost in order to survive. This awareness probably explains the behavior of the subjects in the scenarios described in the paper.

THE SUPPLIER EVALUATION PROCESS

An industrial customer is highly dependent on its suppliers of components and parts that the customer will use in its manufactured products. Similarly, any firm, whether it is product or service-oriented, depends on its suppliers for high-quality products and/or services.

Researchers Lyn Purdy and Frank Safayeni developed a framework with potential advantages and limitations of supplier evaluation processes. They essentially divided the supplier evaluation processes in two dyads. The first dyad is in terms of process or product evaluation, and the second dyad is in terms of direct or indirect evaluation.

Process and project evaluation is self-explanatory. By direct evaluation they mean evaluation of the process directly by the customer through direct observation, data collection, interviewing, questionnaires, and so on.

Indirect evaluation involves use of information collected by the customer or by other outside parties or organizations.

Although the above provides four sources of supplier evaluation, it does not mean that any one source is preferred over the other. Sometimes all sources may be utilized and in other cases one source may be sufficient. It will all depend on the context in which the supplier information is required and collected.

The key advantages to the four supplier information processes are described below. Indirect process information provides the advantages of extensive documentation, good fit for large bureaucratic customers, and a mechanism for supplier pool reduction. Direct process information provides the advantages of firsthand observation of process, holistic view of supplier organization, and opportunity for active supplier development.

The key advantages for indirect product information processes consist of summarized product information provided to the customer, minimized expense for product testing, and ability to rely on supplier reputation. And the key advantages for direct product information processes consist of firsthand knowledge of testing procedures, increased organizational learning for customer, and an additional level of product quality control.

The choice of supplier information process will be influenced by the content in which the information is required. The main one is the relationship between the customer and the supplier. If there are problems in the quality or specifications of the products supplied, one can expect that there will be a strong focus on direct product and direct process information. If the material supplied is of a standardized nature or when a new supplier is being considered for standardized materials, one would expect that just indirect product information will be the first step in the supplier information process.

Finally, there is no perfect method of supplier information collection. Each one of the four strategies outlined in this paper has its advantages and limitations. A major determinant, however, is the depth of the relationship between the customer and the supplier.

SUPPLIER DEVELOPMENT THROUGH TECHNOLOGY ENHANCEMENT

One way to enhance the supply network is through development of the capabilities of suppliers by the buying companies, which buy from the suppliers. Researchers Fiona M. Reed and Kathryn Walsh studied this through case studies in two large companies in the U.K. aerospace and defense sectors. Each company had numerous suppliers and both companies had programs for supplier development.

The common practice in supplier development was to focus on process development as opposed to product development. This result is not surprising since the common short-term objective in supplier development is the improvement of quality and the reduction in cost of operations. However, the long-term objective was to develop strong partnerships.

From the two case studies the researchers arrived at four propositions. They are:

1. Direct interventions to improve supplier technological capabilities through supplier development tend to be given lower priority than direct interventions to improve capabilities relating to quality, cost, and delivery.
2. Sustained supplier development leads to improved trust between buying firms and their suppliers, which in turn leads to increased communications of strategic technological information.
3. The communication of strategic technological information between buying firms and their suppliers is positively related to the involvement of customer engineers and technologists in the supplier development process.
4. Engineers and technologists in buying companies are less likely to participate in supplier development where it has a negative impact on individual performance measures.

In summary, supplier development programs were found to be enhancing technological capability of the small suppliers but largely in the process technology area. Also, for the process to be effective, the large buying companies need to ensure that senior technological personnel are actively involved in the supplier development process. Also, it is important that strong channels of communication are established and maintained between the buyer and the seller.

RELATIONSHIP BETWEEN INFORMATION TECHNOLOGY AND BUYER–SUPPLIER RELATIONSHIPS

There is little doubt that information technology has had a significant impact on the flow of information and on the relationship between buyers and suppliers. What is not so clear is what the types of information technology that have affected the relationship are. Professors Amelia S. Carr and Larry R. Smeltzer have investigated this question in detail. They asked three specific research questions. They are:

1. What is the relationship between the use of information technology and frequency of information shared between buyers and suppliers?
2. What is the relationship between the use of information technology and the richness of information shared between buyers and suppliers?
3. What is the relationship between the use of information technology and buyer–supplier trust?

The researchers followed three methods to find answers to the three research questions. First, they conducted an exploratory study. Second, a case study was conducted with semi-structured interviews. Third, a separate mail survey was conducted to further examine the relationship between the use of information technology and the buyer–supplier relationship.

The exploratory study was largely required to design the questionnaire that was to be used in the case study interviews. The case study involved interviews with 36 representatives from companies in 27 different industries ranging from auto parts to utilities. The mail survey consisted of a questionnaire, which was responded to by 175 companies with usable results. Statistical analysis was performed on the data derived from the study to find answers to the stated research questions.

In the case study, the interviewers were asked to describe the type of technology they had been using and the extent to which it had increased over the past 2 years. The categorization used was: (1) transactional management systems, (2) electronic commerce, (3) purchasing information management, and (4) decision support systems. Based on the case study interviews, a set of questions was prepared for use in the survey questionnaire.

After the data produced by the survey questionnaire was analyzed by statistical methods, it revealed the following information:

1. At least three of the four types of information technology are related to the frequency of communications between buyers and sellers.
2. It is not clear if the use of information technology is related to the richness of information shared between buyers and sellers.
3. Only one of the three types of information technology is related to the trust between buyers and sellers. It is the purchasing information management system.

REFERENCES

Carr, A. S., & Pearson, J. N. (2002). The impact of purchasing and supplier involvement on strategic purchasing and its impact on firm's performance. *International Journal of Operations and Production Management, 22*(9), 1032–1053.

Carr, A. S., & Smeltzer, L. R. (2002). The relationship between information technology use and buyer-supplier relationships: An exploratory analysis of the buying firm's perspective. *IEEE Transactions on Engineering Management, 49*(3), 293–304.

Diekmann, K. A., Tenbrunsel, A. E., Shah, P. P., Schroth, H. A., & Bazerman, M.H. (1996). The descriptive and prescriptive use of previous purchase price in negotiations. *Organizational Behavior and Human Decision Processes, 66*(2), 179–191.

Krause, D. R., Scannell, T. V., & Calantone, R. J. (2002). A structural analysis of the effectiveness of buying firms' strategies to improve supplier performance. *Decision Sciences, 31*(1), 33–55.

Purdy, L., & Safayeni, F. (2000). Strategies for supplier evaluation: A framework for potential advantages and limitations. *IEEE Transactions on Engineering Management, 47*(4), 435–443.

Reed, F. M., & Walsh, K. (2002). Enhancing technological capability through supplier development: A study of the U.K. aerospace industry. *IEEE Transactions of Engineering Management, 49*(3), 231–241.

Tan, K. C., Lyman, S. B., & Wisner, J. D. (2002). Supply chain management: A strategic perspective. *International Journal of Operations and Production Management, 22*(6), 614–631.

Tracey, M., &Tan, C. L. (2001). Empirical analysis of supplier selection and involvement, customer satisfaction, and firm performance. *Supply Chain Management: An International Journal, 6*(4), 174–188.

CHAPTER 10

TOTAL QUALITY MANAGEMENT

This chapter summarizes eight papers on the status of total quality management (TQM). Although this area no longer receives as much attention as it did a decade ago, it still is an area where firms can find ideas for improvement.

The first paper addresses top quality management practices, performance, and customer satisfaction. The researchers addressed the question of the impact of TQM practices on customer satisfaction and plant performance, and the impact of plant performance on customer satisfaction. As a source of data they surveyed executive MBA students who all had considerable management experience. The results showed that TQM practices in manufacturing plants are geared largely toward customer satisfaction, and only to a limited extent to plant performance.

The second paper focused on the competitive advantage of TQM adoption. The research focus was on general medical hospitals in 19 metropolitan areas. The important result of this study showed that only hospitals operating with high structured controls exhibited a strong relationship between implemented TQM practices and financial performance.

The third paper looked at the impact of quality improvement speed on quality-related costs. The focus of the study was on two automotive industry supplier plants. Data was collected covering a 5-year period. The researchers found that when quality improvement speed increases, the rate of

Proven Solutions for Improving Supply Chain Performance, pages 123–137

growth in prevention and appraisal costs will decrease but the rate of growth in failure costs will be unaffected. Also, slower quality improvement was more closely associated with reductions in quality-related costs.

The fourth study evaluated a number of TQM constructs. A construct is a collection of several items, which together provide a better measure than a single item. The study focused on the motor vehicles parts and accessories industry. A survey questionnaire was used to collect data. The study suggests that effective TQM requires that various quality management strategies act in synergy to positively affect product quality.

The fifth study looks at the effect computer-based technologies (CBT) have on quality. The study's base is Hong Kong. The researchers collected data with a questionnaire addressed to public companies and government departments. The results of the study indicated that CBT's usage to support quality in Hong Kong is low.

The sixth study addresses the relationship between just in time (JIT) and TQM. Data was collected from both U.S. and Japanese manufacturers by means of a survey questionnaire. The results indicated that the combination of JIT and TQM further heightens firm performance.

The seventh study addresses the effects of human errors on service quality. The study population was a large group of college business students. The students were asked to respond to a scenario on which they could make three kinds of errors: knowledge, rule, and skill-based. The most significant error the subjects made was rule-based, about 60 percent. Skill-based errors accounted for 30 percent, and the remaining errors were categorized as latent errors. No knowledge-based errors were made.

The eighth and final study looks at the impact of quality on learning. Data was collected from two leading manufacturing firms. The study showed that both cumulative defective and good output explain learning curve effects. The critical implication is that quality-related activities can lead to the discovery of inefficiencies in the production process.

This chapter gives an overview of the status of total quality management and how it impacts on the cost of the supply chain operation.

TOTAL QUALITY MANAGEMENT PRACTICES, PERFORMANCE, AND CUSTOMER SATISFACTION

Total quality management involves everyone in an organization in a continual effort to improve quality and to achieve customer satisfaction. Although TQM has a direct impact on customer satisfaction, does it necessarily have a direct impact on plant performance? A study done through the Department of Management at Bowling Green State University shows that TQM has a stronger impact on customer satisfaction than on plant performance.

Researchers Thomas Y. Choi and Karen Eboch of Bowling Green State University compiled a list of TQM activities from a literature survey on the subject and divided the activities into four areas: (1) process quality, (2) human resources, (3) strategic planning and control, and (4) information analysis. Executive MBA students and plant managers at six manufacturing sites in the targeted industries were interviewed while they reviewed the questionnaire to identify any language ambiguities and perceived omissions from TQM practices in manufacturing plants but not in the survey. The two researchers had three propositions for the study:

1. TQM practices have a strong impact on customer satisfaction.
2. TQM practices have a moderate impact on plant performance.
3. Plant performance has a weak impact on customer satisfaction.

The authors used a list of electronics parts manufacturers in Ohio as the target segment. The SIC code was used, which shows groups of common manufacturing processes and technologies, to identify the organizations. Plant managers were chosen to be the respondents of the survey as they are most familiar with the operating process of their plant. According to the responses to the questions regarding principal products and plant size, the sample was a general representation of the targeted industries.

The authors began the measurement analysis by first establishing the convergent validity and discriminant validity of three key factors: TQM practices, plant performance, and customer satisfaction. They evaluated the data with a statistical tool called LISREL 8.10. Process quality, human resource management, strategic quality planning, and information and analysis were all tested in order to measure their validity. These factors were then examined with plant performance with 10 indicators, and customer satisfaction with nine indicators. The validity of the scales was an important focus in the research and each of the TQM items were analyzed separately. The process quality item included maintenance issues, problem-solving activities, and quality data. The human resources item included rewards, training, idea generation, and feedback. Finally, the strategic planning item included top management commitment, mission, and product layouts. From these data, relationships between TQM practices were analyzed.

The results supported the three propositions made about TQM. The correlations of all three components of the model were positive. The results gave a correlation level of 0.63 for customer satisfaction and TQM, which is very high. Plant performance was also correlated with TQM but at a much lower level of 0.10.

The study showed that there is no correlation between customer satisfaction and plant performance. One of the many reasons for this is due to internal conflict. This means that a plant's goals for plant performance may conflict with its external goals for conformance (quality practices), and this can slow down productivity on the production line.

This study showed that TQM practices in manufacturing plants are geared more toward customer satisfaction. The implications should make us question what can be done to improve productivity of the plant while at the same time maintaining a high level of customer satisfaction. We must think of how many TQM practices are implemented because of customer requests. If these practices are solely put into place without actually analyzing how they will affect production, it is a major problem.

TOTAL QUALITY MANAGEMENT: ADOPTION AND COMPETITIVE ADVANTAGES

Many organizations have adopted TQM practices. A considerable number of organizations have failed to achieve much of a competitive advantage, yet others have achieved great success. Specific reasons for poor success rates have not been identified in the past. Recent research suggests that the degree to which total quality management is adopted by an organization is related to the achievement of competitive advantages.

Researchers Thomas J. Douglas, of Clemson University, and William Q. Judge, Jr., of the University of Tennessee, surveyed 38 chief executive officers, and 101 directors of quality control from 193 general medical hospitals in 19 metropolitan areas containing at least 15 general hospitals. Their research explored the measures taken by hospitals to implement total quality management practices and the degree to which the practices have been implemented.

The researchers asked the CEOs and directors of quality to evaluate their organization's TQM practices (TQM teamwork, quality philosophy, TQM-oriented training, customer-driven, continuous improvement, management by fact, and total quality methods), perceived financial performance relative to competitors over the previous 3 years, and structural exploration and control.

Prominent studies of the hospital industry addressed the need for control variables. Organizational size, hospital ownership, measure of market growth, and the level of competition were the control variables used in the study. Each component was evaluated based on data in well-known publications. In an effort to prove or disprove any relationships, the researchers calculated the mean, standard deviation, and correlation for each variable.

The research confirms that there is a statistically significant and positive correlation between an employee's perceived financial performance and the industry expert–rated performance. This supports the hypothesis pertaining to the degree of implementation of TQM practices in a hospital being positively related to the hospital's performance.

The researchers also evaluated the conditional effects on the relationship between TQM practices implemented and financial performance. Structural control and structural exploration were used to evaluate the conditional effects. The results of the evaluation indicated that hospitals operating with high structural control exhibited a stronger relationship between the TQM practices implemented and financial performance. Conversely, hospitals with low structural controls did not show a statistically significant relationship between TQM practices and financial performance. The result of this relationship suggests that the degree of TQM implementation and financial performance is influenced by levels of both structural control and exploration.

This research has begun to address the relationship between the degree to which total quality management practices are adopted and the gain of competitive advantages. Organizations that choose to partially adopt TQM practices will not achieve maximum benefit from the program. Complementary variables have shown that the higher the degree of implementation, the more enhanced the effect of the practices will be on competitive advantage.

THE IMPACT OF QUALITY IMPROVEMENT SPEED ON QUALITY-RELATED COSTS

For many North American firms, quality improvement has proven to be a difficult, yet essential undertaking. Customer-driven quality requirements, as well as a strongly competitive market, pressure firms to either improve quality or lose business. American companies have dropped some of the quality improvement processes, viewing them as unprofitable and slow in meeting high expectations. Yet research suggests that continuous quality improvement will result in decreased quality-related costs.

Researchers S. Thomas Foster, Jr., and Everett E. Adam, Jr., of the University of Missouri–Columbia gathered conformance-related data from five separate plants of an auto parts manufacturer. Their study tested the hypothesis that continuous quality improvement will result in an overall decrease in quality-related costs. On the other hand, a rapid speed of quality improvements will yield smaller decreases.

Foster and Adam chose the period from January 1987 through March 1992 from which to collect data. Consistency in the collection was very important, so quality checklists were used to tally the data for the 5-year period. Twenty-two years' worth of data were compiled due to the absence of 3 years of data between two different plants. Conformance cost, prevention and appraisal cost, and conformance data for each plant were divided into 22 separate 1-year data sets and placed into a table.

Statistics for speed of quality improvement were from the 1-year slopes of the data. Rates of change in prevention, appraisal, and failure costs were also provided. These were used to further analyze the relationships between these variables. Hypothesis testing relating to quality-based learning effects shown by earlier research was done using rate-of-change statistics. Observations consisted of 22 conformance slopes paired with 22 prevention and appraisal cost slopes and 22 failure cost slopes for the five plants. Least-squares regression was used to determine the relationship between rate of growth in conformance and changes in quality-related costs.

The hypotheses tested by Foster and Adam were validated. First, when speed of quality improvement increases, the rate of growth in prevention and appraisal cost will decrease. Results also confirmed that when speed of quality improvement increases, the rate of growth in failure costs will be unaffected (statistically insignificant). The next theory supported was that the association between rapid speed of quality improvement and unadjusted prevention and appraisal costs were not statistically significant. Also, the statistically significant association between the rapid speed of quality improvement and failure-related costs was validated. Therefore, rapid speed of quality improvement resulted in reductions in the rate of improvement in quality-related costs. In addition, slower quality improvement was more closely associated with reductions in quality-related costs.

In order for managers to understand and accept that quality improvement is accompanied by statistically significant organizational learning, they must also realize that the variable affecting the permanence and extent of this learning is time. The effort required to achieve quality improvement declines as a result of organizational learning over time. As prevention activities become more focused on specific problems and less general in nature, prevention related costs decline. One pitfall managers may face is increased internal failure costs because the measure of quality conformance is related to final inspection quality. If managers set goals for a reduced number of defects without having systems in place to achieve these goals, costs will increase. In summary, a slower, continuous improvement in a learning environment may be the best approach to achieve quality improvements at manageable costs.

QUALITY MANAGEMENT STRATEGY CONSTRUCTS

Over the last two decades, U.S. manufacturers have been challenged by overseas competitors to produce higher quality products at lower prices. This strategy was first introduced by W. Edwards Deming in Japan, and Japanese firms began cutting into the revenues of U.S. manufacturing firms. Many U.S. firms have adopted this TQM strategy, but their implementations have not been equally successful. Some of the failures of these U.S. firms have been the result of a shift in emphasis from improving product quality to unfocused improvement efforts, such as installing a piecemeal statistical process control (SPC) system, or starting training programs without understanding their impact on quality.

Researchers Sanjay L. Ahire and Damodar Y. Golhar, both of Western Michigan University, and Mathew A. Waller, of Arkansas University, surveyed 371 manufacturing firms. Their research questioned these firms' implementation and progress with the 12 constructs of integrated quality management strategies. They then empirically tested and validated each of these constructs and suggested what the effects of these quality management strategies are on a firm's product quality.

A strategy construct is a collection of several strategy items that together provide a better measure than a single item. As such, each of the 12 constructs listed below are made up of several items.

This study focused on one industry, the motor vehicle parts and accessories industry. They selected this industry because it has been a leader in implementing progressive quality management strategies in the United States. They surveyed plants with only 100 or more employees, and received a 37 percent response rate from the 1,000 firms to which they sent their questionnaires. They surveyed only the plant managers in their questionnaires, asking them to rate their firm on a seven-point Likert scale for each of the 12 constructs of quality management that they identified. The scale ranged from 1= Worst in Industry, to 4 = Average, to 7 = Best in Industry.

The 12 constructs of quality management that were enumerated in their survey were developed from an intensive study of the literature on the topic. Each of these constructs was then developed into scales to determine management's commitment to each of the constructs. The first construct was Top Management Commitment to TQM. This was broken down into the following six-item scale:

1. Clarity of quality goals for the organization.
2. Relative importance given by top management to quality as a strategic issue.
3. Relative importance by top management to quality versus cost.

4. Relative importance given by top management to quality versus production schedule.
5. Allocation of adequate resources to quality improvement efforts.
6. Performance evaluation of managers based on quality.

They also surveyed the managers on customer focus, supplier quality management, design quality management, benchmarking, SPC usage, internal quality information usage, employee empowerment, employee involvement, employee training, product quality, and supplier performance. They broke each of the categories into scales, much like that of top management commitment's scale.

Their research indicates that while top management acts as a driver for progressive quality management, its commitment must be translated into a set of strategies and their effective implementation. These strategies must be implemented with a clear focus on the three integral parts of the organization: customers, suppliers, and employees. Superior quality from suppliers is the most important of these parts because it is impossible to make quality products without quality raw materials. Their research also suggests that designing quality into products, ensuring in-process quality through defect prevention techniques, and judicious use of internal and external quality information as being the more important aspects of TQM. In essence, this study suggests that effective TQM requires that various quality management strategies act in synergy to affect product quality.

This study has important implications for manufacturing firms across the globe. It suggests that implementation of only a couple TQM strategies will not be a cost-effective policy. TQM requires that all of its components be implemented with complete commitment from top management for any of them to be effective. Once all of the components are in place and given complete commitment, then and only then can management expect to reap the benefits of TQM.

COMPUTER-BASED SYSTEMS TO SUPPORT OPERATIONS IN HONG KONG

Businesses realize that the key to increasing market share in the global market lies in the ability to improve their product and service quality. To prompt industry to recognize the importance of improving product and service quality and to promote the use of computers to address quality issues, the Hong Kong government initiated a quality awareness campaign at the beginning of this decade. The usage of computer-based technologies to support operations management (OM) in Hong Kong has been the subject of a number of studies during the past decade. A brief report on the latest survey conducted to examine the usage of computer-based technologies to support OM in Hong Kong follows.

The survey conducted by Ngai and Cheng represents a first attempt to examine the real-life usage of CBTs in Hong Kong in support of quality. The key objective of the survey is to examine the status of the use of computer-based technologies and to uncover the extent to which they are being used to support quality in Hong Kong industry. The survey covers many facets of quality, including quality control, quality assurance, and quality management. The findings identify great potential of using CBTs to enhance the practice of quality management in the local industry.

The research is based on empirical data collected through questionnaire surveys with quality practitioners working in different types of service and manufacturing organizations in Hong Kong. A random sample of 750 company addresses is drawn from the following sources:

- Public companies quoted in the Hong Kong Stock Exchange and other selected companies listed in the *Business Directory of Hong Kong* (1992).
- Selected departments of the Hong Kong Government from the *Hong Kong Government Telephone Directory* (1993).
- Private hospitals and other hospitals under the control of the Hong Kong Hospital Authority.

The questionnaire was first pilot-tested with practicing quality consultants and quality managers. Data were collected through a postal survey to the above-selected groups of organizations. A cover letter, which describes the objectives of the research and procedures for completing the questionnaire, and a stamp-addressed envelope were enclosed to facilitate returning of the questionnaire. A reminder was sent to nonrespondents 3 weeks after the questionnaires were mailed. Of the 750 questionnaires mailed, 179 were returned and used for analysis.

The findings indicate that CBT usage to support quality in Hong Kong is low, particularly in terms of expert systems and artificial neural networks. This is partly due to a lack of awareness of the potential of CBTs in supporting quality among their potential users, and partly because of a lack of availability of suitable software to support their use.

Another reason suggested by the surveys is that most Hong Kong manufacturing companies have moved their production facilities to the People's Republic of China or to nearby South East Asian countries, while retaining only their non-production functions such as marketing and distribution in Hong Kong.

The main findings of the survey study show that 93 percent of the respondents use office computers for word processing. The functional area that is most extensively covered by computer system applications in the surveyed organizations is accounting, with a usage rate of 85 percent. About two-thirds of the company's computers are not in a networking environment. CBT usage to support quality is at a low level in Hong Kong: Over one-third of the respondents indicate that they have no plans to use or develop them in the near future. Surveyed organizations are not fully aware of CBTs and their benefits. The most commonly cited reason by the respondents is that they perceive no advantages in using computers to support quality.

The main implications and recommendations of the study are awareness about potential of CBTs to support quality, the need for CBTs to support quality, collaboration between academics and industry in development of CBT projects to support quality, conduct more periodical survey research, and to compile more case studies. More empirical research needs to be conducted to learn how companies explore CBTs to achieve better product and service quality.

RELATIONSHIP BETWEEN JIT AND TQM

In building a world-class manufacturing facility, it is important to incorporate integrated manufacturing practices to obtain the highest desired competitive performance possible. Some beginning empirical evidence from this study seems to indicate that an integrated function between JIT and TQM exists, and these practices are indeed jointly supportive in improving performance.

The three researchers for this study were Barbara Flynn of Iowa State University; Sadao Sakakibara of Keio and Gakushin Universities in Tokyo, Japan; and Roger Schroeder of the University of Minnesota. These three academics surveyed 42 world-class manufacturing plants in the electronics, transportation components, and machinery industries from both the United States and Japan. Their research examined the overlapping relationship between JIT and TQM in terms of their practices and performance. For example, the use of TQM leads to improved JIT performance through inventory reduction and decreased cycle time.

The researchers of this study contacted plant managers of these selected facilities and set up an on-site research coordinator to help collect information and to administer surveys that would examine employees' assessments on the degree that TQM and JIT practices were utilized in their respective plant facilities. Information was gathered and incorporated into nine different questionnaires relating to performance and management practices. Each survey was specialized and targeted different groups within the facilities such as laborers, supervisors, and managers. The responses given by the employees through the surveys were measured on Likert scales ranging from 1 to 5, 1 strongly agreeing and 5 strongly disagreeing.

The research that was completed in this study does indicate that there is indeed a relationship between TQM and JIT practices on performance. Both TQM and JIT are already known to be very effective in enhancing performance in isolation from one another, but the results of this study illustrate that when TQM is coupled with JIT, performance will be heightened much further. The first interaction between TQM and JIT illustrates that TQM, while interacting with JIT, successfully reduced cycle time or reduced the number of items requiring rework. This is accomplished by lessening the amount of time it takes to rework defective items and scrap. Remember, this occurs by maintaining specific quality levels within the production process with the ultimate goal of reducing rework time. On the other hand, JIT interacted with TQM practices to improve performance by revealing areas that need process improvement and by diminishing the possibility of inventory spoilage through inventory reduction. With a reduced amount of time in inventory, finished goods are less likely to be damaged through handling and movement; thus, the quality of the product is maintained.

This study has shown that there are positive effects on performance when TQM and JIT practices are combined together. The authors believe that this is just a framework and future studies should improve on the limitations of this study, specifically in the area of how quality performance is measured. The authors do agree that there cannot be one perfect combination of JIT and TQM in the workplace. More importantly, they believe it is the manager's task to find a mix that combines these two practices together while fitting them to the organization's overall culture.

HUMAN ERRORS AND SERVICE QUALITY

A difficult challenge for service operations is creating service systems that reduce errors in the service delivery process. The challenge arises from the misunderstanding of the types of errors that arise in the performance of service functions. Service quality is commonly referred to as the variance in the service delivered to the customer and the customer's perception of the service performed. Since people predominantly perform service functions, service errors are usually due to human error.

An article written by Douglas M. Stewart and Richard B. Chase attempts to address the inadequacies in error research in various service companies, and seeks to recognize the customers' perceptions of the errors. The two authors of the article sampled customers from a population in which actions and/or decisions made by the service provider adversely affected customer satisfaction.

The population was comprised of undergraduate business students enrolled in a required introductory operations management class at a large private university. The specific population was chosen because the business students would be able to easily communicate their experiences relevant to business concepts such as customer contact, recovery actions, and process time lines. The researchers captured the data by giving the students take-home surveys in which they explained, in detail, a dissatisfying service encounter caused by human error.

The data captured was only the first step for the two researchers. The data had to be transformed into useful information, a procedure that was very time-consuming and involved quite a few phases. The two researchers first had to isolate the errors within the responses. Since many questions were in essay form, extraneous information had to be eliminated. If a respondent's comprehension of the actual process was inadequate to identify the cause of the error, expert opinions were elicited to fill in the blanks and additional information was solicited from the surveyed student. For example, if a medical error was identified, a nurse or doctor was questioned to determine the responsibility and cause of the error.

The third step in the process was to interpret the information into categorized results. A framework was used to classify the errors into skill-, rule-, or knowledge-based errors. Common activities that need little conscious intervention were handled at the skill-based level of control. For example, making a cup of coffee or driving to work becomes routine after numerous times, and requires little thought for the most part. When faced with a more unusual situation or problem, rule-based control is used to respond to the situation at hand by matching the current situation with a situation from a past experience, and basing the decision on previously made choices. If a person had had no previous experience with the situation at hand, knowledge-based control was used to decide what to do based on what they thought would yield the best result. In addition to human errors, more complex errors could occur in which the consequences of the errors were not immediately realized. Latent errors usually occur in highly complex organizations, which make them unpredictable and dangerous.

The results of the research yielded very interesting data. There were no knowledge-based errors associated with any of the errors studied. On the other end of the spectrum, rule-based errors were the most significant type of error encountered; they accounted for about 60 percent of the errors. In addition, about 30 percent of the errors were skill-based, and the remaining 10 percent of errors were latent errors.

From the conclusions made by the authors, one must conclude that many of the skill-based and rule-based errors encountered in the research could have been avoided with a combination of increased communication, technology, and training of employees. For instance, many skill-based errors discussed were results of data entry errors. The systems in which these employees work could be made more foolproof, and the employers could further train these employees to inspect data for errors to improve customer satisfaction and error reduction. To reduce rule-based errors, the companies can build powerful database systems in which solutions to previous problems would be stored for future reference. A simpler alternative to the database approach would be to train employees to communicate with each other. For example, the communication system through which physicians and airline pilots interact allows them to work as a tightly knit team, aware of each other's every move. Communication systems between employees can be set up in many instances that would reduce rule-based errors. The research done on human error opens new opportunities for productivity advancement and the understanding of how and why errors occur in organizations.

THE IMPACT OF QUALITY ON LEARNING

Learning curves have been recognized for a long time in industry and in academia for their ability to measure the rate of learning and cost reduction, but little is known about the huge difference in rates at which different firms learn. Recent studies from Japanese manufacturers support the notion that quality-related activities are a major factor explaining the difference in learning rates. Three important questions arise when the impact of quality on learning is considered: (1) How well does cumulative output of objective or good units explain learning curve effects? (2) Do effective units explain learning curve effects better than good units? (3) How should cumulative experience be represented in the learning curve model when the quality level may have an impact on learning effects?

Researchers George Li and S. Rajagopalan collected data from two leading manufacturing firms, referred to as firm A and firm B. Firm A is labor-intensive and produces tire tread by extruding and pressing rubber. Firm B is more labor-intensive and manufactures a variety of medical instruments used in critical-care units in hospitals to monitor vital signs. For both firms product quality is an important factor but for firm B it is a critical factor.

Li and Rajagopalan collected monthly data at firm A for a major product over a period of 3 years, which started at the same time of initial production. The data they collected included the output of tire treads each month, total direct labor hours worked, and a monthly count of the defective output by the quality control department. At firm B, they collected monthly data for one major medical instrument over a period of $2\frac{1}{2}$ years from the initial date of production of this product to the end of 1993. The data included the number of instruments produced each month, total direct hours used, and a monthly count of the number of defective units.

The statistical analysis was broken down into four models. The four models are learning from cumulative units, learning from good units, learning from defective units, and incorporating the quality level in the learning curve model.

The study shows that the evidence from the two manufacturing firms indicate that both cumulative defective output and cumulative good output are statistically significant in explaining learning curve effects. Also, the results indicate that defective units may be more statistically significant than good units in explaining learning effects. In firm A, which is the plant making tire tread, workers noticed one of the machines producing a high level of defects in October 1992. The workers then developed some revised procedures for loading the machine and checklists for ensuring the completion of all activities before running the machine. This reduced the number of defects as well as the average time for loading the machine. For firm B, the plant producing medical instruments, specialized assembly kits and fixtures were developed and standard operating procedures were adopted. This resulted in lower defects and eliminated wasted time searching for parts and fixtures.

This study has critical implications, that is, performing quality-related activities can lead to discovery of bugs or inefficiencies in the production process, thus providing opportunities for learning and thus gaining more knowledge about the production process. It also provides some initial evidence that cumulative production volume is not the only variable to be considered in explaining learning curve benefits, as is implicitly assumed in many economic models deriving implications of the learning curve.

REFERENCES

Ahire, S. L., Golhar, D. Y., & Waller, M. A. (1996). Development and validation of TQM implementation constructs. *Decision Sciences, 27*(1), 23–47.

Cheng, T. C. E., & Ngai, E. W. T. (1998). Computer-based technologies to support operations management in Hong Kong. *International Journal of Operations and Production Management, 7*(18), 654–660.

Choi, T. Y., & Eboch, K. (1998). The TQM paradox: Relations among TQM practices, performance, and customer satisfaction. *Journal of Operations Management, 17*(1), 59–75.

Douglas, T. J., & Judge, W. Q. (2001). Total quality management implementation and competitive advantage: The role of structural control and exploration. *Academy of Management Journal, 44*(1), 158–169.

Flynn, B. B., Sakakibara, S., & Schroeder, R.G. (1995). Relationship between JIT and TQM: Practices and performance. *Academy of Management Journal, 38*(5), 1325–1360.

Foster, Jr., S. T., & Adam, Jr., E. E. (1996). Examining the impact of speed of quality improvement on quality-related costs. *Decision Sciences, 27*(4), 623–635.

Li, G., & Rajagopalan, S. (1997). The impact of quality on learning. *Journal of Operations Management, 15*(1), 181–191.

Stewart, D. M., & Chase, R. B. (1999). The impact of human error on delivering service quality. *Production and Operations Management, 8*(3), 240–251.

CHAPTER 11

MARKETING AND SALES MANAGEMENT

Marketing- and sales management-related papers will be covered in this chapter. The marketing function is another link in the supply chain. The marketing link is typically at the end of the supply chain and therefore quite often is the driver of supply chain activities.

The first study describes the development of a taxonomy of the processes in electronic retailing. The taxonomy development is based on data collected from 255 electronic retailers. The taxonomy produced seven clusters, each describing a group of retailers. For instance, the first cluster consisted of retailers who used mail, phone, or fax to communicate with their customers.

The second study posed the question ofwhether satisfied employees produced satisfied customers. The result of the study showed that job satisfaction comes from an opportunity to grow. Under these conditions employees are more satisfied and perform to the best of their ability, and thus effectively satisfy the customer.

The third paper describes a study of customer satisfaction in Denmark. The study focused on eight industries from telecommunications to food retailing. The interesting result of the study shows that image has a strong impact on customer satisfaction. Other items that are important for customer satisfaction are customer expectations, product quality, and service quality.

Proven Solutions for Improving Supply Chain Performance, pages 139–150

The fourth study focuses on reactions of small companies to dynamic market environments. The basis of the study is data from 70 small United Kingdom companies. The research showed that companies in a declining market tend to reengineer their systems to reduce costs while companies in stable markets tend to follow the lead of large companies.

The fifth study describes product variety and price sensitivity with a focus on alignment of marketing and manufacturing strategies. The empirical setting was a chemical manufacturing plant. The two parameters evaluated were price sensitivity and batch volume. The conclusion of the study shows that proper alignment of marketing and manufacturing strategy can be a great determinant of whether competitive advantage can be gained.

The sixth study evaluates intimate computer-based exchanges and self-disclosure. The results of this study are based on the outcomes of two psychological experiments where the subjects were college students. The results of the study show that it is possible to perform efficient customer profiling and build long-term customer relationships and develop more personalized products.

The seventh paper describes a study of the impact of the national economic, social, and cultural environment on price-quality strategies. The data for the study were obtained from senior executives of 57 companies in four major consumer product industries, followed by a survey of 120 MBA students at an American university. The study demonstrates the need for companies to know the environment in which they are marketing their products.

The eighth and final study describes an improved quality function deployment (QFD) model. QFD is able to translate the desires of customers into product design and engineering characteristics. The researchers made certain modifications to the traditional QFD model to make it easier to use. The modified model will enable firms to have a better understanding of what leads to more customer satisfaction.

The summaries below provide the reader with an appreciation of how subtle changes in marketing and sales management can improve firm performance.

TAXONOMY OF PROCESSES IN ELECTRONIC RETAILING

This paper describes the development of a taxonomy of service processes in business in electronic retailing. The taxonomy consists of eight service process configurations.

Professors Heim and Sinha, respectively from Boston College and the University of Minnesota collected data from 255 electronic food retailers and then applied cluster analysis to map the electronic retailers on the process configurations.

The authors point out that flexibility is the most important strategic capability that should be considered for electronic retailing. Flexibility enables firms to sense and respond to evolving customer needs in a quick and timely way, adapt to technology shifts and respond to competitor actions.

A framework is developed for examining the electronic service process flexibility dimensions relevant to electronic retailers. The flexibility dimensions consist of (1) product and customer interactions, (2) intraservice process flexibility or processes of an individual electronic retailer, and (3) interservice process flexibility, or processes connecting multicompany alliances.

The three flexibility dimensions in turn consist of subdimensions. Product and customer interactions consist of: (1a) ability to vary products within a specified period of time, (1b) ability to offer secure transactions, and (1c) ability to changing the ordering and paying processes. Intraservice process flexibility consists of: (2a) ability to respond to demand at the aggregate level, and (2b) ability to add or subtract from the product mix over time. Interservice process flexibility consists of: (3a) ability to manage and modify partnership to participate in other networks, (3b) ability to manage partnership to allow other companies to participate in the company's own networks, and (3c) ability to manage partnerships to participate in other companies' networks and allow other companies to participate in a company's own network.

The authors then developed a conceptual classification scheme for service processes on the basis of degree of flexibility service stages measured from lowest to highest. The lowest service stage was called customization and joint allowance service customization, the service stage with the highest level of flexibility.

The collected data from the 255 electronic retailers was then used to form clusters on the basis of the degree of flexibility service stages and on the service process configurations.

The results of the cluster analysis produced seven clusters. Clusters 1, 2, and 3 were in the service kiosk service stage, clusters 4 and 5 in the service mart service stage, and clusters 6 and 7 in the mass service customization service stage.

On the basis of service process configuration, cluster 1 consisted of mail, phone, or fax retailers; cluster 2 consisted of phone-only retailers; cluster 3 consisted of retailers using unsecured order forms; cluster 4 consisted of retailers using secured order forms; cluster 5 consisted of retailers with a secure shopping cart, cluster 6 consisted of service mart retailers; and cluster 7 consisted of retailers classified as mass service customizers.

The authors conclude their paper with the statement that the developed taxonomy will be able to aid researchers and practitioners in comprehending the complex mix of technologies that provide the service processes in electronic retailing and their association with customer satisfaction.

DO SATISFIED EMPLOYEES PRODUCE SATISFIED CUSTOMERS?

When dealing with customers and employees, managers wonder if satisfied employees directly correlate with satisfied customers. It seems as though it would make sense. A recent study found a relationship between Hertzberg's two-factor theory and quality implementation.

Researchers Dawn Utley, Jerry Westbrook, and Susan Turner conducted a study in 1997. They conducted a survey in nine organizations to see if such a relationship existed. The hypothesis was that organizations that motivate employees are much more likely to emphasize the Hertzberg theory to improve performance. In the study, it was determined that lack of job satisfaction was directly correlated to lack of advancement or alternatives.

Part of the project was a questionnaire that was designed to assess the level of success in implementing a quality management program. The responses were similar among the nine companies that participated. The second part was also a questionnaire designed to collect data for the Hertzberg evaluation. All responses were then grouped together to see if there was a correlation.

The result that was most interesting to the researchers was that job satisfaction comes from an opportunity to learn and grow. If this condition were prevalent, the employee would be more satisfied, and more likely to perform to the best of their ability and effectively satisfy the customer.

CUSTOMER SATISFACTION AND LOYALTY IN DENMARK

As business becomes more and more competitive, the problem that most managers face is how to analyze what drives customer satisfaction. Companies gain more market share mostly on the basis of how customers perceive their products or services. Managers who have a profound knowledge about what drives customers and loyalty can help companies optimize the allocation of limited resources. This knowledge will thereby have consequences for the company's priority-setting and strategy development.

To study the above, a study was performed in Denmark by researchers Martenson, Gronholdt, and Kristensen. The study includes eight industries, consisting of the telecommunication industry, the soft drinks industry, the fast-food restaurant industry, banks, and supermarkets.

The study shows that a strategy is successful if it creates satisfied and loyal customers mainly by having a good service-minded image. Industries such as retail banks and soft drinks show that image has a strong impact on customer satisfaction.

The research shows that for areas such as cable TV and supermarkets, the four drivers of customer satisfaction are expectations, image, product quality, and service quality. Of these four, image is the main driver for customer satisfaction. Expectation is the least important for customer satisfaction. The consequences of image being the main driver for satisfaction are that companies within these industries should use this result in their future strategic planning and priority setting. This can be accomplished by devoting special attention to marketing communication and to what the company is achieving by satisfying the needs and the expectations of the local, national, and international community.

The research confirms that a company's success comes from its strategy for promoting its products or services. No matter what industries the business is in, large or small, the market reactions are the same. The largest impact on loyalty comes from image, followed by service. Other drivers are not as important as image because a product's quality has only a minor impact on loyalty. Products can be easily duplicated by competitors.

In conclusion, the main purpose for the study is to emphasize that companies should focus more on drivers that lead to customer satisfaction when they are implementing strategies. The point is to initiate or continue activities, improving the company's image, such as image advertising and sponsorship, and support activities at the local and national level. Companies should keep up to the industry standard regarding product and service quality by implementing continuous improvement activities. These improvement activities will also have a positive influence on image.

REACTIONS OF SMALL COMPANIES TO A DYNAMIC MARKET ENVIRONMENT

When the market environment in one's line of business changes, what can management do to respond to this problem? Reengineering is one approach that can be used. By identifying and streamlining processes that add value to your product, one can make an entirely new product or modify the original product. Or management can decide to adjust its production operations to reduce costs. But what is the best change to make when the market environment rapidly changes?

Rodney McAdam, a Senior Lecturer at the School of Management for the University of Ulster, did a study on 70 small companies. He wanted to find out what these companies did to improve their processes and reengineer their systems to figure out what the best scenario is to follow if the market environment changes rapidly.

The researcher selected companies that had between 50 and 100 employees, because he felt that with a company this size they are consistently growing, but no longer in the embryonic stage. These companies functioned in different markets that were constantly changing and had production systems that were still developing. These 70 companies were then narrowed down using a process of putting them through a filter. Eight companies were selected from the filter results.

The research results showed that companies that are in a declining market tended to reengineer their systems in an attempt to reduce costs, while companies in stable markets tended to follow the lead of large companies. Management generally felt that manpower training and development of new processes were important to improve their products. They also attempted to enter new markets with their products, to reduce lead times in their production, and to develop new products. The companies also had a strong focus on the role of leadership.

These findings suggest that companies should always be aware of their market environment. They should always understand and follow the market that they function in, so that if it changes they know they have to make an adjustment. The best way to do this is to plan ahead. Companies should think about how they can reengineer their systems when the market environment changes. If the market changes rapidly, a prepared company will have a plan on how to improve their system or to fix the problems that arise. The best reactions are to try to reduce costs in the production cycle, have strong leadership in the company, extend existing products, and create new products.

Reacting in the above ways ensures the continuation and the growth of the company.

PRODUCT VARIETY AND PRICE SENSITIVITY

There has been a trend recently in manufacturing firms toward product variety. This is a result of catering to more specific customer needs. To meet this specialized demand, more production lines are needed with less volume for each. More batches and changeovers are needed. But are manufacturing firms prepared to accommodate this new business trend to the point where the increased sales revenues from satisfying the new demands comfortably exceed the increased manufacturing costs needed to meet these new demands? Put another way, is a financial impact felt from misalignment of marketing strategies with manufacturing strategies?

William L. Berry of the Ohio State University faculty of Management Sciences and Martha C. Cooper of the Ohio State University faculty of Marketing set out to observe this potential misalignment by conducting exploratory field testing of a proposed marketing–manufacturing framework and methodology at a chemical manufacturer's plant.

The framework compared the price sensitivity of a particular product (marketing) with the batch volume used to make different products at the facility. Both variables were dichotomized into low and high categories, yielding a 2 × 2 grid. Along the vertical axes of the grid, price sensitivity was measured from low to high. The horizontal axes measures batch volume also from low to high.

The ideal situation for a company is the case where batch volume is low and price sensitivity is also low. Low batches require less changeover cost, and low price sensitivity means that the prices can be raised significantly without significant loss in demand. This combination will maximize profits. The two cases where either price sensitivity is high with batch volume low or the opposite are manageable but not ideal situations. The case where both price sensitivity is high and batch volume is high should be avoided. High batch costs coupled with high market-based prices do not allow for high margins. This situation is most likely to result in negative outcomes.

The researchers created a number of hypotheses and conducted regression analysis to see at what levels and where on the framework the company studied was operating.

Results of the research showed that production batch size has a major impact on productivity. Also, the proposed methodology can indicate those process conditions where variables such as batch size do not affect manufacturing performance.

The conclusion that can be drawn from this study is that the proper alignment of marketing and manufacturing strategy can be a great determinant of whether competitive advantage can be gained through a strategy of increased product variety. Batch size and price sensitivity must be analyzed, however, to determine if the two strategies are aligned.

COMPUTER-BASED INTIMATE EXCHANGES AND SELF-DISCLOSURE

While there is substantial evidence that, on a person-to-person level, intimate self-disclosure can be triggered by using reciprocity principles, is this also true for the use of a computer instead of a human as the questioner? Moreover, can a computer elicit intimate information from a person? What are the patterns in such a scenario and what are the effects on follow-up interactions?

Assistant Professor Yongme Moon of Harvard University conducted two experiments with a total of 84 undergraduate students. The objective of the first experiment was to test a hypothesis that people tend to disclose more intimate information about themselves when the computer interacts in a human manner. Sixty students participated in this experiment. The second experiment was designed to give information about how an intimate self-disclosure affects subsequent attitudes and behaviors. Twenty-four students participated in this experiment.

The first experiment consisted of two parts. The first part contained four questions, while the second contained eleven questions. The questions were put together into six different interview formats (with reciprocity, long, without reciprocity) and all of them either in a gradual manner (following proper social sequence of disclosure) or abrupt (not following this sequence). Reciprocity means that the computer disclosed some information about itself/himself and then showed the question: "Sometimes this computer is used by people who don't know how to operate it. It ends up crashing and having to reboot. What are some of the things that make you furious?" Without reciprocity, just the question was presented. Finally, the long version was a general introduction to the question and then the question: "You will now be presented with the next question in the interview. This question is about the things that make you furious. What are some of the things that make you furious?" Each of these three basic interview formats were now organized either with or without gradualism. The 60 students were then interviewed by the computer with one of the test formats (meaning 10 students per format).

Experiment two consisted of three parts. In the first part, an interview format from experiment one was applied (reciprocity questioning in the gradual manner). The next part was a paper-and-pencil puzzle (for distraction purposes), and the last one employed a shopping task. The students were split into two groups—one group got the same computer to work with for parts one and three, whereby the other group had to do the parts on two different computers. The procedure required that the students finish part one at the computer. Afterwards they were taken to another room to finish the paper-and-pencil part. Once they completed this part, they returned to the first room, using either the same or another computer to finish part three.

The results for both experiments were very interesting. They suggest that computers can be used to simulate person-to-person interaction. While the quality of the disclosures varied only slightly between the non-reciprocity and the long format, they varied much compared to the reciprocity approach. The best results were gained by employing the reciprocity approach for both the gradual and abrupt formats. However, looking at the overall results, the study indicates that the qualitatively best results can be gained by employing the reciprocity-gradual format. This means that the interviewed students disclosed the most intimate information by getting a self-disclosure from the computer and got interviewed in a socially appropriate sequence.

The second experiment delivered also remarkable results. The research paper puts it into the following words: "participants in the same-computer condition had higher purchase likelihood scores ... than participants in the different-computer condition." This means that the particular candidate established some kind of connection with the computer he or she was working on. In the same computer approach this relationship led to a better buying likelihood.

Whether these findings could be validated in a real world setting (where the interview takers do not know that it is an experiment) or not is still questionable. Even the author notes that drawing conclusions from the findings should be done with caution. But one thing becomes obvious by looking at the reciprocity setting. The interview taker was given a context for each of the questions. As a result, the responses were qualitatively and quantitatively better, compared to responses without the particular context (e.g., nonreciprocity setting). Since humans act normally in a particular context, it would be a logical next step if this behavior would also apply to a computer. But, this has still to be shown by research.

The implications for the general business world are tremendous. With these techniques, it will not only be possible to perform efficient customer profiling in a company, but also to build long-term customer relationships and build more personalized products. On the other hand, it remains questionable to what degree these techniques should be used from a moral point of view. Whether completely backed by research or not, a company can already make use of these findings. Since Internet surveys are nearly at no cost for the company, one could design a survey in a context-question format. In theory, the quality of the responses should improve in this setting. This can be determined by comparing results of old surveys to the data derived from the new survey. It remains to be seen if the quality improves in this real world setting.

PRICE/QUALITY PRODUCT STRATEGIES AND NATIONAL ENVIRONMENT

With increasing competition and globalization, companies find it harder to achieve high profits. Companies in all industries choose their corporate strategy for any number of reasons. Do certain strategies work best in certain situations? This research attempts to prove a relationship between a firm's price/quality ratio to the strategic fit of the country in which that firm is located. A strategic fit is the best strategy to adopt in a given country depending on its competitive advantage, current products, and other environmental factors.

The researchers who conducted this study were Lance Eliot Brouthers of the University of Texas at San Antonio, Steve Werner of the University of Houston, and Erika Matulich of the University of Tampa. They sent questionnaires to CEOs of United States, Japan, and European Union firms (consisting of Italy, Great Britain, The Netherlands, Sweden, France, and Germany) and surveyed MBA students. This data collection process was to get information about the quality of products made by a select group of firms.

The firms selected were in one of four industries: consumer electronics, automobiles, tires, and beverages. The CEOs were expected to respond by commenting on their competitors' price/quality as perceived by the CEOs. Over 70 percent of the surveys were returned in completed form and consisted of 57 firms. Next, they surveyed 120 MBA students at an American university on their perceived price and quality of products from the 57 firms. If a firm's price/quality perceptions were not the same between the students and the CEOs, then the firm was not included in the final sample. This procedure reduced the number of firms to 46. The researchers used the *Fortune 500* database to collect price data for a 14-year period from 1982–1995 and used pooled cross-sectional and time series analysis. This type of analysis is used since the sample is across different firms and covers many years.

They ran a regression analysis on this data using return on sales, return on assets, and growth rate as dependent variables. They also used dummy variables for the year, region, and industry.

Price/quality relationship can be segmented into three main categories. These are economy, value, and premium. Economy is a low price to low quality relationship, premium is high price to high quality, and value is low price relative to competitors and high quality relative to competitors. Their hypotheses are that certain countries have innate price/quality relationships for various reasons. Intuitively, these make sense and are based on such things as costs, demand, competition, corporate climate, and politics. The other hypothesis they made was that these advantages will lessen over time due to better competition and globalization.

According to the researcher's hypotheses, Japan has a superior value strategy, the European Union has a premium strategy, and the United States has an economy strategy. When firms follow a strategy that is aligned with the above list, it tends to perform better than the competition that is not aligned in the same manner. Sixty-three percent of the firms sampled show a significant positive relationship with the home country strategic fit defined earlier. Also, only 33 percent of those firms would fit by chance. Thus, this shows that most of the firms perform better than others when aligned with the strategic fit of their home country. They also found that the idea of strategic fit was less accurate in the last 5 years of the sample. This provides evidence that their second hypothesis is correct.

This study demonstrates the need for companies to know their environment. However, this is only a starting point. Once the firm knows which price/quality strategy will best fit with its environment, it is up to the managers to decide if that strategy should be followed. The company should not blindly decide to follow a strategy without further analysis, even if 70 percent of the firms that use it perform better than average. For example, in Japan where a high quality strategy seems to fit best, there is still a need for low price/low quality products, even if that demand is small. If a company can be the absolute low cost provider, then it is possible that the company can achieve better than average returns. This study is only a place to begin and companies need to take into account all factors, internal and external, before making a strategic decision.

AN IMPROVED QUALITY FUNCTION DEPLOYMENT MODEL

To advance in the competitive market, companies have adapted the usage of total quality management (TQM). One of the total quality management methods is quality function deployment (QFD), which is used to translate customer needs and wants into technical design requirements by integrating marketing, design engineering, manufacturing, and other relevant functions of an organization.

The basic concept of QFD is to translate the desires of customers into product design or engineering characteristics, and subsequently into parts characteristics, process plans, and production requirements. Each translation uses a matrix, called the house of quality, for identifying customer requirements (CRs) and establishing priorities of design requirements (DRs) to satisfy the CRs. The downside to QFD is it does not calculate the priorities of DRs and does not determine appropriate DRs for a design problem. Taeho Park and Kwang-Jae Kim introduced a modified QFD model to correct this problem.

The modified QFD model gives a new interpretation to QFD and employs a new rating scheme for the relationship between CRs and DRs using a very commonly used multi-attribute decision method.

There are five phases to calculate QFD. The first phase is to collect the data, the second phase is to calculate the importance of CRs, the third phase normalizes the rating relationship between CRs and DRs, the fourth phase calculates the importance of DRs, and the last phase selects the appropriate DRs.

Studies showed that there is much concern on indoor air quality for non-industrial buildings. Designers, owners, and operators have tried to minimize unwanted air infiltration because of the high cost involved. The Business Tower building at San Jose State University contained such a problem. Employees complained of stuffiness, dust particles, poor ventilation, odors, and flies. There are many recommendations suggested to improve the mechanical Business Tower heating, ventilation, and air conditioning operating system. To find the most appropriate improvement to use for the Business Tower, the new QFD model was used. A survey was conducted to collect data on the building ventilation problem, then these data were used for the QFD model. According to the results, upgrading an air delivery system is most important for improving the building occupants' satisfaction.

By using the modified quality function deployment model, firms will be able to have a better understanding of customer satisfaction. The modified prioritization procedure employs a multi-attribute decision method for assigning relationship ratings between CRs and DRs instead of a conventional relationship rating scale. Utilization of the new QFD model allows firms to have a more efficient management system.

REFERENCES

Berry, W. L., & Cooper, M. C. (1999). Manufacturing flexibility: Methods for measuring the impact of product variety on performance in process industries. *Journal of Operations Management,17*(3), 163–178.

Brouthers, L. E., Werner, S., & Matulich, E. (2000). The influence of triad nations environments on price/quality product strategies and MNC performance. *Journal of International Business Studies, 31*(1), 39–62.

Heim, G. R,. & Sinha, K. K. (2002). Service process configurations in electronic retailing: A taxonomy analysis of electronic food retailers. *Production and Operations Management, 11*(1), 54–74.

Martenson, A., Gronholdt, L., & Kristensen, K. (2000). The drivers of customer satisfaction and loyalty: Cross-industry findings from Denmark. *Total Quality Management, 11*(5), 5544–5554.

McAdam, R. (2002). Large scale innovation—Reengineering methodology in SMEs: Positivistic and phenomenological approaches. *International Small Business Journal, 20*(1), 33–52.

Moon, Y. (2000). Intimate exchanges: Using computers to elicit self-disclosure from consumers. *Journal of Consumer Research, 26*(3), 323–339.

Park, T., & Kim, K. (1998). Determination of an optimal set of design requirements using house of quality. *Journal of Operations Management, 16*(4), 569–579.

Utley, D., Westbrook, J., & Turner, S. (1997). The relationship between Hertzberg's two-factor theory and quality improvement. *Engineering Management Journal, 9*(3), 5–13.

CHAPTER 12

MANUFACTURING MANAGEMENT—DOMESTIC

This chapter covers the area of manufacturing management in North America. Manufacturing, whether done internally or externally (outsourced), is an important and critical area in the supply chain.

The first paper describes a production and distribution planning model. The model is essentially a decision support system (DSS) for production and distribution planning where the sellers and buyers are electronically linked for frequent data exchange. The results show that implementation of such a model could significantly increase throughput and reduce inventory levels.

The second paper is a study of the impact of random production disruptions on manufacturing process costs. To minimize the impact of these disruptions, optimal safety stock levels need to be determined in order to minimize total production cost. This was a study that used mathematical modeling and the above is essentially the outcome of their study.

The third study describes production scheduling and enterprise resource planning (ERP) systems. The objective of the study was to design a system that can select and propose the best computer-based scheduling model for every possible combination of production systems and production characteristics. They evaluated several existing computer-based scheduling systems and concluded that it is difficult to arrive at one scheduling model that fits all possible applications.

Proven Solutions for Improving Supply Chain Performance, pages 151–164

The fourth paper describes an evaluation of flow shop scheduling rules. The three rules the researchers evaluated were the greatest total processing time (GTPT) rule, the least total processing time (LTPT) rule, and the random assignment rule. Using computer simulation, the researchers came to the conclusion that there was no significant difference in the performance of the three rules.

The fifth paper is a study of flexibility management practices and performance. A survey questionnaire was sent to manufacturing managers and 158 usable responses were received. The results of the study show that certain work force management practices and performance are related to flexibility in terms of product variability in order to achieve a competitive edge.

The sixth paper also addresses flexibility but as process mobility. The study is based on the definition of flexibility as the ability to change quickly among a group of known products. The main conclusion of the study was that flexibility is affected more by human aspects than by technological aspects. Whatever management deems as important will receive the attention of the work force.

The seventh study addresses the implications of process commonality. What are the benefits of high process commonality, and what are the sources of process commonality. The researchers concluded that process commonality has managerial implications because it has a major impact in such areas as product/process selection, scheduling, lot sizing, just-in-time implementation, and quality.

The eighth paper describes the benefits of group technology. Group technology is a philosophy based on the principle of grouping similar parts into families, which then leads to economies in the manufacturing process. The advantages of group technology are especially important in cellular manufacturing.

The ninth and final paper is a study of advanced manufacturing technology (AMT) and organizational culture. The researchers collected sample data from 97 manufacturing plants in 11 industries. They examined how organizational culture is related to the outcomes associated with AMT implementation. The results of the study indicate that there is some correlation between organizational culture and AMT implementation. However, the data reveal the link is not convincing.

This chapter shows the types of studies that continue to appear in the manufacturing management research journals. They all have some relevance to the manufacturing sector.

A PRODUCTION/DISTRIBUTION PLANNING MODEL

In today's competitive business world, every company is trying to get the upper hand. The problem described in this article is that many companies have invested in information technology (IT) and have pushed for faster and better technology, but this competitive advantage does not necessarily let companies get the upper hand.

Researchers Sudhir Mallya and William G. Bistline have proposed a DSS for production/distribution planning where the sellers and buyers are electronically linked for the frequent exchange of important data.

The DSS calculates the production requirements of all products at a plant for a week. Production requirements then determine plant deployment needs. The decision-makers have the ability to make any changes to the calculations if they see fit. The DSS then recalculates the production/distribution plan based on the modifications made.

After collecting information from different sources, they enter the data into Microsoft Excel spreadsheets, which then are used to update the database. Excel is used to overcome compatibility problems between different software applications that are used between each source. Also, imported models for forecasting are included in the Excel application.

The solution from the linear planning model is then presented to the decision-makers. The decision-makers use the data to create reports. Using these reports helps the decision-makers in doing "what-if" analysis.

This DSS was tested using real data from a large firm. The firm distributes multiple products to retail outlets such as Wal-Mart, K-Mart, and Target. The results were very positive. The results showed that a company could significantly increase the annual throughput and reduce the average inventory level with this DSS. These positive results would not increase costs for the company. Also, by doing a "what-if" analysis, the company could increase the annual throughput. Another positive aspect of this DSS is that the decision-maker does not need to understand the DSS completely. After testing this DSS, decision-makers gave favorable comments on the data the DSS provided.

This DSS uses production planning and inventory control decisions but does not use vehicle routing decisions in the system. A potential improvement would be to use a multiple-period production-planning model with a single-period distribution model. Development of another system to integrate production planning, warehousing, and distribution decisions under one DSS to solve a multiproduct facility problem would be another possible extension of this DSS.

IMPACT OF RANDOM PRODUCTION DISRUPTIONS ON MANUFACTURING PROCESS COSTS

As manufacturing organizations increasingly move toward just-in-time (JIT) production processes and total quality ideals in order to maintain their competitive edge, they become more and more susceptible to negative impacts arising from production, inventory, and supply system disruptions, such as in the form of machine (or parts) failure, labor strikes, and the general unavailability of raw materials. For this reason, the appropriate determination of optimal safety stock levels is extremely important in minimizing total production cost.

The significant results of the research suggested that in unreliable productions systems (those subject to random disruption), reducing setup cost is less effective in reducing total operating cost and results in higher optimal safety stock levels.

In addition, setup costs decrease as safety stock increases. Further research indicated that the average total cost rate is more sensitive to the safety stock levels than to the target stock buildup levels. It was observed that as the setup costs increased, the system became more reliable.

Researchers Moinzadeh and Aggarwal analyzed an unreliable bottleneck facility that was subject to random production disruptions. The assumptions were that the production rate, demand rate, and restoration time were constant while the time between breakdowns was exponentially distributed, the production setup cost and/or setup time was positive, and the excess demand was backordered. For measuring reliability of the production system, expressions for the operating characteristics of the system were developed within a production policy in which production was started if on-hand inventory fell to a specified threshold level (and the process was idle and capable) and was stopped if either on-hand inventory reached a maximum specified level or a breakdown occurred. Finally, a heuristic, or general guideline, was devised and implementing it produced near optimal results with respect to total costs. In addition to the parameters set forth in their experiments, the authors extend their approach regarding the issue of random disruptions to the cases of production start-up costs after a breakdown being lower than the setup cost and of a positive internal production time being present in the system.

There has been considerable research and literature on production and inventory control. Much of it has involved the impact of uncertainties in production, such as in the form of uncertain demand, lead times, process quality, process yields, and manufacturing capacities. Other research has centered on unreliable production systems in which supply mechanisms fail, resulting in lost sales, or in which random breakdowns occur, resulting in lost excess demand. The inherent limitations in such models were, respectively, that lost sales were possible even when the system had stock on hand and safety stock could accumulate unchecked. The research attempts to address some of the shortcomings of previous research and set the course for further study. Extensions of the research model may include cases in which demand is lost, demand and/or production rates are random, and the duration of the disruption in production is variable.

PRODUCTION SCHEDULING AND ERP SYSTEMS

Currently, in a competitive manufacturing environment, companies face a number of challenges such as achieving high efficiency, customer satisfaction, reliable delivery dates, high quality of products or services, and quick response to customers' demands. Recently, to help improve their efficiency, firms have adopted enterprise resource planning (ERP) solutions. ERP is a software system where the integration of operations, business processes, and functions, through common data processing and communications protocols, are enabled. However, most of these systems do not support the production scheduling process that is of great importance in today's manufacturing and service industries. Some current problems associated with current ERP scheduling systems result from the fact that scheduling uses mathematical techniques that may vary according to the machine environment. In modern industries there are many different combinations of machine configurations and production systems, job processing is often subject to unique constraints, and many different types of objectives are important in operations scheduling.

Researchers Kostas S. Metaxiotis, John E. Psarras, and Kostas A. Ergazakis of the Institute of Communications and Computer Systems, National Technical University of Athens, in Greece, conducted a study of current ERP intelligent system qualities and drawbacks. They mainly used the results of several highly acclaimed surveys on the effects of expert systems (ESs) in manufacturing among the largest industrial companies in the United States. This study included responses from 98 companies listed in the Fortune 500 with a mean number of employees of 19,000 and average gross annual sales of $6.2 billion. In this study, scheduling emerged as the most common application area of expert systems. Some of these systems included: OPIS; PEPS; PATRIARCH, a hybrid expert system developed at the University of Houston; neural networks; and genetic algorithms to deal with the different modes of scheduling in manufacturing and job shop scheduling problems.

There were three stages in the researchers' study upon which they based their solution to the current ERP and ES shortcomings. The first stage was the acquisition of high-level knowledge concerning the different approaches (dispatching rules or sequencing algorithms) that are used in production scheduling. This knowledge was acquired through interviews with experts and from specialized sources, but the main source was the latest papers published during the period from 1980 until May 2001.

The second stage was the evaluation and selection of the approaches that would finally be used in the system. The main criterion for this selection was the reported efficiency of each approach through an experimental procedure in real problems and in combination with the running time of its application. High-quality research papers were used for the evaluation and for the final selection of the most appropriate algorithms and rules.

In the third and final stage, each approach was classified and attributed to each particular problem. This attribution has been done after a thorough examination of the latest experimental results and conclusions. The main purpose of this is to determine the best utilization of the shop with different objectives, such as the minimization or maximization of these objectives.

The objective of their study was to design a system that can select and propose the best scheduling model for every possible combination of production systems and production characteristics. This system is designed to contain as many production systems and characteristics as possible. However, for many scheduling problems there are no solutions. So they designed the system in a way that prevents the user from choosing any possible combination by limiting the number of choices the user can use. At each stage the data provided by the user is evaluated by the system and in the next stage it allows the user to choose among the data that will lead to a feasible combination. The experimental system showed reduction of the total number of late production orders by 18 percent, reduction of the total number of early production orders by 6 percent, and an increase in the average machine utilization rate by 7 percent. It also increased flexibility by using various scheduling criteria and gave the production manager dynamic intervention in the proposed production schedule in order to make potential modifications.

There are many positive implications of this study for the manufacturing community. Since production scheduling is the most difficult part of production planning, the introduction of such a system would be of great benefit to any industry needing complex production planning. With the use of a knowledge-based or expert system incorporated into a customer ERP system, many complex scheduling problems could be handled. Because of the many variables found within the framework of production scheduling, this process can be so complicated that it is almost impossible to optimize production planning without the use of an in-depth software package. The authors, in cooperation with the Greek software house Singular SA, are now working for the integration of such a module in commercial ERP packages. This software has the potential to be very useful because of the complexity of the problem. However, no software package will have all the right answers or be all capable. Human intuition will always be important in the production planning process.

EVALUATION OF SCHEDULING RULES

It is generally well accepted how important scheduling is to operations management. Scheduling problems exist in all types of industries and have different levels of complexity. How one deals with scheduling problems is to model them as a job shop. There are two types of job shop models. First, there is the general job shop model, where there are no restrictions in the form of technological constraints. Each job may be processed through the plant independently of any other job. Second, there is the flow shop model, which is a special case of the general job shop. This model arises when all jobs share the same technological order. In other words, all jobs must sequence through the plant in the same order.

The researchers Caffrey and Hitchings describe how the flow shop model is a very difficult one in regards to scheduling. Basically, as the number of *n* jobs goes across *m* machines, the problems associated with scheduling these jobs and machines goes up. It also talks about how flow shops could also be looked at as a network of queues. It states that queuing theories have been used often but because of the nature in which jobs pass through these shops, this approach is too complex to succeed. A method that seems to be able to solve some of these problems is a computer simulation method that the paper describes in great detail.

Basically, what the authors did was to set up a flow shop model where there were five jobs going across five machines. Their goal was to minimize the makespan of these jobs. The makespan is defined as the total waiting time plus the total processing time of each job across each machine. The bottom line was that the makespan was the overall schedule of the flow shop. The study broke down each job and each machine from a processing standpoint and ran numerous statistical tests against the findings.

The researchers then discussed three priority rules. The first priority rule they looked at was the greatest total processing time (GTPT) rule. Second, they looked at the least total processing time (LTPT) rule, and lastly they looked at a random assignment rule. Basically, the study used these three rules to evaluate schedules generated from a computer-based simulator. Once these schedules were generated, more statistical analysis was done on the data. The basic or fundamental finding of the study was that the GTPT and LTPT rules did not perform any better than the random assignment rule. The bottom line was that flow shop scheduling and makespan minimization are difficult things to accomplish in any situation.

FLEXIBILITY MANAGEMENT PRACTICES AND PERFORMANCE

With increased global industrialization, U.S. companies are beginning to face competition from many opponents outside the United States. Companies are adopting numerous techniques such as just-in-time production to achieve maximum smooth production with little work-in-process (WIP) inventory to produce low-cost products. For this reason, it is pivotal that U.S. manufacturers adopt and implement flexible manufacturing systems to handle product variability in order to achieve a competitive edge. In order to achieve this, however, management must be compliant, focused, and dedicated.

Past research has indicated that certain workforce management practices contribute to better managerial performance when emphasis on flexibility is high. Researchers Kathuria and Partovi decided to test the earlier research results by an empirical study of many manufacturing plants using a wide variety of independent variables. They wanted to test the effects of these independent variables on the dependent variable plant performance when the emphasis in flexibility is high.

Data was collected from five manufacturing managers at three different levels of each plant. Given the amount of data collected, they anticipated a low response rate and therefore identified a large potential pool of manufacturing plants. Different industries were selected to create a diverse sample that would facilitate a generalizable conclusion. Five questionnaires of three different types were then sent to each of the 158 participating plants.

The plant manager of each plant was used to obtain data on the performance of manufacturing. Data from manufacturing managers were then collected for assessing their plants' emphasis on flexibility. The emphasis on flexibility was then measured. A contingency model was created to then depict the effort of the emphasis on flexibility on the relationship between workforce management practices and managerial performance.

The results of the experiment show that all manufacturing practices, except monitoring and delegating, are positively correlated with managerial performance. These management practices include team building, mentoring, inspiring, recognizing, and planning. The results of the regression analysis show support for the hypothesized effort of flexibility on the relationship between workforce management practices and performance.

The results indicate that some practices, such as relationship-oriented practices and participative leadership practices, are more effective in managing work when the emphasis is high on flexibility. The results of the study provide an instruction format for manufacturers to follow in order to achieve flexibility. The findings of this study can help assess the training needs for manufacturing managers in plants that emphasize flexibility. The ideas provide a good starting point for further empirical research on flexibility and workforce management.

FLEXIBILITY AS PROCESS MOBILITY

In his article "Flexibility as Process Mobility: The Management of Plant Capabilities for Quick Response Manufacturing," Professor David M. Upton from Harvard University argues how manufacturing flexibility can be increased by exploring the effects of plant operation policies, structure, infrastructure, and managerial emphasis on flexibility.

One of the most important shortcomings in the research related to flexibility has been the ambiguity about the concept and how it should be used. Therefore, Professor Upton starts with the definition of flexibility as the ability to change quickly among a group of known products and focuses on this specific aspect of flexibility throughout this study.

The research was carried out in 52 plants of the North American uncoated fine paper industry. The main reason for choosing this specific industry was the evidence that the product was simple and it was always manufactured by the same fundamental process. None of the plants had some peculiar processes that would make any type of comparison between the plants unrealistic. Another important reason for choosing this industry was the fact that the industry was facing a demand for a broader variety of products. The product variety and product proliferation were making inventory-holding an infeasible method to achieve quick response. Thus, flexibility in production was becoming the main concern.

The research focused on the effects several factors had on the process of grade change. Grade change was basically defined as changing the composition of pulp and the density of the paper. The time spent for these changes was the main concern of the study. The changes were made on an ongoing basis, without stopping the production, where the production between the two acceptable standards would be viewed as waste and would usually be discarded.

In this research, Professor Upton concludes that the magnitude and the frequency of the change have no effect on the change times. Surprisingly, both the recentness of the technology and the degree of computerization installed for making grade changes affect the time negatively. Older technology has less accounting value and therefore the operators feel safer experimenting with the equipment to come up with shorter change times.

Likewise, a computerized change focuses on operating with minimum failure risks. The additional effort to avoid any failures increases the time needed to perform the process. The results should be viewed keeping in mind that flexibility is defined as the time spent in making changes. If uniformity after the changes was the main concern, the two factors explained above would most likely have a positive effect on flexibility. Speed comes out to be the only structural factor that affects the time of change positively. An important result worth mentioning is the fact that plant size is not affecting flexibility negatively. This contradicts with the general belief that larger plants are less flexible and opens up a new discussion about how this result should be capitalized on in the industry.

The most interesting conclusion is that flexibility is affected more by human aspects of the manufacturing facility than by technological aspects of the plant. The most important factor that affects the change times is what the management communicates as being the priority for them. If the management emphasizes uniformity, the change speed slows down. On the other hand, if the management focuses on speed, so do the workers. Another significant result is that the more experience the workers have, the longer the change times. One explanation for this interesting result is that, experience comes usually with age, which also brings some physical limitations with itself. So the main reason of the increase in change times may not be the experience of the workers, but the physical limitations they encounter with age. Another explanation is that workers training in an area where quick response was less important may fall short of seeing the changes in the market structure and the competitive advantage gained by speed.

The challenge at this point is that the fact that these factors explain only half of the variation in flexibility across plants. Thus, the next step should be to question whether all the important factors have been included in the study. Another interesting point is whether these results can be generalized to other industries. Professor Upton concludes that this study should be viewed as a stepping stone for further investigation about the concept of flexibility and its relation to the manufacturing industry.

IMPLICATIONS OF PROCESS COMMONALITY

The problem at hand is the issue of commonality of processes. There are benefits to high process commonality but this research identified the sources of developments of measurements and the discussion of the managerial implications of process commonality. Three sources of process commonality are short set-up times, flexibility to change from one operation to another, and the flexibility in making quick decisions.

A researcher on this problem is Roque and he defined the degree of the mean number of applications per component, and suggested possible resource savings through a decrease in complexity. Later, a researcher named Collier renamed the mean number of applications as the degree of commonality index (DCI) and used a limited situation to show possible resource savings. Wacker and Treleven expanded upon this index by showing that there are many different indices depending on the management decisions facing the organization.

The study on process commonality breaks down to a study of the sources of process commonality, which are: (1) short set-up time for each operation, (2) flexibility to change from one operation to another, and (3) expediting flexibility. A firm having a short set-up time is not penalized for having small lot sizes and, therefore, can closely match the output demand. Also, shorter set-up time is associated with higher process commonality, and has capacity as well as scheduling implications. This shorter set-up time increases the effective machine capacity by that same amount of time, since additional production (run) time would be available. As set-up times approach zero, the system becomes a better candidate for the implication of JIT.

The sequencing flexibility portion of process commonality refers to differences in the penalties for changing any two operations. Flexibility is at its highest when the set-up times for two operations are identical. But there is no penalty for choosing a different order in the sequence of shop orders. The last area of process commonality is expediting flexibility, which refers to the ability to expedite particular shop orders. This is important because being able to change lot splitting to meet schedules lowers the capacity for additional set-up times. To have zero set-up time, the lot-sizing criterion must be met but flexibility and expediting criteria are not important because the set-up time is zero.

Process commonality has a major impact in such areas as product/process selection, scheduling, lot sizing, JIT implementation, and quality. Therefore, it is extremely important that workable measures of process commonality be developed. The researchers on this problem feel that the research that they did was the first major step in a line of other research into process commonality.

Process commonality has managerial implications because the indices of process commonality have the potential to become powerful tools in the management of operations. They can be used in a proactive mode to guide management in its decision making at various levels and in a reactive mode to evaluate the impact of those decisions.

BENEFITS OF GROUP TECHNOLOGY

Layout decisions are a crucial part in any production system. These decisions are vital for management because they greatly affect operating costs and efficiency. After all, it is almost always the top priority in any business to reduce costs and improve efficiency. Managers are responsible for implementing the best possible layouts, whether they are product layouts, process layouts, or fixed-position layouts. Technologies, especially computers, facilitate the manufacturing process.

An excellent case of how group technology principles are integrated from a range of elements of computer-integrated manufacturing comes from a paper by Professors Suresh and Meredith.

The article deals with group technologies (GT) and computer-integrated manufacturing (CIM) and the observations made regarding the state of batch manufacturing at that time period in the United States. The authors discuss how there has been a great amount of change in the technological aspects of the manufacturing industry. These advances, while being extremely beneficial to managers, have at the same time caused some confusion for managers concerning the difficulties in identifying which managerial concepts should be kept and which should be abandoned.

According to the authors, group technology is a manufacturing philosophy based on the principle of grouping similar parts into families, which leads to economies throughout the manufacturing process. GT is used to reduce set-up cost and time by capitalizing on similarities in recurring operations. For instance, parts that are similar in shape may require very similar set-ups. Keeping these like components physically near one another aids in reducing manufacturing time and improving efficiency. To get a better understanding of GT we should look at the components that are part of the process, such as

1. part family identifications
2. engineering design rationalization and variety reduction
3. process planning
4. cellular manufacturing
5. materials management and operation scheduling
6. quality control

The advantages of cellular manufacturing are the major reasons for undertaking GT. This case study has proven that the main reason for adopting GT has been to achieve the benefits of group layout over all else.

ADVANCED MANUFACTURING TECHNOLOGY AND ORGANIZATIONAL CULTURE

Does a company's organizational culture affect the outcomes in the implementation of advanced manufacturing technology (AMT)? Companies have a variety of cultures ranging from traditional to flexible. These various cultures react to AMT implementation quite differently and perhaps even affect its success.

Researchers Christopher M. McDermott of Lally School of Management and Technology and Gregory N. Stock of Frank G. Zarb School of Business collected sample data from 97 manufacturing plants in 11 different industries. They used their data to examine how organizational culture is related to the outcomes associated with AMT implementation. McDermott and Stock grouped cultural characteristics together by utilizing a two-dimensional space. The first dimension showed flexibility versus control. A flexibility orientation shows spontaneity, whereas a control orientation reflects stability, control, and order. The second dimension focused on concerns for activities occurring within (internal) or outside (external) the organization. Four cultural groups were formed: (1) Group culture had high flexibility and high internal activities, (2) developmental culture had high flexibility and high external activities, (3) hierarchical culture had high control and high internal activities, and (4) rational culture had high control and high external activities.

The researchers used three hypotheses as a basis for their research. The first was that a flexible organization (group and/or developmental culture) in perceived organizational culture will be positively associated with operational benefits of AMT implementation. The second was that a flexible organization (group and/or developmental culture) in perceived organizational culture will be positively associated with organizational benefits of AMT implementation. And finally, that a flexible orientation (group and/or developmental culture) in perceived organizational culture will be positively associated with managerial satisfaction in AMT implementation.

A questionnaire was mailed to 470 plant managers and vice presidents and 97 responses were received. The questions asked the respondent to consider a specific AMT implementation project in answering the questions. The instrument collected data for variables measuring organizational culture, implementation outcomes, and satisfaction. The survey also measured each of the four cultural groups by listing organizational attributes and utilizing a five-point response scale. Other organizational information was also measured in this fashion. Scores were calculated from the analysis and then a multiple regression was used to test the relationships predicted in the above hypothesis.

The regression showed that there was no statistically significant difference in the operational or organizational variables as compared by the four cultural groups. Some significant data was found with managerial satisfaction and competitive variables. This information was used to challenge the three hypotheses that were created. The first two hypotheses were not supported, but the third hypothesis was supported by the group culture group but not for the developmental culture group.

This study begins to show some correlation between organizational culture and AMT implementation. It is not clear though, based on the lack of support for the hypotheses, if management should align its culture to be more flexible in order to reap the most organizational and operational benefits from an AMT implementation. Other studies are necessary to prove any significant correlation between an organization's culture and successful AMT implementation.

REFERENCES

Caffrey, J., & Hitchings, G. (1995). Makespan distribution in flow shop scheduling. *International Journal of Operations and Production Management, 15*(3), 50–58.

McDermott, C. M., & Stock, G. N. (1999). Organizational culture and manufacturing technology implementation. *Journal of Operations Management, 17*(3), 521–533.

Ergazakis, K., Metaxiotis, K. S., & Psarras, J. E. (2001). Production scheduling in ERP systems. *Business Process Management Journal, 9*(2), 221–247

Kathuria, R., & Partovi, F. Y. (1998). Work force manager practices for manufacturing flexibility. *Journal of Operations Management, 18*(1), 21–39.

Mallya, S., Banerjee, S., & Bistline, W.G. (2001). A distribution support system for production/distribution planning in continuous manufacturing. *Decision Sciences, 32*(3), 545–556.

Moinzadeh, K., & Aggarwal, P. (1997). Analysis of a production/inventory system subject to random disruptions. *Management Science, 43*(11),1577–1585.

Suresh, N. C., & Meredith, J. (1995). Achieving factory automation through group technology principles. *Journal of Operations Management, 5*(1), 152–161.

Upton, D. M. (1995). Flexibility as process mobility: The management of plant capabilities for quick response manufacturing. *Journal of Operations Management, 12*(2), 205–224.

Wacker, J. G., & Treleven, M. (1986). Component part standardization: An analysis of commonality sources and indices. *Journal of Operations Management, 6*(1), 219–244.

CHAPTER 13

MANUFACTURING MANAGEMENT—INTERNATIONAL

This chapter illustrates the globalization of the supply chain. Much of what was at one time manufactured locally is now supplied from other countries. Because of this the supply chain manager must be aware of foreign manufacturing approaches. Nine international cases are covered in this chapter.

The first paper addresses the global spread of production. The paper points out that manufacturing is not leaving the developed world. In fact, it is expanding both abroad and locally. The paper provides a solid background and destroys the myth that manufacturing is a dying industry in the developed world.

The second paper presents a comparison of American and European manufacturing practices with a focus on the small machine tool and non-fashion textile industries. The study utilized a survey questionnaire. The results indicated that there were differences in the operational practices between the two regions but the differences were relatively minor. The researchers pointed out that firms moving into either region for the first time should be aware of the differences so they can plan accordingly.

The third paper addressed the issue of just-in-time practices and performance in Mexican manufacturing plants. The researchers utilized a survey

Proven Solutions for Improving Supply Chain Performance, pages 165–182

questionnaire and based their results on 137 usable returns. They found that just in time adoption in Mexico was associated with superior performance in Mexico.

The fourth paper compared operations managers in Canada and Australia. The study utilized a survey questionnaire approach in both countries. The results revealed that managers in both countries faced similar problems. This indicates that manufacturing is becoming more global even in management practices. One interesting result is that managers in both countries needed to focus more on developing their human resource skills versus their technical skills.

The fifth study has an Australian and New Zealand setting. The study focused on the link between total quality management (TQM) utilization and firm performance. The researchers utilized a survey questionnaire and received 1,024 usable responses. The results of their study indicated that application of TQM techniques is a valid predictor of firm performance. They also found that the strongest predictors were leadership, human resource focus, and customer focus.

The sixth study addressed computer integration in Chinese manufacturing. The study is based on the benefits and problems experienced by a number of enterprises in China. The researchers found that China has made much progress at computer integration but substantial improvements still await. They believe that strategic management and concurrent development processes will need to be applied by many firms to lead them to the point where they can garner all of the benefits of computer integration.

The seventh study poses the question of what the relationship is between a resource-based view (RBV) of a firm and a transaction cost economics (TCE) view of a firm in terms of global sourcing. The researchers utilized a survey questionnaire sent to 600 manufacturers in 20 countries. The conclusion of the study was that firms use global sources of supply to exploit and enhance technical capabilities. And firms reduce transaction costs through local sourcing and freezing of production schedules.

The eighth study provides a review of the term *international operations management*. The author states that there are real differences in the practices between countries and regions of the world. For that reason he advocates that the area of international operations management should remain a field of study in management training across the world.

The ninth and final paper is an international survey of operations management practices. The study is based on surveys in Korea, China, Europe, and the United States. The results showed that there are wide differences from country to country and from region to region. However, there is also a common body of concepts, language, and techniques in operations management practices around the world.

This chapter has revealed that manufacturing management has many similarities and differences as we move from one country or region in the world to another.

THE GLOBAL SPREAD OF PRODUCTION

Domestic manufacturing is changing rapidly toward transnational manufacturing. For instance, it is becoming very difficult to tell where things are made. Products once being manufactured in one country are now manufactured in two or more countries. This article describes the response of this transnational manufacturing shift and answers four of the most common manufacturing myth-based questions.

One of the biggest myths is that manufacturing is leaving the developed countries. This is largely false. However, the notion that manufacturing is moving to developing nations is true. Media has a large impact on what we think. When a company invests in a developing economy it is recognized by the media. However, if a manufacturing firm invests in a developed economy it receives little attention from the media.

Manufacturing is increasing both in the developed economies and in the developing countries. It is true that the increase in developing countries is greater than those of developed countries, but that is because developing countries are starting out at a much lower base. It is a fact that investment in developed countries is not declining.

Another question pertaining to manufacturing is if manufacturing in developed economies will employ fewer people. Manufacturing has been growing faster than any other sector of the developed economies during the past few decades. However, fewer people have been needed to supply the output and the number of manufacturing jobs has been declining. This is not necessarily a bad result. The average U.S. hourly wage in manufacturing in 1993 was $12 an hour. This wage was higher than in the wholesale trade, finance, or the retail trade. This wage level is going to employees where only about 20 percent have more than a high school education. Although the number of jobs is declining, the wages are satisfying and stable.

Also, manufacturing jobs are changing. The trend is moving away from the more traditional assembly line jobs to more jobs where employees work in teams, help design new processes and products, and deal with customers directly. This is beneficial because it requires greater investments in education, technology, and working conditions. Even with a lower amount of manufacturing jobs, the manufacturing industry still thrives.

Does manufacturing really matter in developed economies? This is another common manufacturing question. There is a comparison between manufacturing and agriculture. Based on productivity improvements, we need few agricultural workers to produce our food supplies. Similarly, we need only a few production workers to make the goods we need. This argument is one-dimensional, because it does not focus on the potential of adding value to manufacturing.

There are at least three ways manufacturers can generate more wealth. First, manufacturers can generate new technologies to produce higher performance products. This advancement would be highly beneficial. New ideas would increase sales and ultimately revenue and profits. Second, manufacturers should produce more customized products. This increases their profitability. Also, manufacturing companies should learn to quickly respond to rapidly changing customer needs. The faster you can make customized items, the faster gross margins are going to increase. Third, manufacturers should provide better servicing for the products they produce.

If a manufacturing company could initiate all three of the value-added strategies, they would quickly improve their production efficiency. Since we are moving from the industrial age to the information age, manufacturers should implement the aforementioned ideas to prevent the demise of manufacturing sectors. After all, manufacturers comprise the largest share of exports from developed economies.

The final manufacturing myth is that manufacturing abroad is just a substitute for investing at home. For the majority of the cases, this is not true. It is obvious that companies will set up factories where labor is cheap, tariff walls are high, and subsidies are offered, but most companies expand primarily at home. In fact, one of the chief reasons for investing abroad is to ultimately benefit the factories at home. Also, many companies invest abroad to better serve customers. The top 10 developing economies that have the greatest increase in manufacturing investment are some of the most populous, hence serving the largest amount of people.

In conclusion, manufacturing is not slowly fading away. In fact, it is still a major part of our way of life, perhaps with new twists to it. Manufacturing has the potential to stay updated with increasing technologies with prominent local and geographical investment, and will retain its prestige through increasing wages. Manufacturing is not outdated; it may become the wave of the future, again.

AMERICAN AND EUROPEAN MANUFACTURING PRACTICES: A COMPARISON

Comparing and documenting manufacturing practices in various parts of the world has become an important concern. Due to globalization and the falling of trade barriers, manufacturers have found themselves in competition with companies found on the other side of the planet. Increasing numbers of manufacturing companies are relocating and establishing ventures in other countries, often with different cultures and economic systems. These differences may be reflected in the manufacturing practices and subsequently hinder attempts of collaboration between firms in order to be more competitive. Recent research has uncovered various differences and identified them. This has allowed for a better understanding and possible correction of any differences that could and will impede manufacturers looking to become partners with companies in other countries or to expand in foreign regions.

Researchers Gyula Vastag of the Budapest University and Clay Whybark of the University of North Carolina administered a survey in several countries. Data was gathered on practices in several areas of manufacturing, ranging from forecasting and planning to shop floor control. Firms in the small machine tool and nonfashion textile industries were surveyed. In addition to having different manufacturing processes, these two industries are found virtually everywhere. The data was gathered from Australia, Austria, Belgium, Bulgaria, Canada, Chile, China, Finland, France, Germany, Holland, Hungary, Ireland, Japan, Mexico, South Korea, Sweden, Switzerland, United Kingdom, and the United States.

The researchers surveyed manufacturing executives by telephone. In order to encourage participation the executives were told that if they completed a thorough questionnaire they would be furnished with a copy of the results. About 50 percent of the executives that agreed to participate actually returned the completed form.

All completed questionnaires were usable, although some information was missing on some of the responses. The final sample represented 45 machine tool firms and 50 textile firms. Canada and the U.S. West were slightly underrepresented in the sample. The sample used for this study is consistent with other studies conducted on manufacturing activities.

Much of the research done has shown that differences in manufacturing practices between companies can largely be explained by regional or cultural differences, differences in the industry, and differences regarding whether the market is market-oriented or centrally planned. The results used all 119 variables to compare manufacturing practices between North America and Western Europe. Only the variables that could be identified as having a pure regional effect were discussed.

It was shown that Western European companies' exported sales are greater on average than the North American ones. Similarly, a higher portion of total sales are exported by Western European firms than those in North America and the capacity utilization is higher in Western Europe as well.

North American firms have significantly more production planners with a college education than do Western European companies. There were also shown to be regional differences in what firms consider to be the two most important uses of the production plan. In North America, operations scheduling is combined with inventory or manpower planning while facility planning is combined with subcontractor utilization or operations scheduling in Western Europe.

One of the responses to a question concerned with reducing capacity in the firm was laying off extra workers. This response was frequent in those firms surveyed in the United States while not as common in Western Europe. Layoffs are an important alternative in North American firms, while they are not useful in the Western European ones.

No differences were found in the sales forecasting or materials management, leading the researchers to conclude that the manufacturing practices of Western Europe and North America are more similar than different.

European firms have always had a concern for the design, maintenance, and use of capital equipment. This is illustrated by the historical quality image of European machine tools, the cleanliness of their factories, and technical competence of the factory management. It is not surprising that it was found that there were higher levels of capacity utilization in European plants.

The fact that the production planner in North America is more likely to have a college degree while a high school degree will suffice in Western Europe is partly a reflection of the differences in the formal educational systems. Another reason may be the European apprentice system that places young people in a program of practical skills training and work experience as preparation for a job in a manufacturing company.

The differences that were found and analyzed could be of importance to firms trying to establish joint ventures or other forms of manufacturing cooperation. This study can help those companies that are looking to expand or aid them in understanding why there may be difficulties in their operations in other parts of the world.

JUST-IN-TIME ADOPTION AND PERFORMANCE: THE MEXICO EXPERIENCE

In the early to mid-1990s, multinational companies (MNCs) had greatly increased their manufacturing operations as well as investments in Mexico. With that trend expected to increase due to the easing of trade restrictions thanks to the North American Free Trade Agreement, there is a growing concern to keep costs to a minimum. The question being asked is can adopting a just-in-time (JIT) philosophy in Mexico improve responsiveness and quality and further reduce costs in MNCs operating in Mexico.

Researchers John J. Lawrence of the University of Idaho and Michael P. Hottenstein of Pennsylvania State University used a mail survey to investigate the relationship between JIT manufacturing and performance in Mexico. Multi-item scales were developed and used to measure key components of JIT. The four dimensions of performance measured were productivity, quality, lead time, and customer service.

Lawrence and Hottenstein sent questionnaires to all 504 plants listed in the American Chamber of Commerce of Mexico's 1991 Directory of American Companies Operating in Mexico. The three types of information desired from these questionnaires was information that would permit an assessment of the extent to which the responding plant was using JIT; information that would permit an assessment of plant performance; and characteristics of the plant and the person responding to the questionnaire.

The final version of the questionnaire contained 49 different items to be used to determine the extent to which the responding plants were using JIT. As earlier stated, the four dimensions of plant performance that were measured were quality, lead time, productivity, and customer service. Characteristics of the plant and the person responding to the questionnaire were collected so that their possible influences on the relationship between JIT and performance could be accounted for in the analysis.

Of the 504 questionnaires sent out, 31 did not fit certain criteria, 137 returned usable questionnaires, giving the study a 29 percent response rate. From the results of the 137 questionnaires, JIT is found to be associated with superior performance in Mexico, at least under certain circumstances. Significant positive relationships were found between JIT and each individual dimension of performance. From these results, one can conclude that JIT principles can be used successfully in Mexico.

With the recent growth in investment in Mexico, these results could be very important. The research shows that the use of JIT in Mexico tends to be associated with superior performance. Despite the existence of obstacles in its use, JIT was significantly positively correlated with performance among the responding plants. The results of this study provide guidance for managers considering or attempting implementation of JIT.

OPERATIONS MANAGERS: CANADA VERSUS AUSTRALIA

In today's global economy, managers in all areas must be well educated and must be able to adapt to uncertainty and deal with pressure. This research paper studies the environment of production/operations managers in small to medium enterprises (SME) in Canada and Australia. A major problem is that the operations management field has been somewhat unsuccessful in attracting a quality workforce. This has become a major problem because of today's business world, which requires a change of roles and responsibilities from a single department focus to a cross-functional approach with other departments. This study shows the result of how some organizations must reexamine their management of the production/operations function in order to be successful in a competitive market. Organizations may find the problems difficult to deal with due to the tough demands of working for a SME. Some of the challenges employees in SMEs face include working long hours, lack of staff support, and also limited opportunities for advancement.

Researchers Sohal and D'Netto conducted a survey of Australian production/operations managers and researchers Fitzpatrick and Noori conducted the Canadian part of the study.

The Australian study investigated small to very large organizations, while the Canadian study is restricted to small to medium enterprises. Although the organization sizes were different, the research instruments and questionnaires were the same. The purpose of the study was to establish whether the changes in production/operations of Australian managers could be found in a different industrialized country such as Canada.

The study is based on several data sources including collected data on company and personal background, respondents' career progression, present job responsibilities, and reward perceptions. Included in the study were sample profiles, backgrounds, past careers, and annual salaries of production/operations managers.

Examination of the data revealed that the average age of respondents was close to 45 years. The data not only revealed that the managerial position is middle-aged dominated but it also showed that it is a male-dominated profession. The research study also explored areas of educational background, age at first employment, and managers who are members of professional organizations. The study showed that only 36 percent of the respondents had membership in a professional organization. A small number of participants were included in membership of a management-based organization, but the most common type of membership was in an engineering or a science-based organization.

A major part of the study focused on job content, reward perceptions, discussion, and implications for the production/operations management function. The research study also asked managers if they had any defined targets or programs for improvement within their business. If the managers answered yes, they were asked if there were explicit programs and/or organization resources exclusively or primarily allocated to performance standards.

This study was conducted to verify that the demands of globalization and the need for continuous improvement have transformed the nature of the operations managers, and as a result have transformed the person managing these functions.

The research confirms that there had been many changes in the production/operations manager's job not only in large organizations, but also in small to medium enterprises. It also showed that SMEs must continue to attract and recruit highly competent and motivated people. As noted above, there is a low level of membership in professional organizations, which may result in managers being unable to maintain current trends. The lack of continuing education may further explain why dealing with human resources and labor difficulties were the highest cause of dissatisfaction among managers. Results also concluded that the production/operations managers do in fact play a critical role in many functions of the organization. The study showed that 80 percent had total and direct control of production/operations.

Results pertaining to areas in which production/operations managers can improve indicated that cost reduction was cited as the highest priority of improvement. Following that, productivity and organization of work were also noted as responsibilities for improvement by the production/operations manager. Referring to the percentage of time spent on different activities, managers noted that more than one-quarter of their time is spent on direct production/operations. Planning for these operations is a major factor of the manager's job, taking up on average 18 percent of their time. Managers' perceptions of rewards were very positive, with over half the respondents feeling that the compensation they received was above average.

Overall, respondents seemed satisfied with their jobs, and the research concluded that the managers derive high satisfaction from opportunities for improving efficiencies, innovating, and for personal initiative. In summary, the most prominent discovery of this study is that production/operations managers are highly qualified and motivated individuals, even considering the challenges that SMEs face.

This study has significant implications because it indicates that a lot of problems including mostly human resource problems of the production/operations area have been overcome. The results of high rewards and personal satisfaction will make it easier for businesses to attract qualified candidates. Although insider views are positive, the operations field must make a positive and more optimistic perception to potential recruits and the public in general. There are still areas that can boast improvement, such as the opportunity for advancement, which will not only help to attract individuals but also primarily retain them.

Comparing these Canadian results with the Australian results exposes a tendency that technical skills alone will not be enough to perform the job. This situation is inevitable due to the quick increase in technology and the need to develop distinguishing human resource skills in order to compete in the global business world.

TOTAL QUALITY MANAGEMENT AND OPERATIONAL PERFORMANCE

Companies around the world are always looking for ways to become and remain more competitive and TQM has been a popular way to try and achieve this goal. There has been mixed success with the use of TQM and this has prompted questions about the effectiveness of the method. Research has been done to determine if the elements of TQM are reliable for measuring and predicting how an organization will perform and if so, which elements are the best predictors.

The researchers, Danny Samson of the University of Melbourne, Australia, and Mike Terziovski of Monash University, reviewed over 1,000 articles on TQM philosophy and methods. Only a few of them attempted to test the relationship between TQM and the performance of an organization. The researchers sent approximately 4,000 surveys, 3,000 in Australia and 1,000 in New Zealand, to random manufacturing sites in an attempt to find a link between TQM and the performance of an organization. They also wanted to determine which TQM elements were the most important for the success of a company.

The survey was 17 pages long and consisted of 246 questions. It was developed by managers, the Chairman of the Australian Quality Awards Foundation, and one of the authors. They used a number of sources to develop the questions, including the Malcolm Baldrige National Quality Award Criteria, the Deming Prize Criteria, the European Quality Award Criteria, the Australian Quality Award Criteria, and the Made in Britain Award Criteria. Only 1,289 responses from the original 4,000 surveys were received and 265 of those responses had to be ignored because there were too many unanswered questions. This left 1,024 responses to be used and analyzed. The use of factor analyses, multiple regression, and other statistical calculations were used to process the collected information.

The researchers had seven criteria that they adopted as the TQM model elements, including leadership, people management, customer focus, strategic planning, information and analysis, process management, and performance. Performance was the dependent variable and all the other elements were independent variables. Information about the validity and reliability of the seven elements had to be investigated to determine if they were stable and accurate and if they measure what they were meant to do. After being tested for content validity, construct validity, criterion validity and reliability, it was determined that the seven elements did form a construct from both a theoretical and statistical perspective.

The information that was gathered and processed did confirm that the TQM model is a reliable and valid instrument for predicting a company's performance. They also found that the elements that are the strongest predictors of performance were leadership, human resources management, and customer focus. The other systems and analytic-oriented criteria (information analysis, strategic planning, and process analysis) were not strongly and positively related to a company's performance. The results show that managers should concentrate on people management, leadership, and customer focus if they expect to improve performance. They also concluded that if TQM fails, it is not the content of TQM and its elements but how it was implemented.

This research information is important for businesses today because it gives managers some very useful information that allows them to become and remain successful. If managers concentrate on implementing TQM and concentrate on the vital elements (leadership, human resources management, and customer focus), they will have a much greater chance of prospering and gaining the competitive edge.

COMPUTER INTEGRATION IN CHINESE MANUFACTURING

The last two decades have seen an increased interest in computer-integrated systems (CIM) in China. The overall aim of CIM is to enable different computer-based functions and processes to be integrated into coherent systems to achieve the business objective of the firm. This paper describes the benefits and problems experienced by a number of enterprises in China based on an article by Yuejin Zhou and K. B. Chuah in the *International Journal of Operations and Production Management.*

Since the early 1970s, CIM has been playing a major role in the industrial sector of China. The Chinese are trying to integrate new CIM techniques to provide computer assistance, control, and automation for all types of manufacturing industries. This is because the CIM process is one of the most technologically sophisticated processes in the world. It is basically a closed-loop feedback system that tries to optimize every process in order to minimize the need for input and maximize the quality and quantity of the output.

A CIM system generally includes four subsystems: an engineering information subsystem (EIS), a management information subsystem (MIS), a quality information subsystem (QIS), and a production planning and control subsystem (PPC or MRP II). The engineering information system mainly consists of four subcomponents, which are computer-aided design (CAD), computer-aided engineering analysis (CAE), computer-aided process planning (CAPP), and computer-aided manufacturing (CAM). MIS is composed of a decision-making support system (DSS), finance and account system (F&A), human resource management system (HRM), and marketing and sales system (M&S). QIS is made up of computer-aided quality assurance, quality management, quality planning, and quality improvement system.

This decade-long endeavor has led to some striking achievements. Increasing numbers of enterprises have adopted or are going to adopt CIM technologies to improve product quality and meet the needs of the market. However, China has not been able to exploit the CIM technology to its full extent. Extensive surveys have revealed that improvements need to be made to realize the full potential of CIM. The authors put forward strategies and suggestions that the Chinese can implement to improve their CIM applications.

Over the past decade, Chinese industry has made much progress in CIM implementation. They initially started the implementation of CIM in a select few plants, which were reputed for being technologically superior but in the following years they saw to it that the CIM technology trickled down. They have been able to improve the quality of the goods they produce. There is a striking reduction in the use of raw material used. The plants that have implemented CIM have time and again been able to beat their estimated production goals.

But the picture is not all that rosy. The authors still believe that the Chinese need to go through a lot of change in order to fully utilize the potential of CIM. Considering the Communist nature of the country, management was never considered an important part of manufacturing. Primarily, the roles of the managers were to write reports and report to their superiors. As far as CIM goes, the manager has to play a more dynamic role in implementing this technology. CIM demands that management make decisions using the information CIM provides and steer the company toward success. This was not happening in China where the managers were not making any decisions, although all the information they needed was available to them. The authors found that although CIM provides excellent tools for the human resources division to create job designs that motivate the employee and help the company, management was not making use of it. Also, the quality-maintaining functions that form an integral part of the CIM were not implemented, as the outdated management philosophy did not really care about the quality of the product.

Because of the above problems, the authors came up with three strategies or models that can help the Chinese fully utilize CIM. They include a knowledge-based model of organizational structures, an enterprise model, and an implementation model. These models will help the company tackle various problems that are occurring at different levels of the organization.

The enterprise model proposed will help the companies analyze themselves and figure out where the problems are occurring in the company. The solution will eliminate problems such as bottlenecks and production process problems. This is because the enterprise solution defines the job of every employee who works on the production line and gives him access to a dictionary that has answers to every possible problem that he can come across. The authors have so far identified about 200 different activities, which their attributes clearly explained. The model views an enterprise as a complicated system with defined boundaries and divides the enterprise into three main components: (1) management, (2) technology, and (3) internal environment.

A knowledge-based model of organization, on the other hand, divides the entire manufacturing function into small, functional units, which are independent and autonomous. All these units have their personal agendas and goals but at the same time work toward a common goal of the company. The units communicate and pool resources using intricate networks of computers. The managers are provided with intelligent and informative reports that help the managers make decisions to make their unit profitable and efficient.

The implementation model for this strategy mainly covers six important milestones:

1. Strategic decisions
2. Activity analysis
3. Technological employment
4. Organizational changes
5. Human roles (teams)
6. Evaluation and improvements

The authors believe that strategic management is important as it forms the integral part of a company's functioning. Activity analysis helps the company identify the validity and need of every activity that takes place in the company. Others are concurrent development processes that work together. They can be controlled and optimized by seeing to it that there is proper flow of information to management so that they do not experience any hindrance when it comes to making decisions.

Implementation of CIM is a slow and transitional process. Although it takes a lot of time to be fully functional, care has to be taken that each stage is consistent with the final goal of the entire project. The companies can use the best-suited strategy from the ones described above in order to improve their current state of CIM. Although some companies have gone ahead and implemented the new strategies, it will take them time to reach their intended goals.

TECHNOLOGICAL AND OPERATIONAL EFFECTS ON GLOBAL SOURCING

What is the relationship between the resource-based view (RBV) of the firm and/or the transaction cost economics (TCE) view of the firm on global sourcing? Researchers John E. Ettlie of the Rochester Institute of Technology and Kannan Sethuraman of Australia's Melbourne Business School posed this question and then designed and implemented an empirical study to find answers to the question.

To find the RBV's impact on global sourcing, they posed three hypotheses, consisting of: (1) research and development intensity and global sourcing; (2) investment and commitment to new, computer-controlled production technology and global sourcing; and (3) sales from new products and global sourcing.

The researchers then posed three hypotheses to find the TCE impact on global sourcing, consisting of: (1) degree of vertical integration and global sourcing; (2) commitment to total quality infrastructure and global sourcing; and (3) length of frozen manufacturing schedules and global sourcing.

The study is based on mail survey data from 600 durable goods manufacturers in 20 countries. For each of the six hypotheses mentioned above, data was collected for the six main independent variables and also for the dependent variables, global sourcing. For each of the seven variables, one or more items were used to obtain a valid representation of that variable.

The statistical analysis revealed that all six hypotheses were statistically significant in the hypothesized direction.

For the RBV hypotheses, it was found that: (1) the degree of research and development intensity was positively related to degree of global sourcing; (2) the degree of automation used and planned was positively related to degree of global sourcing; and (3) the percentage of resources derived from new products was positively related to degree of global sourcing.

For the TCE/resources hypotheses, it was found that: (1) the percentage value added in manufacturing was negatively related to degree of global sourcing; (2) the quality index was positively related to degree of global sourcing; and (3) the percentage of resources derived from new products was positively related to degree of global sourcing.

In summary, based on this study, firms use global sources of supply to enhance and exploit technical capabilities. But also, firms reduce transaction costs by local sourcing and freezing production schedules.

INTERNATIONAL OPERATIONS MANAGEMENT: A SEPARATE PERSPECTIVE?

Does the term *international operations management* even make sense? Does this phrase imply that there is domestic operations management or even north, south, east, and west operations management? In the United States, managers and scholars alike seek more knowledge on the topic of international operations management. Some people argue that there should not be a separate field of study for international operations management. The author, D. Clay Whybark, feels that there should be continued study of international operations management as a separate field of study. The interest in this topic is strong in the United States where people wish to gain more knowledge on the topic of international operations management.

Whybark documents some of the attention being devoted to international operations management in the United States. He intends to show that there are real differences that distinguish management activities around the world. Whybark illustrates some differences in the development of international activity between Europe and the United States as an example of why there are differences and he presents a model of operations management that will help managers understand those differences.

There is a perception overseas that U.S. firms do not know how to do international business. The perceptions of European and Asian businesspeople is that somehow or other, Americans are not as skilled or experienced in the international business arena as people from many other countries. U.S. operations managers have plants overseas that are more problematic than all of their U.S. plants put together. All of these perceptions point out the difficulties that U.S. managers have with coordinating international activities and running overseas plants. There recently has been a lot of attention given to improving international management capabilities. Many U.S. companies have been treating international activities separately from all other management activities. This interest, however, is almost exclusively a United States phenomenon.

To deal with the inexperience of U.S. managers overseas, the American Assembly of Collegiate Schools of Business mandated an internationalization of the business curriculum for accredited colleges. Now, there are a number of international management courses at American universities. There have also been many published articles on international operations management. This concern for international options management problems seems to be largely confined to the United States. There have been numerous conferences around the world that deal with this subject. However, these conferences do not address international operations management as a separate, distinct area of operations management. There are some real differences in management activities in different parts of the world. These differences are sometimes larger than differences between different industries.

There are many differences between the way companies grow in Europe and the way they grow in the United States. In the United States, companies have a huge domestic market; on the other hand companies in Europe have much smaller domestic markets. United States firms can grow large and expand rapidly all within the domestic market. European companies must cross borders in order to expand significantly. The market and physical size of European countries would account for the differences in patterns of international activity and development. European managers are frequently crossing borders for business and pleasure. Many U.S. managers do not even have a passport. Even in schooling European managers are better trained than their U.S. counterparts. Europeans have substantially more language training. Europeans have also had more opportunities to be exposed to other cultures than American managers do.

This research shows that there are indeed real differences in practices around the world that need to be taken into account when managing international facilities. U.S. managers do suffer a startup disadvantage in the international arena. U.S. managers consider international operations management to be different. U.S. managers are looked upon as being not good at international operations management. This can be helped by teaching material, assignments, and international exposure in operations management courses. Direct exposure to international differences is valuable. By including real international exposure in courses, managers will be able to handle international operations successfully.

By taking his study into consideration, international operations managers should have the tools at hand to be successful when managing overseas facilities. The implications for business in this article are significant. The study of international operations management should continue, separately from the study of regular operations management. This is clearly shown to be a problem for U.S. managers; by studying international operations management, they should be able to successfully run overseas operations. Despite the feelings of foreign businesspeople that Americans are not good at international business, it can be overcome.

INTERNATIONAL SURVEY OF OPERATIONS MANAGEMENT PRACTICES

The main objective of this study was the design of a survey that could be used to assess and compare manufacturing practices globally. Rather than examining performances in operations management, this study focuses on specific practices. The Global Manufacturing Research Group (GMRG) conducted the study through a survey. The data analysis from the research results reveals a multivariate relationship in manufacturing practices that can be linked with manufacturing performance.

This project was undertaken following a presentation at the 1985 Pan-Pacific Conference in Korea by Professor Boo-Ho Rho of Sogang University in Seoul. Indiana University Professor D. Clay Whybark started a joint research project to learn more about manufacturing management globally, and hence, the Global Manufacturing Research Group was started.

There was no specific hypothesis in mind when this project was started because this project was based not on the performance of operations management, but on its practices. Whybark wanted to find similarities and differences in various operations management theories practiced around the world to determine whether or not cultural/societal values had an effect on these theories' overall effectiveness in operations management.

Representatives of the Korea Productivity center conducted the first survey in the form of interviews with representatives of Korean companies. In China, the Shanghai Institute of Mechanical Engineering helped to distribute questionnaires on management concerns in China, and mail surveys were sent out to firms in Western Europe and the United States by the International Institute for Management Development. Revisions on the original survey were made after this initial testing and sent out again to various companies in their respective formats.

The survey indicated that there is a wide range of differences from country to country and region to region. However, data analysis also reveals that although many practices and policies differ, there is also a common body of concepts, language, and techniques in manufacturing management around the world.

What does this imply? It suggests that as globalization becomes more of a necessity than an option and it may not be as difficult a transition as one may believe. The core values behind successful operations management do not seem to differ widely between countries, cultures, or society. Therefore, although it will not be easy for companies to build successful plants around the world, or to find improvements on their existing plants, there is some reassurance that the most basic ideas of operations management have a lot of commonality around the world.

REFERENCES

Ettlie, J. E., & Sethuraman, K. (2002). Locus of supply and global manufacturing. *International Journal of Operations and Production Management, 22*(3), 349–370.

Ferdows, K. (1997). Made in the world: The global spread of production. *Production and Operations Management, 6*(1), 102–110.

Lawrence, J. J., & Hottenstein, M. P. (1995). The relationship between JIT manufacturing and performance in Mexican plants affiliated with U.S. companies. *Journal of Operations Management, 13*(1), 4–11.

Samson, D., & Terziovski, M. (1999). The relationship between total quality management practices and operational performance. *Journal of Operations Management, 17*(3), 393–409.

Sohal, A. S., D'Netto, B., Fitzpatrick, P., & Noori, H. (1995). The roles and responsibilities of production/operations managers in SMEs: Evidence from Canada. *Technovation, 21*(1), 437–448.

Vastag, G., & Whybark, D. C. (1994). American and European manufacturing practices: An analytical framework and comparisons. *Journal of Operations Management, 12*(1), 1–10.

Whybark, D. C. (1997a). Does international operations management need a separate perspective? *Production and Operations Management, 6*(2), 122–131.

Whybark, D. C. (1997b). GMRG survey research in operations management. *International Journal of Operations and Production Management, 17*(7), 686–696.

Zhou, Y., & Chuah, K. B. (2002). Computer-integrated manufacturing in China, *International Journal of Operations and Production Management, 22*(3), 271–288.

CHAPTER 14

TRANSPORTATION AND LOGISTICS MANAGEMENT

Transportation and logistics is a critical area in the management of the supply chain, especially in those cases where supply sources are far away from the manufacturing site or the customer. In this chapter we cover nine papers on the topic.

The first paper covers an investigation of the experiences firms have had with the use of electronic data interchange (EDI). Data were collected from four countries including Germany, Italy, Japan, and the United States. The results of the study show that the use of EDI will improve on-time delivery, and especially in times of production instability.

The second paper addresses the problem of transport risk of hazardous materials. The researchers used five different risk models for comparison. The results of their study indicate that each model has a best fit with a particular situation, and for that reason the proper model should be selected for each hazardous material shipment.

The third paper looks at operations safety in commercial aviation. The focus of the paper is on improving safety. Data was used from over 160,000 commercial aviation pilots. The one area the researchers focused on was the driving while intoxicated (DWI) status of pilots. One of the risk measures they used was DWI status. Their conclusion was that the FAA's DWI program was ineffective in improving airline safety.

Proven Solutions for Improving Supply Chain Performance, pages 183–197

The fourth paper focused on operational efficiency at airports. The researcher found that airport hubs for major air carriers were more efficient than those without hubs. Also, airports not located in the Snow Belt were more efficient than airports in the Snow Belt.

The fifth paper asked the question if there is a difference between inbound and outbound logistics. A survey was used and sent to firms in Western Europe. A total of 418 usable responses were received. The results indicated that there is no difference between the two types of the geographic markets for customers and suppliers. However, on average the firms have more customers than suppliers. Also, the number of suppliers is decreasing while the number of customers is increasing.

The sixth study centers on which factors are associated with improved delivery speed and reliability. A survey questionnaire was used that produced 193 usable responses. The results showed that delivery speed and reliability are two unique manufacturing strategies in the make-to-order environment. Delivery speed can best be achieved through design, supplier interface and process layout. Delivery reliability can best be achieved through meeting production plan and master scheduling goals.

The seventh study explored the relationship between a customer and the supplier/provider and how the relationship affected customer satisfaction. The study is based on a questionnaire survey directed at major customers of the U.S. Postal Service. The results of the study show that customer satisfaction is strengthened by the customer/provider relationship if the customer is already satisfied. But if the customer is not satisfied then the customer/provider link can worsen customer satisfaction.

The eighth study presents an evaluation of third-party reverse logistics providers. The evaluation model used is called an ANP decision model, which is a general form of the analytic hierarchy process (AHP) model. The example required that the best of three candidates be selected. The process worked but it was quite laborious.

The ninth and final paper asked the question what makes automobile buyers loyal to the brand and to the dealer. The researchers used a survey questionnaire and received 659 usable responses. The research revealed that automobile owners are tolerant toward one negative incident with the automobile but are not tolerant toward more than one incident. Also, a bad service job by the dealer can be as destructive to loyalty as a problem with the vehicle. This chapter covered nine papers in the transportation/logistics area, an area of importance to and an important link in the supply chain. Below follow the nine paper summaries described above.

USE OF ELECTRONIC DATA INTERCHANGE AND DELIVERY PERFORMANCE

Electronic data interchange (EDI) is a computer-based system that connects two organizations such as a supplier and a customer together electronically. It is also called an interorganizational system and has been in use for over 25 years by numerous organizations. It is used for placing orders, making payments for orders, and for other routine and special interorganizational communications on technical issues, quality issues, delivery-time issues, and so on.

Authors Ahmad and Schroeder, respectively of St. Cloud State University and the University of Minnesota, investigated a number of issues regarding the experiences firms have had with EDI including nonmanagerial factors such as product diversity, product customization, production instability, and organizational size and managerial factors such as just-in-time and quality management.

The authors collected data from the World Class Manufacturing (WCM) project, which covered four countries including Germany, Italy, Japan, and the United States and in such industries as electronics, machinery, and automobiles. The final data set, or sample size, consisted of 85 plants nearly equally distributed among the four countries and three industries.

Four hypotheses were posited by the researchers. Hypothesis 1 stated that plants that used EDI will have higher delivery performance than plants that do not use EDI. Hypothesis 2 stated that in plants that use EDI, the extent of EDI use is positively related to delivery performance. Hypothesis 3 stated that for a given level of production instability, the higher the extent of use of EDI, the higher will be the achieved delivery performance. And finally, hypothesis 4 stated that the extent of use of EDI combined with delivery performance achieved will be moderated by the size of the plant.

Following considerable statistical testing of the dependent and independent variables used in the study, the following conclusions were found in relation to the hypotheses stated above. Hypothesis 1, EDI use provides better delivery performance, was proven correct. Hypothesis 2, extent of use of EDI provides better delivery performance, also was proven correct. Hypothesis 3, for a given level of production instability, extent of use of EDI provides better delivery performance, was proven correct. And finally, hypothesis 4, plant size moderates extent of use of EDI combined with achieved delivery performance, was rejected.

The overall results of the study show that the link-up between suppliers and customers through EDI, and the extent of the use of EDI, will improve on-time delivery performance, and especially in times of production instability. Also, even if plants already are utilizing just-in-time and quality management practices, the additional use of EDI will still show improvements in delivery performance.

TRANSPORT RISK OF HAZARDOUS MATERIALS

Determining risks associated with the transportation of hazardous materials is crucial in identifying optimal paths between sets of origins and destinations. The question arises, does it matter how risk is quantified for hazardous materials (hazmat) shipments? Research suggests that transport models perform differently under varying conditions. The research recognizes the importance for careful risk modeling in hazmat transport.

Researchers Erhan Erkut of the University of Alberta, Edmonton, Canada, and Vedat Verter of McGill University, Quebec, Canada, analyzed prevailing transportation models. They then compared the models using their own empirical research that asked two questions: How similar are the paths found by different risk objectives for a given origin–destination pair? How does the optimal solution for one objective perform under the other objectives? They used a computational analysis approach for different risk models and objectives.

Five different risk models are used; traditional risk, population exposure, incident probability, perceived risk, and conditional risk. Eight cities were chosen and 28 possible origin–destination pairs were modeled. Six objectives were considered in the risk analysis: shortest travel distance, minimum population exposure, minimal societal risk, minimal risk as determined by Department of Transportation (DOT) standards, minimum accident probability, and minimum incident probability. The researchers used the professional software package PC*HazRoute as their comparison tool. The software maintains a vast database of road information and related population densities, which are the independent variables. In turn, accident and release probabilities and an impact radius can be adjusted as dependent variables. After a computational analysis, the result is an optimal hazmat transport path for a given pair of cities for the associated objective.

The first question asked, how similar are the paths found by different risk objectives for a given origin–destination pair? The results show that there are very few similarities between different paths that are selected using different criteria. Two instances of similarity did occur between accident and incident probability minimization and between societal risk and DOT risk minimization.

The second question asked, how does the optimal solution for one objective perform under the other objectives? The results show that two models are in conflict. These become special cases of the traditional transport risk model when faced with population exposure minimization and incident probability minimization. Research infers that the shortest path determined is usually a poor choice under other criteria. Also, the minimum societal risk paths do not perform very well under several other criteria. For example, these paths are approximately 70 percent longer than the shortest paths, and incident probabilities are 3.5 times as high as minimum societal risk paths.

Because of the large number of hazmat shipments, it is expected that there will be some probability for accidents and incidents. Risks can be reduced if hazmat producers and transporters account for the different forms of risk when planning and selecting transportation routes. Many researchers agree that risk determination needs to be considered in selecting a route for hazmat shipments, but very few agree on how this risk should be modeled. Erkut and Verter conclude that a significant amount of attention must be given to the risk modeling of hazmat transport. Their reasoning is, and their research proves, that different objectives cannot be used interchangeably. Different paths are determined by different models for the same origin–destination pair, and these models do not tolerate each other very well.

For management, specifically operations managers, questions remain on which model to use for planning and mapping of an optimal path for hazmat transportation. The researchers suggest that several models be used for determination and several alternative paths be identified. Decision-support systems can be very useful to select the final path when it is based on the manager's utility function. The most important aspect of the software is its information base, which assists in the informed decision making of the manager.

OPERATIONS SAFETY IN COMMERCIAL AVIATION

Operations safety has always been an important issue when dealing with operations management. In the past, many studies have been conducted that focus on the operational performance of a specific industry while ignoring the efficiency of any type of safety program. One sector in particular is the airline industry. Have government airline safety programs really been effective in preventing the number of accidents that occur in commercial aviation?

Researchers Kathleen McFadden, from the Department of Operations Management and Information Systems, and Balarishna Hosmane, from the Division of Statistics at Northern Illinois University, conducted an empirical study that evaluates a commercial aviation safety program that sanctions pilots with alcohol-related motor vehicle convictions. They compared a 5-year period prior to the implementation of the government airline safety program against a 5-year period following the implementation. Both McFadden and Hosmane used data that was collected from over 160,000 commercial aviation pilots.

Improving safety has always been a field of interest to those involved in operations management. Total quality management, technological change, cost-saving objectives, regulatory pressures, and customer expectations of social responsibility stimulate the need for incorporating safety as an operating priority. The need for more emphasis on safety program assessment is extremely important and without it, the reputation of such programs could forever be tarnished.

Alcoholism and alcohol-related motor vehicle convictions have always been a risk factor in airline safety. The Federal Aviation Administration's handling of pilots with alcohol-related motor vehicle convictions also has serious implications for safety. In November 1990, the FAA established a DUI/DWI program. Prior to the program, no action was taken against a pilot who had DWI convictions, as long as the pilot reported them to the FAA. Pilots failing to report DWIs to the FAA were suspended and subject to a possible criminal indictment. The November 1990 program moved the FAA away from the self-reporting DWI system to a system that sanctioned pilots with convictions. Pilots with two or more DWI convictions within 3 years were automatically suspended from flying commercial airplanes.

As part of their study, the researchers collected data from two FAA databases: the Civil Aeromedical Institute's consolidated airman information systems (CAIS) and the Aviation Standards' accident/incident database (AID). Both databases were merged for the purpose of this study and only included pilots classified by the FAA as commercial pilots. They then compared a 5-year period (1986–1990) prior to the implementation of the DWI program against a 5-year period (1993–1997) after the implementation. They left a 2-year gap (1991–1992) between the two periods to allow the program time to evolve and become fully operational. There were six hypotheses that the researchers were testing. Has the program been effective in improving a pilot's DWI status, has the program been effective in reducing the proportion of repeat offenders, is there a significant difference in the proportion of pilots with pilot-error accidents in the two periods, are the pilots with DWI convictions at a greater risk of pilot-error accidents before the implementation of the program, and are the pilots with DWI convictions at a greater risk of pilot-error accidents after the implementation of the program?

The methods used for the study involved standard tests for comparing proportions and logistic regression to evaluate hypotheses five and six. The dependent variable used in the study was the occurrence of a pilot-error accident. After much graphing, charting, and using statistical tools to help find the answer to their problems, the researchers came up with some surprising results.

Hypothesis one tested the proportion of pilots with improved DWI status. This was not supported by the research since only about 36 percent of pilots experienced an improved DWI status after implementation. Hypothesis two tested whether or not the program has been effective in decreasing the proportion of pilots who have DWI convictions. Again, since the proportion of pilots with DWIs was greater after the implementation of the program, hypothesis two could not be supported by the research. Hypothesis three tested the proportion of pilots with two or more DWI convictions. This hypothesis was also not supported by the research. The proportion of pilots with multiple convictions actually increased in the later 5-year period. Hypothesis four tested the proportion of pilots with pilot-error accidents. Commercial pilots without DWI convictions experienced an improvement in pilot-error accident rates while those with DWI convictions also experienced an improvement. Hypothesis five tested accident rates of pilots with and without DWI convictions before the program. This hypothesis was supported by the research and coincided with other studies that link DWI convictions to a decrease in flying performance. The last hypothesis tested accident rates of pilots with and without DWIs after the program was implemented. It was shown that DWI convictions were linked to pilot-error accidents, even with the use of a DWI program for pilots.

The FAA's implementation of a DWI program for pilots made it possible to study and examine whether or not pilots with DWI convictions are at a greater risk of having a pilot-error accident and incident. McFadden and Hosmane concluded that the program used by the government along with the airline industry has been ineffective in improving a pilot's DWI status. It does not have a reduced effect on the chances of a pilot receiving either a first time conviction or additional convictions. The research data showed that almost 1,723 pilots (58 percent) received their first conviction after the implementation of the program. Although all of this information is relevant, one thing that it does not provide is evidence to show that the current DWI program has improved airline safety.

Following the completion of this study, many new issues involving operations safety have been brought to light for future research considerations. Whether examining a service industry like commercial airlines or the manufacturing industry, the point of such research remains the same. Improving safety should always be an important issue when working in the field of operations management. If a particular company or industry fails to place a strong emphasis on the safety of its employees and customers, the effects could be tragic, as is the case when an airliner crashes. Despite industry concerns about safety and its importance to operations management, actions must be taken in order to implement programs that are successful at providing safety measures for all members of the business community.

OPERATIONAL EFFICIENCY AT MAJOR AIRPORTS

In recent years, the question has been posed as to how efficient the major airports are within the United States. One would think that since air travel has been such an influential part of American lives due to the type of society we live in, that the airports of today would be running at the most efficient level possible. Recent studies question this notion of efficiency based on several important factors that can alter the efficiency of an airport at a given time period.

Researcher Joseph Sarkis, of Clark University, obtained the results of a mail survey that was sent out to the top 80 U.S. airports based on the Federal Aviation Administration's (FAA) 1993 passenger revenue numbers. Only 44 responses were obtained for years 1991 through 1994. His research tested as to whether any of the three conditions he stressed to be critical factors would either contribute to or deter from operational efficiency at our nation's airports. These three conditions had to do with the presence of hubs at these airports, whether or not a multiple airport system was present, and whether or not the airport laid within a snow belt.

As stated before, Sarkis wanted to test three particular conditions. He incorporated these conditions within three propositions or hypotheses that he would test using several efficiency measures. His first proposition stated that airports that are hubs for major air carriers were more efficient than those that were not hubs. The second proposition stated that airports in multiple airport systems were more efficient than those in single airport systems. And the third proposition stated that airports that were not in Snow Belts were more efficient than those in snow belts.

The efficiency measures that were used to test his three propositions consisted of several statistical functions that took into account four resource input measures, including airport operational costs, the number of airport employees, gates and runways, and five output measures, including operational revenue, passenger flow, commercial and general aviation movement, and total cargo transportation. Airport operational efficiency, in this study, was calculated by using various data envelopment analysis (DEA) models. The models used were simple efficiency, simple cross-efficiency, aggressive cross-efficiency, ranked efficiency, and radii of classification rankings.

The research from this study supported propositions one and three. Airports that were hubs for major air carriers were more efficient than those that are not hubs, and airports that were not in snow belts were more efficient than those in Snow Belts. Apparently, weather plays a major role in operational efficiency. Proposition two, airports in multiple airport systems were more efficient than those in single airport systems, was not supported by this study.

This study has major implications because one of the critical issues, when you look at the specifics of individual numbers, was that many of the nation's airports were not being run at the level of operational efficiency that they were capable of. This is not good news because they are not just hurting themselves, but they are also hurting the people that they serve. In terms of hurting themselves, by not operating at an optimum level, there is a chance they lose out on federal funding that would help them to make improvements in their establishment. The federal government places major emphasis on performance measures when granting funds. Also, by not operating at an optimum level, they are not giving their all to their customers who rely on them heavily for transportation purposes. Within the last 10 years, air industry volume has increased drastically, as many people depend on this industry as a means to get where they need to be in an efficient and timely manner.

DIFFERENCES IN INBOUND AND OUTBOUND LOGISTICS

Is there a difference between suppliers/subcontractors and their related inflow logistics on the one hand and the customers and their related outbound logistics on the other hand? Swedish researcher Goran Soensson of Vaxja University designed an empirical study including a survey questionnaire to find an answer to this research question.

The researcher contacted 251 firms, largely in Scandinavia and Western Europe, and for each firm he approached two managers to fill out a survey questionnaire. One manager, responsible for the inflow logistics and suppliers/subcontractors, was either the logistics or purchasing manager. The other manager, responsible for the outbound logistics and customers, was either the production or sales manager. Different questionnaires were used for outbound and inbound logistics. A total of 418 usable responses were received for a surprisingly high response rate.

Although the results of this study are not surprising, they do reveal the differences in suppliers/inbound logistics and customers/outbound logistics. For instance, on average the firms have more customers than suppliers/subcontractors. Also, the larger the number of suppliers/subcontractors, the higher will be the number of customers. It is also more likely for there to be a single supplier/subcontractor than a single customer.

Opposed to the above results is the finding that the top two customers have a larger share of the outbound logistics flow, then the top two suppliers/

subcontractors have of the share of the inbound logistics flow. Consequently, on average customer concentration is higher than supplier/subcontractor concentration, at least at the top two customer and supplier levels.

Comparing the overall inbound logistics flow and the overall outbound logistics flow revealed that there is no statistically significant relationship between the two logistics flows.

A comparison of the geographic markets for customers and suppliers/subcontractors revealed that there was no statistically significant difference between the two.

Finally, the number of suppliers/subcontractors is decreasing in total terms but also in terms of a particular item, component, or raw material. In contrast, the number of customers is increasing in total terms but also in terms of a particular component or product. Hence, there is a difference in the trend of a firm's inbound logistics and outbound logistics flows.

STUDY OF DELIVERY SPEED AND RELIABILITY

This study, by Robert B. Handfield and Ronald T. Pannesi, attempts to investigate the notion of delivery performance as it relates to manufacturing strategy. Specifically, the research centers on which factors are associated with improved delivery speed and reliability performance. An initial hypothesis given is that improved planning can affect delivery reliability. However, improved process plays a more dependent role in contributing to delivery speed. Gathering empirical data from two studies then validates or nullifies this hypothesis. The study helps those firms with delivery problems focus on specific solutions.

The notion of delivery performance was then defined, along with specific definitions of delivery speed and delivery reliability. Delivery speed was defined as the elapsed time from the receipt of a customer order to final delivery. Delivery reliability was defined as the ability of the company to deliver on or before the promised scheduled due date. In the initial analysis, delivery speed was hypothesized to be dependent on lead times while delivery reliability was thought to be dependent on effective manufacturing planning systems and accurate forecasting systems.

Next, the four possible combinations of speed and reliability were analyzed, the first being a firm with poor speed and poor reliability; second, a firm with good reliability and poor speed; third, a firm with poor reliability and good speed; and fourth, a company with good reliability and good speed. By analyzing the characteristics of these firms' speed and reliability combinations, it was reasoned that delivery speed and reliability capabilities are generally achieved through very different means.

To verify these theories, two empirical studies were then completed. The first study determined which planning-related factors were associated with improved delivery reliability in make-to-order manufacturing environments. The second dealt with a set of semi-structured interviews with a group of managers in make-to-order industries to determine which process-related factors were perceived to have the biggest impact on delivery speed. The first study involved a survey sent to 2,500 manufacturing firms and returned by 285 firms, 193 of which employed job-shop and batch flow processes. This five-part questionnaire focused on the planning mechanisms of each firm, and primarily was answered by the materials manager of the firm. Path analysis was used to analyze the data received. Results of the study indicated that production plan performance, inventory goals met, and master schedule performance all have a significant effect on delivery reliability, while forecasting accuracy did not.

The second study was accomplished through interviews with managers at 13 plants in the state of North Carolina over a 2- to 3-month period. Managers were asked what they believed was the greatest contributor to delivery lead time in their firm. Next, they were asked to describe the three most effective methods for reducing delivery lead time. Results of the study indicated that design activities and implementation of JIT purchasing activities had the greatest impact on delivery lead time of all external factors. Contrary to theoretical operations management research, the effect of decreasing lot sizes was not mentioned as frequently as the other responses.

In summation, it was found that delivery speed and reliability are two unique manufacturing strategies within the make-to-order manufacturing environment. Delivery speed can best be accomplished through design interface, translation of designs into supplier interface, and process layout, while delivery reliability can best be achieved through meeting production plan and master scheduling goals. Although accomplished through different means, delivery speed and reliability are two important factors that firms can maximize to create a competitive advantage.

CUSTOMER–FIRM RELATIONSHIPS AND CUSTOMER SATISFACTION

Unlike a manufactured product, where quality can be readily attributed to measurement activities and entities, service quality has no direct guidelines for measurement. Services tend to be performance oriented, thus making precise specifications for uniform quality difficult to establish and enforce. In most services, quality occurs during service delivery and involves customer contact with the service provider. The focus on organizational involvement and customer satisfaction puts us at the boundary of organization and marketing sciences. Recent research explored both customer satisfaction and its components, as well as how the customer and supplier relationship can affect overall satisfaction.

Researchers Paul S. Goodman, Mark Fichman, F. Javier Lerch, and Pamela R. Snyder, of Carnegie Mellon University, examined customers' overall satisfaction and the relationships among the levels of involvement between customers and suppliers. Their research tested how involvement may change customers' knowledge and familiarity, and how transactions are evaluated.

The researchers sampled companies that did at least $100,000 worth of mail business per year with the U.S. Postal Service (USPS). They contacted 110 customers, and 107 agreed to participate. The participants included corporate, financial, nonprofit, government, professional, and mailing organizations.

The researchers set up an interview schedule, using fixed-response questions to measure satisfaction with specific components of the USPS–customer relationship and overall satisfaction, as the major data collection instrument.

For customers dissatisfied with service performance, high involvement increased overall dissatisfaction. Many firms are building closer, more integrated relationships with their customers. Customer involvement could be profitable if the firms perform well; however, if they perform poorly, closer relationships may amplify overall dissatisfaction.

This study demonstrates that the form of the relationship, in regards to customer satisfaction, affects the overall evaluation process. Consumers form expectations of the specific product or service prior to use. The perceived quality of the services may be confirmed or disconfirmed based on preuse expectations. If disconfirmation is perceived to have occurred, then customer satisfaction decreases. If quality of the services is confirmed, there will be increased satisfaction.

The results suggest that managers should pay attention to both customer relationships and customer satisfaction. As firms build closer relationships to customers, levels of involvement may affect how customers evaluate firms, independent of any other factors.

EVALUATING THIRD-PARTY REVERSE LOGISTICS PROVIDERS

Reverse logistics providers serve retail sales operations by handling the previously purchased materials when returned for whatever reason by the original purchaser. The most common returns are containers on which a deposit was charged as required by law. But any return, whatever the reason, needs to be processed and reverse logistics providers perform that function as a service to retailers.

Researchers Laura Meade and Joseph Sarkis developed and designed a conceptual model to help the retailer in selecting the most desirable reverse logistics provider from a specific but limited number. The number chosen in the example they presented numbered three.

The input to this process consists of six reverse logistics provider functions. The functions they selected for their example were collection, packaging, storage, sorting, transitional processing, and delivery.

The solution model they used for the analysis was the ANP decision model, which is a general form of the analytic hierarchy process (AHP) model. The ANP decision model utilizes quantitative, qualitative, tangible, and intangible factors to arrive at the decision of which of the three reverse logistics providers should be selected.

The ANP decision model also requires the elicitation and determination of relative importance weights for each of the six reverse provider functions. The relative importance weights are determined by pairwise comparisons of each of the possible pairs of the six provider functions.

This comparison process is then repeated for the four elements of the product life cycle, the four elements of the performance criteria, and the six elements of the organizational role. All of these combined generate 396 pairwise comparisons.

The above process then generates a 24 × 24 supermatrix. The supermatrix is then normalized by raising it to the 64th power. The final results after this process then provide the order of preference for the three reverse logistics providers. In the example used, provider C had the largest relative importance weight of 0.384. The other two had weights of 0.348 for A and 0.268 for B.

The process presented in this paper is rather laborious to select the best of three reverse logistics providers. One would think there must be a less laborious way to do so. However, if there is indecision or conflict in the decision process, the ANP approach may well be the best method to use.

WHAT MAKES AUTOMOBILE BUYERS LOYAL TO THE BRAND AND THE DEALER?

When purchasing a large and expensive item such as an automobile, what are the expectations of those buyers? Do the automobile buyers expect a fine quality car with quality services done routinely? And if the owner of the vehicle does not find him- or herself happy with the automobile and the services performed on it, will it have a direct effect on his or her decision-making process the next time he or she is in the market for a new vehicle? Once they drive that new automobile off the lot, customers do expect a close relationship with that dealer in case there are any problems with that vehicle. And recent studies have shown that when the product and/or service is not of the quality level that they had been expecting, customers will tend to change to other makes or automobiles.

Researchers N.P. Archer and G.O. Wesolowsky of McMaster University in Hamilton, Ontario, Canada, obtained names and addresses from several automobile dealers that represented the majority of manufacturers and affiliates of the Canadian Automobile Association. They chose consumers who purchased their automobile at least 4 years ago, excluding leased consumers. They sent out 4,500 surveys, which resulted in 900 respondents producing 659 usable surveys for the study. Their research studied the combined effects of critical incidents involving product and service quality, on owners' intentions to repurchase and recommend purchase from the same automobile company and automobile dealer.

The researchers were trying, with the help of their questionnaires, to determine (1) the amount of critical incidents that happened; (2) of those critical incidents, were they because of the vehicle or because of the dealer; and finally, (3) would the customer purchase another vehicle from the same manufacturer and same dealer. With the inclusion of many variables, dependent and independent, the data required considerable statistical analysis.

After reviewing every survey response and determining all the positive incidents and all the negative incidents that occurred during their ownership of a vehicle, the researchers were then to determine what caused those incidents by going to the source and also figuring in all of the possible variables that could have an effect on the outcome.

From the collection of data that these two researchers acquired, the data suggest that owners tend to have a tolerance toward single negative incidents with regard to vehicle or manufacturer loyalty, but are not tolerant toward more than one such incident. However, negative service incidents can harm owner perceptions of both the automobile dealer and the manufacturer. Thus, critical incidents are likely to play a major role in the formation of customer opinion; it is essential that they be monitored and controlled as well as possible in order to improve the design quality of future products. It is also worth noting that positive critical incidents can counteract negative critical incidents.

The research that was conducted supports the idea that consumers' opinions can change as easily from a bad service job done on their vehicle as from a bad vehicle. This study emphasizes the importance of keeping a close relationship with the customer after they have purchased the vehicle. Even though there might be a problem with the automobile, good customer service and quality repair service can create a positive view of the automobile company as perceived by the customer.

REFERENCES

Ahmad, S., & Schroeder, R. G. (2001). The impact of electronic data interchange on delivery performance. *Production and Operations Management, 10*(1), 16–30.

Archer, N. P., & Wesolowsky, G. O. (1996). Consumer response to service and product quality: A study of motor vehicle owners. *Journal of Operations Management, 14*(1), 103–118.

Erkut, E., & Verter, V. (1998). Modeling of transport risk for hazardous materials. *Operations Research, 46*(5), 625–641.

Goodman, P. S., Fichman, M., Lerch, F. J., & Snyder, P. R. (1995). Customer-firm relationships, involvement, and customer satisfaction. *Academy of Management Journal,* 38(5), 1310–1324.

Handfield, R. B., & Pannesi, R. T. (1992). An empirical study of delivery speed and reliability. *International Journal of Operations and Production Management, 12*(2), 58–72.

McFadden, K. L., & Hosmane, B. S. (2001). Operations safety: An assessment of a commercial aviation safety program. *Journal of Operations Management, 19*(4), 579–591.

Meade, L., & Sarkis, J. (2002). A conceptual model for selecting and evaluating third-party logistics providers. *Supply Chain Management: An International Journal, 7*(5), 203–295.

Sarkis, J. (2000). An analysis of operational efficiency of major airports in the United States. *Journal of Operations Management, 18*(2), 335–351.

Soensson, G. (2003). Sub-contractor and customer sourcing and the occurrence of disturbances in firms' inbound and outbound logistics flows. *Supply Chain Management—An International Journal, 8*(1), 41–56.

CHAPTER 15

TEAMWORK AND PROJECT MANAGEMENT

Teams are widely used in industry. They can be formed to work on a project, to solve a specific problem, or to be engaged in ongoing activities. Teams can be within a department or function or they can be interfunctional. This chapter describes nine papers on teamwork and project management.

The first paper focuses on interpersonal aggression in work groups. The researchers conducted a study of 149 employees in 25 health care facilities. The results show that aggression in work groups may be contagious and therefore managers or team leaders should mitigate aggression.

The second paper addresses emotional contagion and its influence on group behavior. Contagion refers to transfer of emotion between individuals. The subjects used in the study were 94 business school undergraduates. The students were assigned to groups and then each group was given a negotiating task. The results indicated that positive contagion led to improved cooperation, decreased conflict, and increased perceptions of task performance. The opposite results were obtained for groups experiencing negative emotional contagion.

The third paper addresses the question if personality heterogeneity in teams affects team performance. The subjects in the study were 59 student teams consisting of 267 students. Each team was given a semester-long process improvement project in a management class. The results of the study revealed that relationships between personality and performance differ

Proven Solutions for Improving Supply Chain Performance, pages 199–216

depending on the nature of the task. Hence, personality traits and the nature of the task need to be considered when forming teams.

The fourth paper addresses the issue of renewal of teams to improve performance. The focus of the study was 23 NBA professional basketball teams. Does performance improve if new team members are brought in to replace departures? The results indicated that a team can significantly benefit from the addition of new perspectives and ideas. The results can also be applied to management teams.

The fifth paper addresses the question if whether the geographic dispersement of team members affects the execution of development projects. The researchers focused on concurrent engineering projects and solicited information from members of the Project Management Institute. They received 82 usable responses. The results indicated that more frequent face-to-face meetings enjoy better success in product development projects.

The sixth paper focuses on the effect of training on team effectiveness. The researchers focused on two project case studies for the research. The results indicated that team training and induction programs are very important. Without team training, teams tend to be ineffective.

The seventh study is a comparison of concurrent engineering in Japan and the United States. The researchers surveyed automotive suppliers in Japan and the United States. They obtained usable responses from 92 Japanese firms and from 119 U.S. firms. The results indicated that there was relatively little difference between the United States and Japan firms in using concurrent engineering.

The eighth study addressed the question of what the effective problem-solving tools are for improvement teams. The data were obtained from a study of 16 improvement teams. The results showed that as many as 11 different problem-solving tools were used by each team with four tools being the most common.

The ninth and final study addresses the issue of conflict perception between departments in an organization. A survey questionnaire was used to elicit responses from a Midwest university health center producing 83 usable responses. The results of the study point to the need for greater attention to the study of negative relationships and their effects in organizations.

This chapter addresses a number of important issues in team utilization and team productivity. Since teams are widely used in supply chain management, the paper summaries below are important to the supply chain manager.

AGGRESSION IN WORK GROUPS

This study demonstrates the impact of group social context on individual interpersonal aggression. Prior research results suggest that the predictors of employees' reports of engaging in aggression include both being the target of aggression and the mean level of aggression in a work group (absent the target individual). Focus will be placed on interpersonal aggression instead of aggressive behavior toward a company.

Researchers Theresa M. Glomb of the University of Minnesota and Hui Liao of the University of Illinois at Urbana–Champaign conducted a cross-level study of 149 employees from 25 different health care facilities, asking respondents to complete a paper-and-pencil survey via on-site administration in conjunction with monthly staff meetings. Their main goal was to extend the prior research of Robinson and O'Leary-Kelly (1998) in three main ways. First, this research studied different behaviors. Earlier research focused on antisocial behaviors, whereas this study examined interpersonal workplace aggression. Second, this study accounted for the influence of individual differences variables relevant to aggression where former research did not. Third, they posited an additional social or dyadic influence on individual employee aggression and tested multiple individual and group influences.

Following an approach similar to that of other researchers, this study tried to capture the behavioral construct space by incorporating the assessment of less extreme aggressive behaviors, such as yelling at another person. Three hypotheses were tested: (1) The level of aggression of a focal individual in a work group will be positively related to the aggregate level of aggression of all other group members; (2) employees' reports of being the targets of aggression will be positively related to reports of engaging in aggression; and (3) individual differences will be related to employees' reports of engaging in aggression. In addition, the study offered an assessment of the extreme behaviors usually associated with workplace violence, such as physical threats. Five theoretical perspectives were used to explain the potential influences of groups on individual antisocial behaviors: social information-processing theory, social learning theory, and the attraction–selection–attrition perspective as well as reciprocal aggression and aggression-related individual differences variables.

Overall research model results explained 46 percent of the variance in employee aggression. Hypothesis one, a positive relationship exists between personal aggression and aggregate work-group aggression, was proven by regression results and explains roughly 5 percent of interpersonal aggression variance. Also proven by research results was hypothesis two, in which a positive relationship between employees' reports of being the targets of aggression and reports of engaging in aggression, explained a little more than 15 percent of aggression variance. Finally, hypothesis three was barely supported by research data. Results suggest that this relationship alone explains nearly 10 percent of aggression variance. Research data also suggested that aggressive behavior exhibited by other members of an individual's work group is a significant predictor of the individual's interpersonal aggressive behavior and that being a target of aggression usually results in reciprocal aggression.

These results show just how important it is for managers or team leaders to mitigate aggression and conflict given that aggression may be contagious. Managers may take preventive action and alter social information disseminated by communicating strong consequences for such behaviors. Also, elimination of aggressive role models and opinion leaders is suggested. Training in conflict management techniques and self-management strategies may prove beneficial insight for managers relating to aggression prevention. Given that the explanations for aggression are dynamic, the solutions are likely to be dynamic as well and will work collectively over time to reduce aggression.

EMOTIONAL CONTAGION AND ITS INFLUENCE ON GROUP BEHAVIOR

Emotional contagion, the transfer of emotion between individuals, and its influence on work-group dynamics was examined in this study. Understanding shared social processes in groups is becoming more important as firms move toward a stronger focus on team orientation. These shared social processes facilitate a variety of group interactions and dynamics that are important to getting work done. Most previous research on the influence of shared social processes has focused almost entirely on its cognitive aspects; that is, how ideas and cognition are shared among group members. Although understanding how people share ideas adds to the knowledge of group dynamics, it does not provide the complete picture. The sharing of emotions, or emotional contagion, that occurs in groups must also be taken into account. The development of group emotion is what defines a group and distinguishes it from just a collection of individuals. The study tested hypotheses on differential contagion effects due to the degree of pleasantness of the emotion, and the energy with which this pleasantness was conveyed. After determining that emotional contagion existed in groups, the influence of emotional contagion on individual-level attitudes and group processes was then examined.

Ms. Sigal Barsade, Associate Professor of organizational behavior at the Yale School of Management, conducted the research. Sigal examined the question of how emotional contagion processes operate within groups, and proposed six hypotheses:

1. Both positive and negative moods are contagious among group members.
2. Unpleasant emotions are more likely to spread within a group than are pleasant emotions.
3. The same emotional valence (pleasant and unpleasant) expressed with high energy will be more contagious within a group than is expressed with low energy.
4. Positive emotional contagion (increase in positive mood) will lead to greater cooperativeness on both an individual and group level.
5. Positive emotional contagion will also lead to less group conflicts.
6. Positive emotional contagion will lead people to rate their own task performance and that of others in the group more highly.

As part of their course requirement, 94 Yale business school undergraduates participated in this study. The participants were randomly assigned to 29 groups consisting of a mix of students from two classes. Group size ranged from two to four participants plus a drama student who was trained to act out various verbal and nonverbal (gestures) positive and negative behaviors. The drama student did not know the hypotheses or the specific purpose of the study.

Two factors, emotional valence (pleasant/unpleasant) and energy (high/low) were considered in the study. Each business student participated in a leaderless group discussion that was videotaped. The students were to act as managers on a salary committee negotiating the allocation of a limited sum of bonus money to their employees. Each student was assigned the role of a department head representing a candidate from his or her own department who had been recommended for a merit bonus increase. Two mixed-motive goals were to be achieved: to obtain as large a bonus as possible for the candidate and to aid the committee in making the best use of the available funds and maximize the benefit to the company as a whole.

At the beginning of the negotiation exercise, the students filled out questionnaires regarding their mood. They were then allowed 7 minutes to read over the negotiation exercise. After that, they were instructed to begin their 2- to 3-minute negotiation presentations. The drama student always spoke first—this minimized differences in the business students' initial exposure to him or her; it may have also helped in generating a stronger manipulation of the group's mood. After the exercise, the students completed another questionnaire that included the same mood items they rated before the exercise.

Results of the study proved all of the hypotheses with the exception of hypothesis 3: there were no significant differences when comparing high versus low energy/pleasantness conditions and high versus low energy/unpleasantness conditions. As predicted, experiencing positive emotional contagion led to improved cooperation, decreased conflict, and increased perceptions of task performance, rated by three groups: self, other group members, and outside video-coders. The opposite was the case when experiencing negative emotional contagion. Due to the automatic nature of emotional contagion, prior theoretical work has indicated that people do not necessarily know that emotional contagion is occurring, nor how it is influencing them. This lack of awareness of the mood-process/performance connection could have serious ramifications for organizations. Unrealistic euphoria spread throughout a group could lead to overconfidence and a feeling of invulnerability. This could create subsequent pressures for group uniformity, which can then lead to poor performance or expectations of performance that the group may not be able to achieve. Conversely, a group could unknowingly be affected by a particular negative group member, who causes the entire group to feel apprehensive, angry, or dejected, leading to possible morale and group cohesion problems, unrealistic cautiousness, or the tendency to disregard creative ideas. A practical outcome of this study is that business group members need to be aware that emotional contagion is occurring and understand its possible ramifications for their group dynamics and decision making.

PERSONALITY HETEROGENEITY IN TEAMS

Is there some magic formula for forming teams that will consistently yield high performance? As organizations rely more and more on teamwork to get things done, forming effective teams has become of increasing importance and interest to managers. The effectiveness of a team is measured by the team's performance. However, team performance often varies from one team to the next and from one task to the next. This problem has caused managers to question what factors affect team performance. If the factors can be identified, perhaps an optimal solution may be achieved. While team member personalities have been well established as one factor affecting team performance, the debate is as to how the mix of personalities on a team affects the team's performance. There are those who believe that similarity between team member characteristics improves team performance. Then there are those who believe that diversity among team member characteristics improves team performance. Which argument is right? The answer to that question is at the heart of the debate. However, recent research suggests the answer may lie in the nature of the task.

Researchers Susan Mohammed of Pennsylvania State University and Linda C. Angell of Industrial Research Ltd., Victoria State University, set out to determine the degree to which variation of certain traits among team members relates to team performance on certain tasks. In determining the study, parameters, findings, and criticisms of past research were taken into account. Based on these considerations, researchers chose the type of tasks and the mix of traits to be considered. The study was conducted in the context of an academic institution, providing a standardized performance evaluation system.

Two types of team tasks were taken into consideration: written and oral. These tasks are relevant as they represent two of the eight basic dimensions that describe job performance. Written and oral tasks also provide a good basis for comparison, as each requires different competencies and different levels of interdependence between group members. Written tasks are more cognitively oriented and may be completed through pooled or sequential individual effort, whereas oral tasks are more socially oriented and require reciprocal interaction between team members.

Five traits believed to be significant indicators of team performance were selected, including conscientiousness, extraversion, agreeableness, neuroticism, and team orientation. Conscientious individuals are thought to be thorough, responsible, organized, self-disciplined, and achievement-oriented. Extraverts are described as talkative, assertive, enthusiastic, outgoing, and sociable. Team orientation refers to an individual's propensity to seek out opportunities to work with others. Researchers did not offer a description as to how they defined agreeableness or neuroticism.

Researchers believed that written performance would be negatively influenced by greater diversity among team members in their levels of conscientiousness, while oral performance would be positively influenced by greater diversity among team members in extraversion and negatively influenced by greater diversity among team members in conscientiousness, agreeableness, neuroticism, and team orientation. Team member traits were measured using widely accepted instruments designed for the purpose.

Data were collected from 59 student teams, consisting of three to six members, totaling 267 students. These students were enrolled in nine different quality management courses offered by the same instructor at a college of business administration of a large public research university in the mid-Atlantic region of the United States. Participants included 133 upper-level undergraduates and 134 master's-level business students. The students were primarily Caucasian males with an average age of 24.4 years and average work experience of 3.5 years.

Each team was charged with conducting a semester-long process improvement project at a sponsoring organization. Teams were required to apply the IMPROVE model, a university-based process improvement model requiring the following seven steps: (1) identify a process for improvement, (2) map the critical process, (3) prepare an analysis of current process performance, (4) research and develop possible solutions to current process problems, (5) organize and implement process improvements, (6) verify and document the results of the improved process, and (7) evaluate and plan for continuous process improvement. Responsibility for the steps was divided appropriately between the instructor (first step), the student teams (next three steps), and the sponsoring organization (final three steps). A completed team project included two interim reports as well as a formal written report and oral presentation delivered at the semester's end. Written performance was assessed by the sum score received for the two interim reports as well as the final report. Reports were graded by the course instructor, with 40 percent based on professionalism of writing style and 60 percent based on content. Oral presentations were judged on clarity and content by an audience of instructors, project sponsors, classmates, and special guests.

As expected, results indicated that relationships between personality and performance differ depending on the nature of the task. With respect to the oral task, results indicated, as expected, that greater diversity between team members in agreeableness and neuroticism resulted in lower team performance, and greater diversity between team members in extraversion resulted in higher team performance. Furthermore, as expected, conscientiousness proved not to be significantly associated with oral task performance. However, contrary to researchers' beliefs, teams with greater diversity in team orientation did not exhibit significantly lower performance. With respect to the written task, results indicated, as expected, that diversity among team members in agreeableness, extraversion, neuroticism, and team orientation was not significantly related to team performance. However, contrary to researchers' beliefs, diversity among team members in conscientiousness was not found to be significantly related to team performance either.

These findings offer several factors managers may use to predict team performance, as well as an option for maximizing work team productivity. To form an effective team, managers must first consider the task for which the team is being formed. The level of social to cognitive orientation as well as the level of interdependence required for the task both emerged as predictors of team performance. If the task involves oral presentation, such as pitching a proposal, a team similar in agreeableness and neuroticism with a wide range of extroversion will produce the highest performance. Whereas, if the task involves written work, cognitive skills remain the best predictor of team performance. The significance of this study lies in the fact that the personality traits examined will not impact written performance. As such, a team with high cognitive skills, similar in agreeableness and neuroticism with a wide range of extroversion, will produce the highest results with respect to both written and oral task performance. While a single optimal composition of work teams may not exist, this research serves to support the argument that team member personality requirements in terms of achieving high performance depend on the task at hand.

TEAM RENEWAL BREEDS COMPETITIVE IMPROVEMENT

Good teamwork and cohesiveness between team members are absolute necessities in the creation of successful organizations, regardless of which business they might be in. However, a recent research study, which focused on the National Basketball Association, reports that teams could incur productivity degeneration with increased team age. The conclusion of the study was that such productivity degeneration could be prevented through the addition of new members, including changes in leadership, at critical times in the life of the team. Such new talent could bring in the benefit of additional tacit knowledge and experience.

In the National Basketball Association study, researchers Shawn Berman, Jonathan Down, and Charles Hill studied the effects of the addition of new tacit knowledge on team performance by following the performance of 23 basketball teams in the NBA through the length of two seasons.

Similar to organizational or business performance, the performance of a sports team depends heavily on the team's human capital due to the fact that external competitiveness requires internal cooperation and effective pooling of resources. The main assumption of the study was that the teams will continue to improve performance with the addition of more tacit knowledge. Therefore, each team's season wins and season assists were recorded, and a pattern of decline in these numbers would be considered as supporting evidence of the belief that the cumulative collection of the team's tacit knowledge of an extended period of time would indeed lead to a decline in performance.

The researchers' underlying belief was that tacit knowledge can be gained through experience instead of study. This applies to both individuals and groups. Such an accumulation of knowledge would, over time, result in high performance in a work team. Also, with time, rapport is built between the team members, which makes them considerably more effective at cooperation in achieving the team's common goals. However, the researchers' hypothesis is that this process does not last indefinitely, but rather after some point in time, this process becomes counterproductive, and instead of increasing performance it begins to lower it.

The research results confirmed the above hypothesis. It was determined that a bell curve is a good representation of the role of increased cumulative experience in the determination of success. The researchers referred to this effect as knowledge ossification, where the teams would become less open to new methods with time, and eventually become counterproductive due to complacency, predictability of the team's strategy by the other teams, and the members' becoming less open to new ideas. Another finding was a relationship between leadership development and performance. When the team had an abundance of new members, it was beneficial for the management to be experienced and well established. On the other hand, when the team had remained the same for an extended period of time, new management would result in more invigorating leadership and increased performance.

Considering how common the use of teams is in the current workplace, these research findings are quite significant. They imply that shared organizational experience is important to each worker's understanding of their implicit routines. However, the team can significantly benefit from the addition of new perspectives and ideas once these routines became mastered. Such results could also help executive recruitment and succession plans for companies, with newer companies benefiting more from experienced leadership, while well-established companies whose workforce has entered into more of a routine could benefit from a management change. In order for teams to stay productive, they need for their members and leaders to rotate in and out regularly, once all the routines and work skills had been mastered, in order to avoid going into the downward-sloping region of the performance bell curve.

PHYSICAL CO-LOCATION AND PRODUCT DEVELOPMENT PROJECTS

In this age of globalization and geographic dispersion of company personnel, one could pose the question of whether this geographic dispersion affects the quality of projects where project personnel are widely dispersed.

The researchers, Anthony Lee Patti, James Patrick Gilbert, and Sandra Hartman, addressed the above question but in a slightly different way. They questioned to what extent is it necessary to physically locate the new product development team in the same place.

The premise of their study is that physical co-location leads to a higher frequency of face-to-face meetings. And the higher frequency of the face-to-face meetings leads to a higher degree of project success. They measured project success in terms of project budget, project schedule, and final product quality.

They decided to restrict their sample to concurrent engineering projects where for instance product design engineers work closely with manufacturing engineers to design a product. They mailed out a questionnaire to Project Management Institute members and asked recipients to participate only if they had been involved in concurrent engineering projects. They received 82 useful responses and used that as their sample.

For their independent variables they used a well-developed measure of co-location by project participants, and the project meeting frequency measure. They found a high degree of correlation between these two variables and therefore used meeting frequency as the main measure.

The researchers then ran a correlation test between meeting frequency and budget performance, schedule performance, and final product quality, respectively. The three correlations were statistically significant at levels ranging from 0.020 to 0.087, thus indicating the benefits of co-location on product development projects.

The results indicate that more frequent face-to-face meetings enjoy better success in product development projects. But a project is a project, and it appears one can extend the results to projects in general. Therefore, co-location should be an important determinant in selecting project team members.

INDUCTION AND TRAINING AND TEAM EFFECTIVENESS

In many project environments, evidence has shown that there are inadequate training and induction programs for project teams. This can lead to poor scope of works and lack of communication between team members and team managers.

Researchers Guinevere Gilbert and Steve Atkins of RMIT University studied two groups of teams and managers to determine why these problems occur and to provide direction as to how these problems can be minimized. The researchers hypothesized that if a comprehensive induction and training plan is implemented within a project, then the effectiveness of a project team has potential to improve.

The researchers conducted their research by studying two cases with noted failures or issues in relation to project teams providing a service to major clients. The two groups which were from the same organization, provided project management services to three major institutes within Australia. The researchers gathered primary data using interviews with team members from the two studies.

In the first case study, the project manager appointed to the project saw an ineffective project team due to lack of support, undefined roles and responsibilities, little scope awareness, and lack of project management experience and knowledge. In the second case, the issues within the team included inadequate individual performances, inability to meet deadlines, lack of experience and knowledge, and lack of communication.

The researchers decided to use observational techniques and interviewing as a way to gather data. This approach of gathering data is exploratory in nature. As the data is collected, it will reveal a pattern regarding the main issue in the study. From that pattern, theories are developed and a hypothesis is made for further testing.

The researchers selected team members from differing hierarchical levels within each case in order to develop a range of perceptions. The types of questions created were aimed at obtaining answers that were concrete and avoided hidden biases. Also, in order to gain useful results, the researchers confirmed that the definition of effectiveness had been established. They also obtained thoughts on the current induction and training program and how it provided effectiveness to the teams. This was done through a pilot interviewing process. The interviews conducted were divided into two sections, induction and training experiences and induction and training effectiveness.

The interviews revealed weaknesses of the training and induction programs implemented for the two cases. The respondents had varied thoughts on the current induction and training process. They ranged from some saying that it needed improvement, to some saying that there was no induction program at all. Questions on the weaknesses of the programs revealed that most team members felt that both projects were allocated little time to plan for any training or induction program.

Also, both projects were assigned with the key focus being to commence the project as soon as possible. This did not provide enough time to train or induct the project team. When asked how to improve this, most respondents said that commitment from the management would enhance the program and would subsequently improve the efficiency of the project. In both cases, a reactive mode instead of a proactive mode was taken by management. Instead of attempting to resolve issues *as* they occurred, management should have identified these potential problems *before* they occurred.

The interviews also provided information regarding the respondents' opinions on the importance of an induction program. All respondents believed that the initial induction was critical for success of the project. They felt that this could be seen as a bonding session, which also would give team members a clear view of the goal and scope of the project.

The researchers asked the question of how often training should be conducted. All respondents agreed that training should be frequent throughout all phases of the project. An ongoing review and change management of the project should also be done.

The researchers also asked questions about the positives and negatives of each case study. Enthusiasm was seen as a positive key to any successful team. With lack of enthusiasm, there lie issues such as demotivation and conflict within the team. One respondent stated that the introduction of procedures and processes improved the project and enabled the team to adapt to these processes and led to improved efficiency. Other positives included team cohesion, learning from mistakes, and ability to adapt efficiently to scope changes.

The negatives of the projects included inability to relate to the client, lack of communication, and inexperience of team members. These positives and negatives gave the researchers a basis for improvement within the teams. It is important for the teams to see their failures and successes as learning experiences. A form of training in future projects to minimize the likelihood of failure could be a project debrief. This could be used as a form of training and benchmark for future projects.

The last part of the interview was an opportunity for respondents to suggest how to maintain and improve the effectiveness of the team following the induction and training program. Responses included ongoing communication, devoting time and dedication to all team members and management support.

In conclusion, the key areas of improvement identified by the research were training methods, project team evaluation, and managerial support. There was also a need for managers to demonstrate full support for induction and training programs in order for them to be successful. The need for the training programs was evident throughout both studies. Also, in team projects, each member must be aware of the project objectives in order to succeed.

The implications of this study on business is that it shows the importance of team training and induction programs. As the research shows, any team without these two programs is likely to be ineffective. Also, other important aspects of teamwork are shown in this study, such as communication, management support, and team enthusiasm. The study of these two cases can be used as a model for any team project. The issues in each case are universal in all team environments. The lessons learned from this study can be applied to any team situation.

STATUS OF CONCURRENT ENGINEERING BY U.S. AND JAPANESE AUTOMOTIVE SUPPLIERS

Concurrent engineering is the term used when product design engineers work closely with production process engineers to design a new product. The close cooperation is necessary to ensure that the product is designed in such a way that it is most economical to produce. Effective concurrent engineering has been able to reduce the cost of products substantially.

Concurrent engineering (CE) can be practiced at several levels, some more effective than others. The lowest level of CE is called point-level CE. Point-level CE involves iterations between separately functioning product design engineers (PDEs) and production process engineers (PPEs). The PDEs will develop a design, send it to the PPEs who will criticize it and suggest modifications, and then return it to the PDEs. This process is repeated until a satisfactory compromise is reached.

The highest level of CE is called set-based CE. Under set-based CE, product design engineers and production process engineers work together side by side to develop not just a satisfactory product design but an optimal product design. Since the two parties work together, the time to design the product is also substantially shortened. Needless to say, set-based CE is considered superior to point-level CE.

Researchers Jeffrey K. Liker, Durward K. Sobek II, Allen C. Ward, and John J. Cristiano developed a research project to discover how Japanese and U.S. automotive suppliers practiced CE, that is, to what extent are they using point-level versus set-based CE.

The researchers developed a survey questionnaire and mailed it to an equal number of Japanese and U.S. suppliers. They received 92 responses back from Japanese suppliers and 119 responses from U.S. suppliers. The two country samples were comparable except U.S. suppliers were twice the size of the Japanese suppliers in terms of revenues. Also, more Japanese suppliers were involved in interior styling components than U.S. suppliers.

The researchers identified and collected information on seven set-based CE indicators consisting of three indicators for communicating requirements, three indicators for exploring solution space, and one indicator for product design-production process communication. The seven indicators were used as dependent variables in the statistical experiment to determine the degree of set-based CE implementation.

They also collected information on seven independent variables, such as product development characteristics, customer communication problems, years of early involvement, component interdependence, company size, Japan versus U.S., and quality function deployment use.

The next step in the statistical analysis consisted of regressing the seven set-based indicators (dependent variables) on the seven product development characteristics. The results of the statistical tests are summarized below.

Quality function deployment provides some support for the set-based approach of CE. Similarly, component interdependence provides some support for the set-based approach, but weakly. Overlapping design also only weakly supports the set-based approach. One of the stronger indicator approaches was years of early involvement in CE activities. Company size has no impact at all on set-based CE. Japanese and U.S. respondents were relatively similar. The prediction that Japanese respondents would be more heavily involved in set-based CE was not materialized.

The authors conclude that set-based CE still holds promises for wider application. Companies need to go beyond greater cross-functional communication to true simultaneous product and process design and development.

WHAT ARE EFFECTIVE PROBLEM SOLVING TOOLS FOR IMPROVEMENT TEAMS?

Continuous process improvement teams (CPITs) have been and are still widely used in industry to improve quality, make operations more efficient, remove bottlenecks, and so on.

Researchers Paul J. Componation and Phillip A. Farrington have attempted to find an answer to this problem by studying CPITs.

They selected a subset of 16 teams from an original selection of 31 teams. The teams were observed over a 2-year period. They came from light manufacturing, logistics, and automotive assembly. The teams observed were expected to work on manageable projects that could be completed in about 5 days. This requirement limited the size, scope, and cost of CPIT activity. Each CPIT was headed by an appointed staff engineer and consisted largely of operators but typically also included a representative from the budget office and the quality control office.

The analysis revealed that as many of 11 different problem-solving tools were used by each project team. Prior to the start of an assignment, the staff engineer would give a lecture of the problem-solving tools that were available. This lecture was especially important for the operators who typically were not familiar with these tools. The tools included among others work flow analysis, process analysis chart, fishbone diagram, facility layout diagram, and information flow diagram, plus a number of others.

The four most commonly used problem-solving tools were fishbone diagram, facility layout diagram, work flow analysis, and difficulty-impact grid. Not surprisingly, the most effective tools according to the CPIT leaders were the above tools plus the process analysis chart and the information flow diagram.

The CPITs focused their efforts on specific manufacturing problems that were easily identified and had to be solved within one week. The above constraints were probably the reason why these teams were successful. Process improvements are always desirable but can become very costly if CPITs are not kept within a fixed schedule and budget.

PERCEPTIONS OF INTERGROUP CONFLICT AND NEGATIVE RELATIONSHIPS

How do members of an organization perceive the amount of conflict between their own departments and other departments in the organization? The quality and frequency of the interpersonal interaction may affect perceptions of intergroup conflict. Likewise, perceived conflict between groups may affect the quality and frequency of interpersonal interaction. These perceptions may be based on direct or indirect interpersonal interactions with people in the other departments. The question that was sought to be answered was if increased frequency of interaction will reduce intergroup conflict. However, as researchers have learned, particularly those in the area of race relations, interpersonal interactions are not always positive, and negative interactions can exacerbate intergroup conflict.

Researchers Giuseppe Labianca, Daniel J. Brass, and Barbara Gray of Pennsylvania State University distributed questionnaires to 108 full-time employees of a university health center in the Midwest, and 83 usable questionnaires were returned. Respondents' questionnaires included communication network frequency questions, interpersonal affect network, and perceptions of intergroup conflict questions.

Following the lead of early theorists on conflict, the researchers noted that perceptual biases and negative images of an out-group increase among in-group members as intergroup conflict increases. As conflict increases, the internal cohesiveness of the groups tends to increase, as does group differentiation. The perceptual biases that are revealed include stereotypes, the complexity bias, the extremity bias, and the out-group/homogeneity bias.

Only laboratory-based experimental research can determine whether perceptions of intergroup conflict have a greater effect on interpersonal interactions, or vice versa. Even longitudinal field studies cannot definitely answer this chicken-or-egg question of causality. Therefore, the researchers assumed that both forces were operating and adopted a reciprocally independent model. They used both the macro and micro perspectives to build their hypotheses and then focused on uncovering the conduits that affect this relationship. The following hypotheses were formed:

1. An individual's number of friendships with an out-group's members will be more strongly related to perceptions of low intergroup conflict with that out-group than will frequency of communication with that out-group.
2. An individual's number of negative interpersonal relationships with an out-group's members will be more strongly related than will the number of acquaintances or friendships with out-group members.

3. The number of friendships with individuals involved in negative relationships with out-group members will be positively related to perceptions of intergroup conflict.
4. In-group cohesiveness will be negatively related to perceptions of intergroup conflict.

The hypotheses were tested by a quadratic assignment procedure (QAP) regression analysis. The results for hypothesis 1 indicate that neither frequency of communication or number of friendships significantly related to perceptions of intergroup conflict. Hypothesis 2 was partially supported. The number of acquaintances in the out-group was significantly related to higher perceptions of intergroup conflict. Hypothesis 3 was significant in the predicted direction and results of hypothesis 4 indicate support for the spillover hypothesis.

The results concerning the importance of negative relationships and amplification effects through indirect relationships provide a foundation for further experiments addressing causality. The results of this study also point to the need for greater attention to the study of negative relationships and their effects in organizations. Recent studies of promotions, performance appraisal, and income attainment have focused on the positive effects of social networks, without considering any possible negative effects. Finally, the results suggest that researchers cannot assume all members of a group are homogeneous in their perceptions of intergroup conflict relationships with members of other groups.

REFERENCES

Atkins, S., & Gilbert, G. (2003). The role of induction and training in team effectiveness. *Project Management Journal, 34*(2), 48–52.

Barsade, S. G. (2002). The ripple effect: Emotional contagion and its influence on group behavior. *Administrative Science Quarterly, 47*(5), 644–675.

Berman, S., Down, J., & Hill, C. (2002). Knowledge as a source of competitive advantage in the National Basketball Association. *Academy of Management Journal, 40*(1), 13–31.

Componation, P. J., & Farrington, P. A. (2002). Identification of effective problem-solving tools to support continuous process improvement teams. *Engineering Management Journal, 12*(1), 23–29.

Glomb, T. M., & Liao, H. (2003). Interpersonal aggression in work groups: Social, influence, reciprocal, and individual effects. *Academy of Management Journal, 46*(4), 486–496.

Labianca, G., Brass, D. J., & Gray, B. (1998). Social networks and perceptions of intergroup conflict: The role of negative relationships and third parties. *Academy of Management Journal, 41*(1), 55–67.

Liker, J. K., Sobek II, D. K., Ward, A. C., & Cristiano, J. J. (1996). Involving suppliers in product development in the United States and Japan: Evidence for set-based concurrent engineering. *IEEE Transactions on Engineering Management, 43*(2), 165–178

Mohammed, S., & Angell, L. C. (2003). Personality heterogeneity in teams: Which differences make a difference for team performance? *Small Group Research, 34*(6), 651–677.

Patti, A. L., Gilbert, J. P., & Hartman, S. (1997). Physical co-location and the success of new product development projects. *Engineering Management Journal, 9*(3), 31–37.

CHAPTER 16

HUMAN RESOURCE MANAGEMENT

This chapter covers nine papers on human resource management (HRM). The HRM function is important because it provides services both to the employee as an individual and to the firm. Any improvements, therefore, in its services are important for firm performance.

The first paper describes the impact of HRM on organizational performance. The study showed on the basis of other research that as HRM became more sophisticated, the firm's market value increased concomitantly. As a result, firms need to consider the services provided by their HRMs as an important contribution to firm performance.

The second paper addresses the reactions of managers to procedurally just performance systems. The researchers used a group of 106 managers as a source of data for their study. They performed two studies before coming to their conclusions. The results indicated that there is a continuing unfairness in managerial decision making, and a manager's bias should be kept out of the decision-making process. Applying these results has the potential to increase employee–manager relations.

The third study looks at the role of incentives and the associated misuse of incentives in an organization. The researchers collected information from 75 graduate business students through a negotiation exercise. The participants had an incentive to misrepresent their actions. The results

Proven Solutions for Improving Supply Chain Performance, pages 217–232

indicated that 55 percent of the participants misrepresented their actions in order to gain the incentive.

The fourth study looks at the organizational consequences of CEO changes. The study is based on 36 large U.S. corporations over a 20-year period. The results reveal that new CEOs are more likely to disperse power, CEO succession is associated with change, succession usually breaks inertia, and a new CEO may bring an organization back to life if it has been languishing.

The fifth study looks at the effects of leave of absence on career success. A survey of 11,815 managers in financial service firms formed the basis of the study. The results showed that the salary of those who took a leave of absence was less than the non-leave takers. Also the majority of leave-of-absence takers were women who took the leave for family reasons.

The sixth paper focused on managerial distancing at layoff time. The study used 98 MBA students with management experience. The students took part in an in-basket exercise taking the role of manager. The results of the study show that the participants tended to distance themselves from those employees who had to be dismissed.

The seventh study explored under what conditions computer monitoring can be successful. Surveys of workers in an aircraft factory were used. The workstations where the workers worked were observed with micro-cameras, which were connected to computers. The objective of the monitoring was for quality purposes only. The results of the study showed that the workers did not find the camera-monitoring intrusive and did not object to it.

The eighth paper is a study on employee turnover and the reason for it. A survey questionnaire was utilized. The subjects were nurses in a hospital setting. The research showed that people use psychological processes when rationalizing reasons to quit. Also, the reasons for quitting are not always rational.

The ninth and final paper looks at firm reputation, social attractiveness, and profitability. The sample used consisted of companies with reputation and attractiveness ratings. Groups of students then were asked to rate each of the selected companies in terms of their reputation and separately in terms of attractiveness as a potential employer. The results showed that firm size influences attractiveness, and its profitability is related to its reputation.

Below follow detailed summaries of the nine papers briefly introduced above. Human resource management is an important contributor to the employees and the firm's well-being and as such is an important service function to effective supply chain management.

THE IMPACT OF HUMAN RESOURCE MANAGEMENT ON ORGANIZATIONAL PERFORMANCE

When human resource management decisions are made, they are rather likely to have some type of impact on organizational performance. This research paper focuses on the link between human resource management and its impact on organizational performance. The researchers, Becker and Gerhart, used extensive material including charts and statistics from previous studies and various other sources.

Although it is apparent that the researchers gained a lot of information from other sources, the research and studies done by them are fairly interesting. They investigated such areas as human resources as a source of sustained competitive advantage. The basic premise of Becker and Gerhart's many arguments and studies is that firms can develop a sustained competitive advantage only by creating value in a way that is rare and difficult for competitors to imitate.

Overall, their studies showed that firms' market values significantly increased as their human resource departments became more and more sophisticated, based on the number of people employed. It is important to note that their study omitted answers to key questions.

Lastly, their studies did provide some very convincing evidence that firms should concentrate on developing their human resource departments to the highest level of sophistication possible, thus lowering operating costs, which allowed them to charge lower prices in the market for their products.

REACTIONS TO PROCEDURALLY-JUST PERFORMANCE SYSTEMS

Management has always been seen as the controlling force of an organization. Many employees have felt that management is almost equivalent to Big Brother, always watching what you do at work, as well as force you to conform to their ideas, without ever letting the employees think for themselves. Now, as companies try to downsize by cutting managerial overhead, employees have found themselves empowered with responsibilities once only belonging to management. Now this is great for employees as well as the finances of the company, but managers in some regards may see this as a shift of power. These two studies will show the results of managers' feelings about just performance management systems.

M. Susan Taylor and Suzanne S. Masterson, of the University of Maryland, Monika K. Renard, of West Virginia University, and Kay B. Tracy, of K. Tracy Associates, conducted two studies which researched managers' reactions to a just performance management system. In study one, 106 managers were split up into one experimental group and two control groups for 3 months to determine the characteristics managers like to see in a just performance management system (experimental group) compared to the old performance-based system (control group). In study two, they researched the same criterion as in study one except that in this study they used only one control group.

In the first study, the managers chosen were split into groups; 70 were in the experimental group, 36 were in the two control groups. The experimental group was the group using the just production management system, whereas the control group used their own. After both groups received the premeasures and the experimental group received the due process performance management (DPPM) training, they each went into a 3-month performance evaluation cycle with one employee each. After the 3-month cycle, they were asked to evaluate their employees using their assigned system.

Statistical methods were used to check the effectiveness of the DPPM training and to examine the control variables. They used multiple regression analysis to test Hypothesis 1, which states that managers who use the just performance management system will report greater satisfaction with the system, improved working relationships with employees, and less distortion of appraisals than those using a less just system. The multiple regression results supported the hypothesis on all three dependent variables.

They used a moderated multiple regression analysis to test hypothesis 2, which states that the unfairness of managers' own recent performance evaluations will positively moderate the relationship between a procedurally fair system and managers' reaction to it. It also says that the more unfair they perceive their own recent evaluations to have been, the more favorably managers will react to the procedurally just performance management system. The results found that DPPM managers who perceived their most recent performance evaluations to be unfair reported more favorable working relationships with their employees than did those who thought their evaluations were fair. Also, DPPM managers who felt their evaluations were unfair showed less tendency to distort appraisal results than did those managers who thought their appraisals were fair.

In study 2 there were 69 managers used in the study. These managers were from different state agencies that were randomly chosen. The methods used in study 2 were the same as they were in study 1 except that there was only one control group, and the conductors of the experiment never contacted the members of the control group in person; rather, they contacted them either over the telephone or through office mail. The hypotheses used for this study were also the same as in study 1. The results of the findings found moderate support for hypothesis 1 and hypothesis 2. So the results of study 2 basically supported the detailed findings of study 1.

The conclusions of these studies show that there is continuing unfairness in managerial decision making, and that we need to come up with ways in which to keep a manager's bias out of the decision-making process. These studies have shown that the just management system has increased employee–management relations, and has made decision making more objective instead of subjective. This also comes with a decline in the managers' overall power in the company on which the managers in this study were split.

The implications that this study has for business is that it gives companies an alternative managerial policy that can be beneficial to the organization in two distinct ways: (1) to increase employee–manager relations and (2) to eliminate manager bias in decision making. These are all very important for the smooth, productive flow of any organization, and it is in every companies' interest to implement these plans or research other management improvement plans that will eliminate bias, discrimination, or any other unwanted behavior from managerial decisions.

THE ROLE OF INCENTIVES AND TEMPTATION IN ETHICS

Misrepresentation by companies' top executives is creating concerns of unethical practices in organizations. Although many discussions have centered on the important question of responsibility, an equally interesting and perhaps more central question is why such misrepresentation occurs in the first place. What led these managers to choose the course of action that they did? What factors were influential in the decision to misrepresent?

Ann E. Tenbrunsel is an Assistant Professor in the College of Business Administration at the University of Notre Dame. Her research mainly focuses on decision making and negotiations, with a special interest in ethics. In this research, she collected a data sample from a group of 75 graduate business students. The students, enrolled in negotiation classes, were required to participate in a negotiation exercise. This study was designed to investigate the role that incentives and temptation play in the decision and decision process of an individual when faced with an ethical dilemma situation.

A negotiation setting was chosen as the context for this investigation. Negotiations are asserted to be excellent breeding grounds for unethical behavior, with deception positioned as a common bargaining tactic. Furthermore, negotiations contain a competitive element that is also present in many ethical dilemmas. Competition has been asserted to increase the prevalence of unethical behavior and thus, studying an actor's decision to misrepresent and expectations of the opponent's misrepresentation in this type of environment is important.

The negotiation involved the dissolution of a partnership formed by two people. The issue was on how to divide up the value of the firm because they were uncertain of the expected value of two new products, one developed by Carlson and the other developed by Barnes. Consequently, the partners had decided to go to an arbitrator who would decide on the total value of the firm and each partner's share of that value. Participants, each of whom played one of the two partners, were told that the relative value awarded to them by the arbitrator would depend on information they submitted to the arbitrator that compared the market share estimate of their new product to the market share estimate of their opponent's new product.

To manipulate the focal actor's incentive to engage in self-serving misrepresentation, she informed the participants that prizes would be given to those awarded the largest amounts of the firm's value. Players had an incentive to misrepresent their estimates as they were told that the higher the estimate of their new product as compared to their opponent's estimate of the opponent's new product, the more likely they were to receive the higher share of the firm and thus to win a prize. The manipulation of incentive took on two levels, low and high. Players were randomly placed into one of two prize categories, either a $1 prize category (low incentive) or a $100 prize category (high incentive). To manipulate the level of the opponent's incentive, each player was also told the incentive category of his or her opponent.

The result indicated that, 54.7 percent of the participants misrepresented their estimates to the arbitrator. Measures related to expectations of opponents indicated that participants expected their opponents to engage in misrepresentation; focal actors on the average expected only a 40.0 percent probability that the opponents would be honest, and they expected opponents to submit estimates that deviated an average of 13 percent from the honest estimate. Analyses determined that the manipulations did significantly influence perceptions of temptation in the direction expected. Focal actors in the high-incentive condition rated themselves as significantly more tempted to misrepresent their estimates than focal actors in the low incentive condition. Furthermore, focal actors whose opponents were in the high-incentive condition rated their opponents as significantly more tempted to misrepresent their estimates than focal actors whose opponents were in the low-incentive condition.

The implications of this research indicate that it is desirable to continue to investigate distortions that occur in ethical dilemmas. This type of research will not only help to better explain the decision process of an individual faced with such situations but may also help to bridge the gap between normative and behavioral approaches to the study of ethics. Although there has been an ongoing debate as to whether these two approaches can or should be integrated, many have argued that the two approaches have been separated for too long and that there is the possibility of a symbiotic relationship, in which there is interplay between the two disciplines, or a fully integrative relationship, in which theory, assumptions, and methodology are merged. The findings presented here provide an example of the type of insight that behavioral scientists may be able to provide to normative theorists by illuminating the behavioral implications of espoused normative rules.

ORGANIZATIONAL CONSEQUENCES OF CEO CHANGES

When CEOs are replaced, what kind of impact does it have on the organization? What is it that new CEOs do differently compared to what the previous CEO did? Was there a change in the concentration of power in the organization? Was there an increase in information processing by means of a greater use of organizational intelligence systems? Was there a decrease in organizational integration? Were there changes in all dimensions of structure and process? These are the questions this paper addresses.

Researchers Danny Miller and Peter Friesen had several hypotheses they tested on the above question. They took 36 large, mostly U.S. corporations and tracked them for at least 20 years and rated them by 17 organizational variables, which were grouped into six dimensions. There were also three environmental variables.

These variables were rated on a scale of one to seven, comparing each firm to another. One meant that a firm rated much lower than the rest, and seven meant that it rated much higher. The entire time frame was broken up into smaller periods of at least 4 years. Periods began when there was a leadership change, strategy changes within the firm, structure changes, and changes in the external environment of the firm. There were also validity test questionnaires, in which top-level executives of many companies rated themselves on the variables. These executives had been with their respective company for at least one time period. There were also many other intricacies in rating the information to be sure that the results were accurate.

There were also control variables used. Date (earlier periods were generally more stable than later ones), age (older firms were generally more conservative), and increases in environmental uncertainty and hostility are all items that were controlled. The data was then put through a series of statistical tests, which included regression analysis.

The results definitely confirmed the hypotheses. New CEOs are more likely to disperse power, and process more information due to poor performance. Succession is associated with change. Increases and decreases in power dispersion, information processing, and competitive aggressiveness are all related to a change in the CEO. It makes sense. Any newcomer will always want to do things their way, to differentiate themselves from previous executives.

There are several implications of the study for business. The results of the study reveal that succession can break organizational momentum. An example of this would be stagnation. A new CEO at the helm would induce changes, and perhaps bring the company back to life. Too many changes, however, could bring unhappy employees. Employees today are difficult to replace, so any CEO, especially a new one, must understand the implications of the changes they are introducing. Employees are the backbone of any organization.

LEAVE OF ABSENCE AND CAREER SUCCESS

What impact do leaves of absence have on management careers in today's workplace? Similarly, what impact do the different types of leaves of absence taken have on career success today? While this matter has not been widely studied, it certainly seems to have an effect on promotions and rewards in managerial positions. In addition to this, how do factors such as age, experience, and gender affect the impact on one's career?

Michael Judiesch and Karen Lyness, both graduate student researchers from Baruch College, surveyed 11,815 managers in a financial services organization. They were trying to examine the relationship between taking a leave of absence and future career advancement. Their research revolved around two main types of leaves of absence: leaves taken due to personal (family) reasons and leaves taken due to medical reasons. They also examined the results of their study and compared them with two theories—the human capital theory and the gender-based theory.

The researchers conducted most of their research through statistical data and surveys. Their statistical data revolved largely around the impact of taking a leave of absence with wages, both in the short term and long term. They compared the wages of someone, regardless of gender, who has worked continuously without taking any leaves with those of someone who has taken at least one leave from work. Based on this data, they hypothesized that people who take a leave of absence from their careers will receive fewer benefits in their jobs than those who have not taken a leave from work. Furthermore, those who take multiple leaves will consequently suffer more than those who have taken fewer, and similarly those who take longer leaves will suffer greater than those who take shorter leaves. They also extended their hypothesis of the impact of taking a leave of absence to the impact of what type of leave was taken, by theorizing that those who take family-related leaves will suffer more than those who take sick leaves.

The research they conducted found that the salary of those in managerial positions who took a leave of absence was less than those who did not take time off from work. In addition to that, the percentage of salary increase was less for those who did take a leave. Part of this is due to the human capital theory, where human capital is experience and education. To take time off is to make a sacrifice in human capital, and therefore there is a sacrifice in career advancement. To take a longer leave of absence is seen as a larger loss in human capital, and therefore has a larger impact on those who take longer leaves. The gap in salaries, salary increases, and other rewards narrowed between those who take leaves and those who do not over time; however, even after a large amount of time there is a noticeable difference.

Another theory that the researchers used to justify their hypothesis is the allocation of energy model, which is an extension of the human capital model. This model is used in part to explain why leaves taken for family-related matters have a larger negative impact than leaves taken for medical reasons. Essentially, the energy model suggests that those who are more able and willing to put a greater amount of time and effort into their positions have a greater chance of career advancement and rewards. Leaves taken due to pregnancy or other family-related matters is an indication that the employee cannot devote as much energy into their job as someone who does not have the same obligations, and consequently suffers more than those who do not take leaves due to family matters. In addition to that, this model affects women more strongly than it does men, as they are more prone to take a leave of absence due to these reasons.

The results of the study coincide largely with their hypotheses and has large implications for employees, employers, and their respective corporations. The largest implication that can be seen is on women with managerial positions who take a leave of absence. While the difference in rewards between men and women who have taken a leave of absence are negligible, the majority of those who take leaves of absence are female, and consequently this affects women greater than men. Organizations are also largely affected by this. While opportunities in managerial positions are increasing, corporations must realize the need for their employees to be able to attend to familial matters in order to compete with rival corporations. This suggests that with time, the negative impact that taking a leave of absence has on advancement in managerial careers will diminish.

MANAGERIAL DISTANCING AT LAYOFF TIME

Downsizing or layoffs are a major concern for organizations. However, the weight of the burden falls on managers. Managers are the ones who are left to deal with the issue of layoffs, such as what approach to take. They are there to relay the information to the employees. They are the middlemen. Research shows that managers often take a curt and abrupt approach when it comes to laying off employees, which is a form of mismanagement. This mismanagement occurs as a result of (1) feelings of discomfort, (2) time designated for dismissal meetings, and (3) anticipation of negative consequences. Recent research suggests that managers abandon sound management principles and distance themselves from employees.

Robert Folger of Tulane University and Daniel P. Skarlicki of the University of Calgary performed a scenario study as well as a field study. The scenario study was designed to explain two hypothesizes: Hypothesis 1—*A manager's feelings of discomfort and distance behavior are greater when the manager is responsible for a layoff decision than when the manager is not responsible for it*; hypothesis 2—*A manager's feelings of discomfort and distancing behavior are greater when a layoff is due to mismanagement by the manager than when it is due to uncontrollable external forces.* The field study was also designed to explain two hypothesizes: Hypothesis 3—*Anticipated accusation will be a positive function of blame for a layoff*; hypothesis 4—*Anticipated harm will be a positive function of blame for a layoff.*

The scenario study used 98 graduate students with management experience at a medium-sized university. Their average age was 26 and 43 of the 98 students were female. On average, these students had 2.63 years of managerial experience. The students were randomly assigned to conditions through an in-basket exercise. Participants took on the role of manager in charge of a particular project and were told how to distribute their time among various duties.

The exercise contained a letter from the CEO that basically stated that their project had been cancelled. The CEO also asked the managers to indicate the form of action that the managers were going to take. The letter included the following manipulations: either the participant or the CEO was said to have decided that the project members were to be laid off or the CEO stated that the layoff was due to mismanagement or market conditions (mismanagement factor). Upon the completion of the exercise, the participants were asked to complete a questionnaire, write how they made the allocation decisions, and then they were debriefed.

The results of the study showed that 92 percent identified that they were in the mismanagement condition. The study also showed that feelings of discomfort and distancing behavior were the main effect for the mismanagement factor, thus supporting hypothesis 2 and not hypothesis 1.

The field study was an extension of the scenario study and it tested the third and fourth hypotheses. This study was expected to show that the mismanagement factor would again predict managerial distancing and discomfort. The study was conducted with 40 middle- to upper-level managers of 37 different companies in various industries. On average, the participants had 15 years of managerial experience and they have done approximately three layoffs in the past 5 years.

The managers were randomly assigned in equal numbers to the mismanagement factor or external forces factor. The scenarios and questionnaires were handed to the managers as extra course credit. Demographic information was also collected for the use of the study. Feelings of discomfort were measured using the scale reported in the scenario study. In addition, the participants responded to four items about how employees would respond to the layoff. Also, an anticipated harm scale was used to measure the manager's perception on the potential harm that could be caused by laid-off employees.

The results of the study showed that blame for the layoffs was related to managerial distancing and the measures of anticipated accusation and harm. Feelings of discomfort were also shown to be related to anticipated accusations but not to the anticipated harm measures. Thus, Hypotheses 2, 3, and 4 were supported. The mismanagement factor produced more anticipation of accusation as well as harm and more distancing. This study was consistent with the first study, indicating that mismanagement is related to the amount of time dedicated to handling laid-off employees.

This study has critical implications on the relationship between managers and laid-off employees. Managers can decrease the negative side effects by demonstrating interpersonal sensitivity. The conditions under which a manager operates directly affects his decision or behavior. This emphasizes that blame is a relevant factor in mismanagement, thus reducing a manager's contact time with layoff victims. However, future studies need to examine ways that managers distance themselves so as to eliminate pressures that lead to poor management practices when implementing tough decisions.

HOW CAN COMPUTER MONITORING BE SUCCESSFUL?

Computer monitoring should not be seen as a way of gathering information about workers, but rather as one part of a production and quality strategy that provides needed information to a diverse team of workers. In its most powerful and effective form, computer monitoring is the use of computers to collect, process, and provide feedback information about work with the intent of improving performance and developing employees.

Unfortunately, in some cases, computer monitoring has also been used to punish employees. Recent research shows that if the computer monitoring program is administered with a pure production quality objective, it can be quite successful and unobtrusive to employees.

Researcher Terri I. Griffith, of the University of Arizona, surveyed workers from the Hughes Aircraft Company. Employees were employed in the following positions at Hughes Aircraft: inspectors, quality engineers, production engineers, and supervisors. Her research tested whether computer monitoring can facilitate integrated production and quality control strategies without having negative effects on employee quality of work life.

The study began when Hughes Aircraft Company, an important manufacturer of microchips for the Department of Defense, installed a computerized video-integrated technology system (CVITS) at each of their microchip workstations. CVITS works through powerful microscopes that act like real-time cameras at each of the workstations, and are connected to computers and video screens. These microscopes produce an image that can be seen by any computer screen connected to the system throughout the company. The main objective of the system is to provide various team members throughout the Hughes organization with information on microchip quality and to create a database with this quality information.

The researcher interviewed employees, who held various positions throughout the organization, as to what their thoughts were about the CVITS. First, the employees were asked about the formal training they received with regards to the different uses of the system. Next, the researcher asked questions regarding the degrees to which team members perceived CVITS to be helpful, how satisfied they were with it, and how committed they were to using the system. Next, employees were asked specific questions about computer monitoring and how they felt in regards to being monitored.

The results showed that the CVITS was a successful monitoring system without being an obtrusive employee social surveillance tool for management. It also showed that training and participation in the design and adaptation of the monitoring system is the key to developing a successful system. The results stressed that the entire production strategy should be considered when planning for the system and its use. When planning the system, the study showed that it is crucial to determine the type of data that employees believe will help them through the use of monitoring.

The study has critical implications since more and more organizations are choosing to move toward computer monitoring of their employees. In order to avoid alienating employees by making them feel that their privacy is being infringed upon, employers need to keep in mind that computer monitoring is just another management tool that needs to be used responsibly. Computer monitoring is only as evil as the management system that employs it. As more and more companies decide to use these monitoring systems, employers need to focus on employee understanding of the monitoring system and employee use of the data.

EMPLOYEE TURNOVER

Understanding reasoning as to why employee turnover occurs was the basis of study on voluntary employee turnover. The paper describes the reasoning and analysis by an employee who is ready to or already has terminated her employment with her employer. The study indicates the different decision paths people go through when deciding whether or not to leave a company.

Researchers Thomas Lee and Terence Mitchell, both of the University of Washington, Lowell Wise of Stanford University Hospital, and Steven Fireman, of the University of Washington, tested Lee and Mitchell's model of voluntary employee departure. They took 49 nurses (48 women, one man) who had previously quit their jobs and put them through individual interviews to collect data regarding thought processes and decisions made as to the reason why they decided to terminate their employment. According to the model, there are four separate decision paths that people go through in their mind when determining reasons to quit.

The study was conducted through questionnaires and interviews. All 49 nurses were asked a series of questions that were directly related to ideas formed from Lee and Mitchell's unfolding model. Questions assessed what decision paths were used by the nurses in their thought process to quitting their job. Questions focused on shock, time to decide, search for job alternatives, and fit judgments. Also interviews conducted were either taped or detail noted to further assess thought processes. Nurses were scored based on the data collection.

The research concluded that people use psychological processes when rationalizing reasons to quit, which sometimes differ from normal existing turnover processes. The focus of the study was the effect that job dissatisfaction has on turnover rates.

Through the research, new ways to rationalize turnover rates have been postulated. First, a good portion of nurses had quit without having a backup plan or job to go to. This diverges from the norm. Second, shock was a major factor in the decision to quit. And lastly the decision to quit appears frequently to involve a process different from a rational choice process.

This study is very important in determining factors such as why employees decide to terminate employment with a company. This study is critical for businesses to know why people decide to leave so they can try to fix problems within the company to minimize turnover rates. In today's economy, turnover rates tend to be very costly and can be avoided when knowing what your employees' wants and needs are.

FIRM REPUTATION AND SOCIAL ATTRACTIVENESS

What is the attractiveness of a company for prospective applicants? Attracting top-quality applicants is becoming increasingly important for organizational success, especially if there are labor shortages or projected labor shortages in the future. Little research, however, has investigated factors that influence applicants' initial attraction to a firm, which in turn influences their decision to interview with a firm.

Both researchers are Associate Professors of Management at the University of Missouri in Columbia. One of the researchers, Daniel B. Turban, received his PhD degree in industrial organizational psychology from the University of Houston. The other, Daniel W. Greening, received his PhD degree in business administration from Pennsylvania State University. They investigated whether firms' actual corporate social performance is related to their reputations and their attractiveness as employers. In other words, they investigated the relationships between organizations' corporate social performance (CSP), their attractiveness as employers, and their reputations.

The unit of analysis for this study was the organization. They used the database that is the largest multidimensional CSP database, which contains ratings for 633 organizations. They determined which company to use for their study with several heuristics, which involved students rating the reputation and attractiveness of the organizations. The researchers chose 161 firms with reputation ratings and 160 firms with attractiveness ratings. From these two samples they selected a study sample of 189 companies.

Seventy-five students in two sections of a senior-level strategic management course rated 189 companies in terms of their reputations on the five-scale rating. Average reputation ratings ranged from 2.74 to 4.87. Another 34 students in two sections of a senior-level strategic management course rated each of the 189 companies in terms of attractiveness as an employer on a five-point scale rating from 1 to 5. Each organization's score for attractiveness as an employer ranged from 2.68 to 4.64.

The results shows that an organization's size influences its attractiveness, although such effects were moderated by applicants' self-esteem and need for achievement. Also, evidence shows that a firm's profitability is related to its reputation. Because they also expected larger and more profitable firms to receive more publicity and to have greater name recognition, they controlled for organization size and firm profitability. They measured firm size as total assets and measured firm profitability as return on assets, using data obtained from the Standard & Poor's Compustat Annual Data tapes.

Total assets, the measure for firm size, was not significantly related to either reputation or employee attractiveness, although it was positively related to community relations and the treatment of women and minorities and negatively related to product quality. Profitability was positively correlated with community relations, reputation, and employer attractiveness, supporting its inclusion as a control variable.

Examination of the correlations indicates that organizations' corporate social performance is related positively to their reputations and attractiveness as an employer. Especially, reputation is correlated significantly with community relations, employee relations, environment, and product quality. Attractiveness as an employer is correlated significantly with community relations, employee relations, and product quality.

Their results highlight the importance of corporate image as an influence on prospective applicants' attraction to a firm. At a time when corporate success depends more and more on a high-quality workforce, firms are becoming increasingly aware of the need to attract the best workers to their companies. Many normative works have stressed the need for firms' positive corporate and social performance; their research suggests that firms may develop competitive advantages by being perceived as attractive places of employment because of their performance in regard to quality products and services, treatment of the environment, and issues of diversity. Firms can do this by signaling potential workers in brochures and advertisements that they offer a work environment conducive to socially responsible activities and by providing a culture and environment that reinforce individual workers' self-concepts and social identities. Their results suggest that corporate social performance may, in fact, be good business.

REFERENCES

Becker, B., & Gerhart, B. (1996). The impact of human resource management on organizational performance: Progress and prospects. *Academy of Management Journal, 39*(4), 779–801.

Folger, R., & Skarlicki, D. P. (1998). When tough times make tough bosses: Managerial distancing as a function of layoff blame. *Academy of Management Journal, 41*(1), 79–87.

Griffith, T. I. (1993). Teaching big brother to be a team player: Computer monitoring and quality. *Academy of Management Executive, 7*(1), 73–80.

Judiesch, M., & Lyness, K. (1999). Left behind? The impact of leaves of absence on managers' career success. *Academy of Management Journal, 42*(6), 641–651

Lee, T. W., Mitchell, T. S., Wise, L., & Freeman, S. (1996). An unfolding model of voluntary employee turnover, *Academy of Management Journal, 39*(1), 5–36.

Miller, D. (1993). Some organizational consequences of CEO succession. *Academy of Management Journal, 36*(3), 644–659.

Taylor, M. S., Masterson, S. S., Renard, M. K., & Tracey, K. B. (1996). Managers' reactions to procedurally-just performance management systems. *Academy of Management Journal, 41*(5), 568–579.

Tenbrunsel, A. E. (1998). Misrepresentation and expectations of misrepresentation in an ethical dilemma: The role of incentives and temptation. *Academy of Management Journal, 41*(3), 330–339.

Turban, D. B., & Greening, D. W. (1997). Corporate social performance and organizational attractiveness to prospective employees. *Academy of Management Journal, 40*(3), 658–672.

CHAPTER 17

ORGANIZATIONAL ISSUES IN SUPPLY CHAIN

This chapter covers nine papers on organizational issues. It is to some extent an extension of the previous chapter because most papers cover employee–organizational relationships

The first paper focuses on the employee–organizational (EO) relationship mentioned above. The researchers identify four types of the EO relationship, consisting of quasi-spot contract, mutual investment, underinvestment, and overinvestment. Information was collected from 10 companies. Of the four types of EO relationships, the mutual investment type was found to create the highest commitment from employees.

The second paper attempts to define what makes a company be a good corporate citizen. The researcher reviewed and analyzed the results of four related studies to arrive at a definition. Although no conclusion was reached, the author recommends the development of an approach to rank the stakeholders in the organization.

The third paper focuses on the multiple roles of managerial women and how those roles interact. The information for the first part of the study was obtained from 61 female managers and executives and for the second part from 276 women managers. The results of the study show that multiple life roles are an indicator of managerial effectiveness.

The fourth paper is a study of affect, which is an individual's feeling or emotion as manifested by facial expression or body language and job satis-

Proven Solutions for Improving Supply Chain Performance, pages 233–250

faction. The research was based on a survey from 120 respondents. The results indicate that positive affect appears to be important in predicting commitment but this result is not true for average affect. Hence, affect in general may not be a predictor in job satisfaction.

The fifth paper focuses on personal initiative (PI) and job success. The paper surveyed past research in the area and provided a summary of that research. The conclusion was that not all jobs require a high level of PI but in a service economy more jobs are looking for PI skills.

The sixth paper addresses the question of how to generate more employee involvement in the work force. The three common ways to generate employee involvement are training, role change by employees, and attainment of job autonomy by employees. The researchers then address the issue of untangling the three ways described above. The authors conclude that organizations may have to alter the nature of employees' jobs and reporting relationships.

The seventh paper addresses the issue of job satisfaction of product and functional managers in matrix organizations. The study is based on information gained from 31 project and functional managers. The results showed that functional managers had lower job satisfaction than project managers. These results provide a challenge to management.

The eighth paper asks the question of whether promotional justice promotes organizational support. The data for the study was obtained from a survey of 450 subordinates and 450 supervisors in a large military hospital. The results confirmed that perceived procedural justice was positively related to perceived organizational support.

The ninth and final study asks the question of whether increased trust could lower contract cost. A survey was used and produced 300 usable responses. The results show that mistrust between a contractor and a customer will increase a project's cost from 8 percent to 20 percent. As a result, increased trust between parties could lower contract cost.

The nine papers summarized below provide scientific-based information to management to lower cost and improve operations, including supply chain management operations.

APPROACHES TO THE EMPLOYEE–ORGANIZATIONAL RELATIONSHIP

In some ways companies are alike in terms of structure, benefits, employees, and so on. But at the same time, these companies can be very different. Organizations are flexible and there needs to be different approaches to fit each individual organization, which in turn will optimize the overall performance of the corporation. There are four different types of employee–organizational relationships. One is quasi-spot contract. This is a relationship that is short term and closed-ended. The second type of relationship is mutual-investment, mutual meaning both parties agree to an open-ended, long-term relationship. The next relationship is underinvestment. Underinvestment involves the employee having broad and open-ended obligations but the employee rewards are based on short-term performance. The last type is overinvestment. This type is just the opposite of underinvestment. As you can see the first two are balanced and the second two are unbalanced. When analyzing all four of these relationships in different areas, the best one came out to be the mutual investment relationship.

Researchers Anne S. Tsui of the Hong Kong University of Sciences and Technology, June L. Pearce and Lyman W. Porter of the University of California at Irvine, and Angela M. Tripoli of the University College Dublin studied employees from 10 different companies. They found that under different types of relationships, employee responses varied.

Tsui and the rest of the researchers developed seven hypotheses, which elaborate on what relationship best fits certain tasks/preferences of employees and employers. The first hypothesis put the quasi-spot contract relationship highest for employee performance of certain tasks. In this type of contract the tasks and rewards are close-ended, meaning they are set at the initial contract between the employer and employee. Rated lowest was the underinvestment. This was because the employee has broad open-ended obligations, and has a variety of tasks that need to be performed, making it harder to achieve all of them. Hypothesis 2 describes organizational citizenship behaviors and places highest the mutual investment relationship. The mutual investment employees' obligations are open-ended, but also the employers' considerations and inducements consist of more than just monetary rewards, giving the employees incentives to work harder toward organizational goals.

In hypothesis 3 dependable continuation of employment was rated highest in the overinvestment. In an overinvestment relationship, the employee performs a set of activities but the employer offers broad open-ended rewards such as training and career opportunities. Hypothesis 4 states that employee attendance will be highest in the mutual investment relationship. It is the highest because of the expectations that are given by the employer and employees will be in attendance when needed. They will also be committed to the organization. Included in this is peer pressure, which is highest among employees in this relationship.

Hypothesis 5 revealed that commitment will be highest in the mutual investment and overinvestment relationships. This is because of the long-term commitment by the employer. Employee–organizational relationships also have some effect on the fairness perceived by the employees. Hypothesis 6 states that employee perceptions of fairness will be lowest in the underinvestment employee relationship. These employees base fairness on the balance of the exchange from employers, such as what employees get in return for what they give the company. Lastly, hypothesis 7 states that coworkers' positive relationships with each other are more important for those employers who offer broad and open-ended obligations. The trust that develops will be greatest in mutual investment employee–organizational relationships.

From these seven hypotheses, about the relationships between an employer's defined employee–organizational relationships and employee performances, the overall relationship that was the highest was that of mutual investment.

Based on the research, companies with employee–organizational relationships need to take into account all aspects and choose the best one that fits not just the organization but also the employees.

DEFINITION OF A GOOD CORPORATE CITIZEN

How does one describe a company as a good corporate citizen? This can be the topic of a spirited class discussion in which there is interaction between economics, business principles, and ethics. As business schools and the business community expand their concept of the good corporate citizen beyond the narrow view of the shareholder as the single major stakeholder, it becomes necessary to define the other important stakeholders. A few of the many models in the literature on this subject are presented here as initial background for a discussion.

One research group described a good corporate citizen as one that treats a mix of stakeholders well. The groups that they included in their model were employees, customers, stockholders, and the community. For each company studied, the groups were quantified using existing databases and an overall rating score was calculated based on equal weighting of each stakeholder group. The five top companies were IBM, Hewlett Packard, Intel, Procter & Gamble, and Herman Miller.

The Canadian Business for Social Responsibility (CBSR), a not-for-profit, nonpolitical organization of businesses committed to socially responsible policies and practices, defined social responsibility as a firm's commitment to operate in an economically and environmentally sustainable manner, while acknowledging the interests of a variety of stakeholders. The base-level guidelines for corporate social performance are community development, diversity, employee relations, environment, international relationships, market practices, fiscal responsibility, and accountability.

In an effort to define the necessary components of good corporate citizenship, Kim Davenport conducted a Delphi Method study with these results: (1) Ethical business behavior: the company is guided by rigorous ethical standards in all of its business dealings; (2) stakeholder commitment: the company is managed for the benefit of all stakeholders: community, consumers, employees, investors, and suppliers; (3) environmental commitment: the company moderates its overall environmental impact through programs such as recycling, waste and emission abatement, and impact assessment via environmental audits.

A fourth study measuring corporate social performance utilized five categories: employee relations, the environment, product quality, treatment of women and minorities, and community relations. In the area of employees the authors were concerned with union relations, employee ownership, and with employee participation in the management decision process. For women and minorities, the concerns were fair hiring policies and opportunities for promotion.

These four research projects present a small sample of a growing literature on the subject of defining a good corporate citizen. They show many differences such that one would encounter in describing an individual as a good citizen. However, there are also strong common elements in the models. Beyond the internal stakeholders of employees, management and shareholders lie many external stakeholders, such as customers, the community, the environment, suppliers, and unions. How one includes and ranks these stakeholders in an ideal model becomes the chalienge of a discussion.

MANAGERIAL WOMEN AND MULTIPLE ROLES

Historically, the relationship between one's professional and personal life was considered to be in conflict. Role scarcity theory asserted that a person has a finite amount of energy to be expended. Commitment to any one life role was seen as detracting energy from all other roles. An outgrowth of this theory is that women are less effective managers than men due to their more complex family roles. Recent research has theorized role accumulation, the direct opposite of role scarcity, and with a record number of women active in today's managerial workforce, the theory of role scarcity is being challenged.

Researchers Marian N. Ruderman, research scientist at the Center for Creative Leadership; Patricia J. Ohlott, research associate at the Center for Creative Leadership; Kate Panzer, a private consultant; and Sarah N. King, Center for Creative Leadership group leader, conducted two studies. Both studies collected data from a group of managerial women: the first built a qualitative framework for the second, which focused on quantitative results. The purpose of the two studies was to add numerical backing to Role Accumulation theory and curtail beliefs that women's natural nonwork roles hinder their professional performance.

To accomplish the goal of identifying skills and outlooks developed outside of work that may act as resources on the job, study 1 involved interviewing the participants about what they believed was the contribution of their personal lives to their effectiveness of managers. The research sample consisted of 61 female managers and executives with an average age of 40 years and ranging from middle management (49 percent) up to top-level executives (16.9 percent). All participants were highly educated, with more than 51 percent holding master's degrees or higher. Also, over 70 percent of the women were married and a little over 50 percent had minor-age children. The participants came from very diverse backgrounds and worked for a variety of Fortune 500 companies. Each participant underwent three 1-hour telephone interviews over the course of 1 year. These interviews were designed to gather data about personal and work life over the course of time. Participants also filled out a research questionnaire and granted the researchers access to all pertinent personal assessment documents from the participant's home company. The researchers used the interview data to identify any themes connecting the women's answers. Preliminary processing identified 13 themes that were then narrowed down to six distinct categories. All excerpts were reviewed again to see if they could be cleanly coded into the six categories. The two most commonly named categories were increased interpersonal skills learned by dealing with family and children and psychological benefits of familial support system.

In study 2 researchers used quantitative measures to examine the relationships suggested by the results of study 1. There were 276 women who participated in study 2, which was conducted over a 4-year period. The demographics of the women involved in this study were very similar to the women from the first, but none of the participants were involved in both studies. Twenty-one independent items were analyzed as independent variables with five key life roles studied: occupational, marital, parental, community, and friendship. The study was structured this way so that researchers had distinguishable data on separate life roles rather than having all roles lumped together as a family. This approach also allowed researchers to study the effects of multiple life roles on each other, which is the main goal of the combined studies. To be more inclusive for all participants, the words *marital* and *spouse* were replaced with committed relationship and significant other, respectively. The department variables being tested in study 2 were managerial skill and psychological well-being. Managerial skill assessment used a specially designed 360-degree feedback survey given to each participant's coworkers. The survey was broken into two overarching categories, one oriented to task skills and the other representing tone. Tone refers to the soft skill one exhibits when dealing with coworkers. Psychological well-being was assessed using three measures, consisting of satisfaction, self-esteem, and self-acceptance. Satisfaction with one's life was measured by a simple personal survey asking each participant to rank questions low to high. Self-esteem was tested in a similar way, but due to the strong relationship between self-esteem and life satisfaction, researchers also examined internal consistency of answers for each participant. Finally, self-acceptance was measured using an outside assessment tool, which rated self-worth on a 28-point system that taps such dimensions as autonomy, positive relationship, initiative, and openness to new experiences. The final component of study 2 was the use of two control variables. Past research shows a strong positive relationship between age and education and managerial effectiveness. So for purposes of control, researchers used chronological age and the highest level of education completed.

The results of study 1 set the framework for study 2 by identifying six distinct themes from personal life roles, which study 1 participants identified as having a positive impact on their managerial effectiveness. These six themes were opportunities to enrich interpersonal skills, psychological benefits of family, familial emotional support, handling of multiple tasks, personal interests, and household leadership. The first five of these themes had agreement ratings among the study participants of greater than 70 percent. Study 2 results show that having multiple life roles is a strong indicator of strong interpersonal and task-oriented abilities. Statistical results showed that these life roles account for about 10 percent of the variance in managerial ability. Although 10 percent is not huge, it is very significant. The psychological indicators, self-esteem and life satisfaction, did show some positive correlation to managerial effectiveness but the relationship was not statistically significant.

The results of this study are a first step toward curtailing the belief that women, or even men for that matter, who occupy multiple life roles outside of work are less effective at work. The studies challenge the current notion of role scarcity showing that multiple life roles can be a good thing. In fact, study results show that multiple life roles actually are an indicator of managerial effectiveness. These findings suggest the need for a theoretical reconceptualization of work–life relationships and the possible application of role accumulation theory for managerial women.

RELATIONSHIP BETWEEN AFFECT AND JOB SATISFACTION

In her paper, Cynthia D. Fisher of Australia's Bond University describes a program of research on real time affect during work. *Affect* is defined as feeling or emotion, especially as manifested by facial expression or body language. The study particularly focuses on the real-time affective experiences while working on the job, in contrast to the positive–negative attitudinal judgments about the job.

The research is derived from Weiss and Cropanzano's affective events theory (AET), in which it is claimed that momentary events cause concurrent positive or negative affective reactions. As an example, the discrete event of encountering a malfunctioning photocopier at 9:50 AM while rushing to prepare for a 10:00 AM lecture may cause one to feel frustration or anger for a short while. For instance, one may snap at a secretary while frustrated about the photocopier. Similarly, an understaffed workplace may more frequently result in minor stressful events. Such actions are called affect-driven behaviors. Over time, a series of momentary affective experiences may cumulate to influence job attitudes. Finally, AET suggests that some behaviors are judgment-driven by attitudes rather than being directly influenced by current affect.

The researcher was particularly interested in learning the real-time affect during work time for which real time data was required. Her rationale was that all prior research on affect in organizations had utilized one-time retrospective measures of mood at work over a prior week or month. These data were questionable because there was evidence of considerable bias in reporting affective phenomena after the fact.

Therefore, the researcher concentrated the data collection efforts over a 2-week experience period. During this period, respondents wore programmed alarm watches and were asked to report their immediate positive and negative affective reactions at random intervals five times each day. One hundred and twenty employees from 65 organizations and many job categories participated in the study. Surveys assessing work environment features, attitudes, intentions, and self-rated behavior were also administered before and after the experience test period.

The researcher tested three sets of hypotheses in a data set comprising 50 reports of momentary affect from each of the 120 respondents. Between- and within-person analyses were used to explore the correlates of aggregated and momentary affect. Her findings suggest that:

1. Average real-time affect at work shares some variance with job satisfaction, but is not isomorphic (having the same structure) with it.
2. Average positive and negative affect have somewhat different antecedents and consequences.
3. Most people experience a strong within-person relationship between momentary affect and concurrent perceptions of task performance.

The findings indicate that job satisfaction and momentary affect while working are related but are not identical, and that standard verbal measures of overall satisfaction are not particularly good at capturing the affective experience of work. Also, the percent of time that momentary positive affect was stronger than negative affect is a better predictor of job satisfaction than the average intensity of positive affect when it was experienced. In other words, it is more satisfying to be at least a little happy most of the time than to be intensely happy from time to time. A possible implication of this finding is that employers should concentrate on providing a work environment free of minor hassles, which tip the balance toward frequent, if mild, negative affect. They might also build in small, frequent, positive reinforcements or uplifts, perhaps through job design and informal reward systems, rather than relying on possibly more intense but less frequent positive feelings created by formal rewards or promotions, in order to enhance satisfaction. AET suggests that some outcomes are affect-driven while others are judgment-driven. In the present study, helping behavior was expected to be predicted by positive affective reactions rather than by attitudes, as individuals may choose to help those around them spontaneously when in a positive affective state. This finding supported the AET conclusions.

The researcher also hypothesized from various behavioral models that individuals monitor their performance against goals or standards. The perception that performance is below the standard produces negative affect, while the perception that one is on track to meet a goal produces positive affect. The findings proved that a considerable proportion (47 percent to 78 percent) of the total variation in affect measures was within-person, demonstrating that individuals fluctuate considerably over time in how they feel while working, thus corroborating the hypothesis that a predictor of momentary affect was self-perceived momentary performance.

The fact that most individuals experience a fairly strong relationship between performances and affect at the momentary level suggests a possible explanation for a long-standing mystery in organizational behavior: why so many people believe that a happy worker is a productive worker. Working varies substantially within persons over time and the average affect also varies significantly between persons. Consistent with the predictions of AET, average affect while working is predicted by affective disposition and work environment features. Average affect while working is not as strong a predictor of job satisfaction as might have been expected. However, positive affect while working does appear to be important in predicting affective commitment and spontaneous helping behavior.

PERSONAL INITIATIVE AND JOB SUCCESS

There is an old adage among people associated with interviewing job applicants that the best predictor of future behavior is past behavior. A very common interviewing protocol in use today is that of behavior-based interviews. Given these facts, there are many traits that are sought by human resource (HR) professionals in the interviewing process. Psychological experts are interested in the course of study that will validate whether a trait such as personal initiative (PI) can be adequately measured (or predicted) based on such an interview. Skeptics consider initiative as a personality trait that is difficult to assess and question whether measurement can be made in a short interviewing process. The results of significant research will either prove the former or validate skeptics concerns. The implications are significant for all organizations; one only needs to watch the soaring budgets that are used today to match job applicants with company objectives. There is great emphasis on a high degree of self-reliance due to a service-oriented economy that is concerned with meeting customer demands. Placing individuals with personal initiative in these positions will increase organizational effectiveness and bottom-line profitability.

Researchers Doris Fay and Michael Frese, both of the University of Giessen, are interested in tying together a vast array of research that had already been published on measuring initiative and add some of their own findings regarding the influence of motivational factors on personal initiative. Given that many of these studies had previously been published, they were concerned with providing a comprehensive paper that would link their findings and show how they are all interrelated. The end result is a practical analysis that provides for in-depth statistical support for generating a disciplined interviewing process that looks for specific tendencies of personal initiative.

The study wanted to evaluate and measure personal initiative using a variety of methods and sources in relation to behavior and personality. One of the primary methods of measuring PI was using interview-based questionnaires. The five scales that they used to structure the interview were:

1. General initiative at work
2. Education initiative
3. Interviewer evaluation of initiative
4. Self-reported initiative
5. Spouse-reported initiative

Each of these scales was used to measure certain aspects of behavior. General initiative looked at past performance at work, education initiative looked at current initiative to increase knowledge in a formal environment unrelated to work, while the remaining three gave perceptions based on given criteria. The importance of this is that they were analyzed for consistency. These questions would seek answers that exemplified actively overcoming barriers to success. Imperative to PI is the ability to take personal responsibility for problem solving and be persistent.

PI has a widely accepted definition as having the attributes of self-starting, proactive, persistent, and procompany. The factors that will contribute to one's level of PI will include cognitive ability, environmental supports, personal orientations, behavior, and skills. For example, a work environment that is complex in nature is more likely to determine a person's level of initiative than a repetitive environment that is less complex. Similar to knowledge and cognitive ability, the more one understands his job, the more likely he or she will use initiative to solve problems and improve vital processes. Using this network of attributes in a work environment, PI will be enabled and those that do not possess the required level of PI will be discovered.

To collect data from a variety of sources, the researchers used results from well-developed countries (Germany and Holland) and developing countries (South Africa, Uganda, and Zimbabwe). They included students, blue-collar workers, white-color workers, and small-business owners. Some of the studies were taken from data sources such as census reports as well as random door-to-door sampling. They also used time-based data such as interviews 6 to 12 months following initial contact.

The implications for this study in business can be used in both the job recruiting process as well as a tool for evaluating those personnel within the organization who will excel in a position that requires a high level of personal initiative. Not all jobs require a high level of PI, but in a service economy, more jobs are seeking this skill. When human resource professionals are forming questions for potential applicants, they should look for specific evidence to support traits that are positively correlated to PI, while they should be weary of examples that do not or negatively correlate with PI. For example, an applicant who attributes lack of personal initiative to his or her poor health or shy personality should be viewed as unlikely to ever become high in PI. However, those who show self-efficacy and aspirations of control should be judged as having a high level of PI. When conducting periodic job reviews, these same attributes should be sought and used to effectively communicate with employees on their ability to perform in current positions or potential positions that require PI.

THE DIFFICULT ROAD TO EMPLOYEE INVOLVEMENT

New manufacturing strategies require that line employees no longer be simply hired hands, but decision-makers, planners, and problem-solvers. But how can organizations encourage line employees to think and act strategically? The participation of employees in organizational management, particularly manufacturing strategies such as total quality management (TQM) and just-in-time (JIT) systems, involves role orientation, strategic orientation, and job autonomy. Some researchers have established that training is important in developing strategic and role orientation, although other researchers believe that training alone is inadequate. There is a direct relationship between role orientation and job autonomy and its implication is vital in empowering employees to attain enhanced implementation of manufacturing processes.

Research by Sharon Parker, Toby Wall, and Paul Jackson of the University of Sheffield, explored how employees develop into strategic actors. Specifically, the researchers investigated whether simply training employees in new manufacturing techniques such as TQM or JIT would enable organizations to meet their strategic goals, or whether additional individual and organizational change might also be required.

There are three different arguments. Some researchers believe that broad changes in employee behaviors can occur solely through training employees in the manufacturing techniques. Theoretically, when employees fully understand the new manufacturing approach, they will develop orientation to the organizational task. Strategic behaviors are expected to follow.

Other researchers argue that training alone is insufficient. These researchers agree that training helps employees understand the new manufacturing techniques. However, they also believe that employees need to change the way in which they consider their own roles and responsibilities in light of broader organizational goals.

Some researchers believe this kind of role orientation requires that employees experience a degree of autonomy over their jobs before they can begin to learn and practice new strategic behaviors. However, this approach requires more extensive organizational changes, including changes in the organization's authority structure, than an organizational intervention that relies primarily on educational initiatives.

The research attempts to untangle the complexities of these arguments and examines the relationship between strategic orientation, role orientation, and job autonomy. The investigation included three separate studies involving employees in British manufacturing facilities. In the first study, the researchers developed their survey instrument for employees to ensure that the written surveys accurately captured the employees' perspectives. The results of that study indicated that the researchers' measures of strategic orientation and role orientation were statistically independent of each other and were consistent with the theoretical concepts of strategic orientation and role orientation.

The researchers then examined the relationship between strategic orientation and role orientation in a second study at a facility that had implemented TQM and JIT initiatives and had trained employees in these techniques. However, the organization did not formally change the authority structure or employee autonomy. Line employees had little flexibility built into their jobs, and a few line leaders retained most of the control. The investigators surveyed line employees in the firm both before and after the implemented changes.

The results of the second study suggested that the implementation of TQM and JIT changed employees' strategic orientation. Moreover, as employees gained additional experience with TQM and JIT over time, their strategic orientation increased. However, there were no changes in employees' role orientation and a significant decrease in employees' recognition of the importance of proactive behaviors such as acquiring new skills.

Finally, the researchers studied strategic and role orientations of employees at a third facility that had both implemented new manufacturing strategies and had consciously redesigned its employees' jobs. This company gave line employees significant control over planning, quality, problem solving, and production scheduling. Again, the investigators surveyed the employees both before and after the organizational changes occurred.

The results of the final study underscore the link between job autonomy and role orientation. For those employees who experienced increased job autonomy, role orientation scores increased. Those employees showed increased ownership of production problems and recognized the importance of a wide range of skills and knowledge for performing their jobs.

Organizations that desire significant strategic change through their manufacturing processes may need to consider altering the nature of employees' jobs and reporting relationships to increase their autonomy and responsibility. Interventions designed to empower employees, such as self-managed teams, may enhance employees' sense of autonomy and improve the implementation of new manufacturing processes. As this study suggests, without the autonomy to learn and practice strategic behaviors, employees are less likely to adopt the sense of ownership essential to achieving the competitive edge.

JOB SATISFACTION OF PROJECT MANAGERS AND FUNCTIONAL MANAGERS IN A MATRIX ORGANIZATION

In a matrix organization, who exhibits greater job satisfaction, a project manager or a functional manager? Although both act as managers in an organization, the corresponding job satisfaction levels between the two groups vary. The causes of satisfaction were identified as those related to the work environment (hygiene) and those related to job content (motivators).

Researchers Susan Turner and Dawn Utley, both of the University of Alabama in Huntsville, surveyed 31 managers within an unnamed government research and development organization. Fourteen of the 31 respondents were project managers and the remaining 17 were functional managers. Their research tested the overall job satisfaction and underlying causes of that job satisfaction in relation to hygiene and motivators.

The researchers asked the managers to provide the following: an example of a situation in her or his current job as a manager where each she or he felt satisfied and internally motivated, and example of a situation in her or his current job as a manager where each she or he felt dissatisfied and frustrated, and which of the aforementioned scenarios best described that manager's feelings toward her or his current position.

In 1959, a group of researchers that included Frederick Herzberg performed a similar study to determine which factors contributed to job satisfaction. Herzberg's group categorized the factors as either hygiene or motivational. The researchers utilized 12 different, distinct factors between Herzberg's two categories, tabulated the results, and compared the results to Herzberg's findings from 1959. Based on findings made in Herzberg's study, they noted that improvement in hygiene factors did not lead to improved job satisfaction for dissatisfied managers. The improvements led to feelings of neutrality toward the job. As such, it appears that job satisfaction is based on motivators.

The research proved the factors that motivated managers in 1959 continued to motivate managers in the late 1990s. The respondents from the November 1996 survey listed accomplishment, teamwork, responsibility, and the work itself as the top motivators, with three of the four motivators being consistent with the 1959 study. Furthermore, the results showed that the top four motivators were the same for project managers and functional managers. The project managers showed a greater emphasis on the satisfying factors than their functional peers did.

The functional managers displayed lower levels of job satisfaction than the project managers. The reduced satisfaction levels result from lower levels of satisfaction derived from the top four motivators coupled with increased dissatisfaction aroused from hygiene factors. As the project managers and the functional managers work for the same government research and development company, it appears that each set of managers is subject to similar hygiene factors. The research proves that the functional managers paid greater attention to the hygiene factors than their project counterparts.

This study proves that the factors that motivated managers in 1959 held true in November 1996. As such, technological advancements and the passage of time have not changed the factors that drive job satisfaction.

The study's results provide a challenge for employers to determine the cost–benefit whereby the benefits gained from improved productivity of functional and project managers exceeds the costs spent to improve the hygiene factors. As the functional managers were not as satisfied as project managers were in the same company, it appears reasonable to assume that the functional managers have lower motivation levels, and ultimately, lower productivity levels than project managers. Furthermore, based on the results of the study, improvements in hygiene that would soothe dissatisfied functional managers would not necessarily improve the productivity of the satisfied project managers. The answer to the challenge for each employer lies within each employer's corporate philosophy.

PROCEDURAL JUSTICE PROMOTES ORGANIZATIONAL SUPPORT

When organizations use their form of procedural justice, does it influence organizational citizenship behavior? That is, does it affect the way an employee feels about his employer? Procedural justice has been found to affect organizational citizenship behavior (OCB) by influencing perceived organizational support, which in turn prompts employees to respond with organizational citizenship behavior. Recent results suggest that procedural justice is a preliminary to organizational support.

Researchers Robert H. Moorman, of West Virginia University, Gerald L. Blakely, also of West Virginia University, and Brian P. Niehoff, of Kansas State University, surveyed 450 civilian subordinates and the supervisors of the 450 subordinates from a large military hospital located in the Midwest. Their research was to test the hypothesis that procedural justice will be positively related to perceived organizational support. It was also to test the hypothesis that perceived organizational support would mediate the relationship between procedural justice and organizational citizenship behavior.

Each of the civilian subordinates was asked to measure procedural justice and perceived organizational support. Meanwhile, each of the supervisors was asked to rate the subordinates on the measure of organizational citizenship behavior.

Supervisors assessed citizenship behavior with a four-dimension scale based on the dimensions of organizational citizenship behavior. The four dimensions measured were: (1) interpersonal helping, which focuses on helping coworkers in their job when such help is needed; (2) individual initiative, which describes communications to others in the workplace to improve individual and group performances; (3) personal industry, which describes the performance of specific tasks above and beyond the call of duty; and (4) loyal boosterism, which describes the promotion of the organizational image to outsiders.

The subordinates were asked to measure procedural justice based on their feelings and on the way they perceive other employees in general to feel. The other employees' feelings were added to combine both an individual and overall experience in the organization. The subordinates were also asked several questions to indicate how much their organization supported them. This would give the researchers an idea on perceived organizational support.

The researchers confirmed that procedural justice was positively related to perceived organizational support. It also confirmed that perceived organizational support would mediate the relationship between procedural justice and organizational citizenship behavior. Data gathered during this research supports both the affirmed hypotheses tested.

This study has critical implications that are more likely to surface as employee satisfaction becomes more and more prevalent. As this study indicates, procedural justice and organizational citizenship behavior are directly related. This information can be particularly useful to those companies that have a low employee satisfaction rating and wish to increase that rating. It is imperative for businesses today to heed the implications of this study.

INCREASED TRUST COULD LOWER CONTRACT COST

When entering into a contract, does your level of trust affect the contracting methods used? There is an apparent level of mistrust between two parties that can be a driver to actually increase the total cost of a project. This was tested in the construction industry in Canada, but appears to be the same throughout North America. Not much research has been done on the advantages of increased trust between contractual parties. The study identified opportunities for better risk allocation mechanisms and contracting strategies. Having a better understanding of this trust relationship can lead to overall project cost savings.

Researchers Ramy Zaghloul and Francis Hartman are in the field of Project Management Specialization at the University of Calgary. The survey was conducted in Canada and the United States through a mailed-out questionnaire. This questionnaire had various forms, including scale type, yes/no, and multiple-choice questions. It also questioned an individual's perception of the most common disclaimer clauses such as uncertainty of work conditions, delaying events, indemnification, liquidated damages, and sufficiency of contract documents. More than 300 people responded, including owners, contractors, and consultants from both private and public industry sectors, all working on various projects.

The construction industry is the single largest nongovernmental employer in Canada, accounting for 15 percent of their gross domestic product. It has been noted that there are considerable cost increases that have been attributed to inappropriate risk allocation in contracts. Since the construction industry is so risky, it is important to note that the amount of risk and how it is allocated has a major impact on the cost of the project. In the past, owners typically appear to avoid risk by allocating as many risks as possible to the contractor. Past studies have shown that disclaimer clauses are the main causes that increase the overall cost of a particular project. Trust is essential in the business world and it can have influence on every aspect of the project management process.

The survey revealed that nearly 75 percent of contracts are prepared by the owners and not negotiated. Of the five commonly used disclaimer clause types, uncertainty of work conditions showed up on 92 percent of the construction contracts. Other clauses such as indemnification, delaying events, sufficiency of contract documents, and liquidated damages showed up 77, 72, 67, and 61 percent, respectively. In every contract with a disclaimer clause, the contractor attached risk premiums to protect himself, thus increasing the total cost of the project. When there is a low trust relationship, the perception of the disclaimer clause's risk was very high, a 4.4 out of 5. When there was a high trust relationship, the perception of the disclaimer clause's risk was low, a 2.3 out of 5.

Because of the mistrust between the contractor and owner, using disclaimer clauses in contracts has shown to increase a project's cost from 8 to 20 percent, based on this survey. On multimillion dollar projects, this increase is huge. Also, the use of disclaimer clauses could present hidden costs such as unnecessary disputes, increased potential for claims, and restricted bid competition.

The results show that the amount of the premium is based on the contractor's perception of the disclaimer clause risk. There is a correlation between the amount of the premiums associated with the disclaimer clauses and the level of trust between the owner and contractor. Basically, if the owners and contractors change the way they currently prepare contracts and change their current perception of each other and trust each other, the cost savings benefit could be substantial.

REFERENCES

Davenport, K. (2000). Defining a good corporate citizenship. *Journal of International Business Studies, 49*(2), 216.

Fay, D., & Frese, M. (2001). The concept of personal initiative: An overview of validity studies. *Human Performance, 14*(1), 97–124.

Fisher, D. D. (2002). Real time affect at work: A neglected phenomenon in organizational behavior. *Australian Journal of Management, 27*(1),1–10.

Moorman, R. H., Blakely, G. L., & Niehoff, B. P. (1998). Does perceived organizational support mediate the relationship between procedural justice and organizational citizenship behavior? *Academy of Management Journal, 41*(3), 351–357.

Parker, S. R., Wall, D., & Jackson, R. (1997). That's not my job: Developing flexible employee work orientations. *Academy of Management Journal, 40*(5), 899–929.

Ruderman, M. N., Ohlott, P. J., Panzer, K., & King, S. N. (2002). Benefits of multiple roles for managerial women. *Academy of Management Journal, 45*(2), 369–386.

Tsui, A. S., Pearce, J. L., Porter, L. W., & Tripoli, A. M. (1997). Alternative approaches to the employee-organizational relationship: Does investment in employees pay off? *Academy of Management Journal, 40*(5), 1089–1121.

Turner, S. G., & Utley, D. R. (1998). Project managers and functional managers: A case study of job satisfaction in a matrix organization. *Project Management Journal, 39*(4), 11–16.

Zaghloul, R., & Hartman, F. (2003). Construction contracts: The cost of mistrust. *International Journal of Project Management, 21*(6), 419–424.

CHAPTER 18

FIRM PERFORMANCE AND SUPPLY CHAINS

This chapter focuses on a variety of triggers on firm performance. Firm performance is commonly measured in financial terms but can also include other performance measures such as market share, revenue growth, new product development, and so on.

The first paper compares CEO compensation and firm performance. The paper covers two studies, one involving 175 firms and a second one involving 243 firms. The results indicated that there is an asymptotic relationship between CEO compensation and firm performance. Also, increased monitoring of CEO compensation causes senior managers to minimize risky decisions.

The second paper explores the link between human resource management (HRM) and firm performance. The researchers studied and evaluated eight prior studies to find an answer. The results indicate that when firms pay close attention to HRM, they tend to be most successful.

The third paper explores the effect of downsizing and/or rightsizing on firm performance. The researchers used data from companies in the Standard & Poor (S&P) 500 to examine changes in employment and financial performance. The results show that downsizing may not necessarily generate the financial benefits sought by management.

The fourth paper asked the question of what the relationship is between corporate social performance and financial performance of the firm. The

Proven Solutions for Improving Supply Chain Performance, pages 251–265

researchers used reputation and financial data from 67 companies that have been rated in surveys between 1982 and 1992. The results show that there is a direct relationship between social and financial performance.

The fifth paper examines the relationship between early retirement programs and firm performance. The researchers utilized data from 51 companies, which utilized early retirement programs. The firm performance factor used was stock market performance before and after the program announcements. The results showed that the performance of the firms increased.

The sixth paper is a study of poor firm performance and CEO's advice networks. A survey was used and 240 usable responses were received. Advice networks are defined as contacts with executives from outside of the company. The results showed that the higher the level of advice seeking, the lower was the subsequent change in corporate strategy. As a result, performance did not improve.

The seventh paper examines firm performance and the utilization of 360-degree feedback programs. In the 360-degree feedback program, senior managers evaluate junior managers, and vice versa. The results indicate that firms utilizing the programs generate decreasing shareholder value.

The eighth and final paper evaluates the impact of e-commerce announcements on the firm's stock price performance. The results of the study show that capital markets react positively to firm announcements of e-commerce initiatives, leading to significant enhancement of the firm's market value.

The following summaries describe in more detail the summarized statements above. The summaries indicate that certain actions by firms will affect firm performance, but not always in a positive way. Senior managers should be aware of this.

CEO COMPENSATION AND FIRM PERFORMANCE

The most common form of business organization today is the corporation. In this form of organization, equity holders have control over the firm's decisions. Most often, the responsibility of the equity holders are delegated to top executives of the firm in the hope that they make decisions in the equity holder's best interest. Although this may be optimal, it is not always the case that what is in the equity holder's best interest is what is done.

Henry L. Tosi, Jr., and Juis R. Gomez-Mejia used a behavioral scale that rated the monitoring of the compensations of CEOs to test two hypotheses. These two hypotheses were derived from agency theory and literature on corporate governance. The first hypothesis stated that a firm's performance is related asymptotically to the level that a firm monitors its CEO's compensation. The second hypothesis stated that the relationship between the firm's performance and CEO compensation monitoring is stronger in management-controlled firms than in owner-controlled firms.

To ensure that management does what is in the best interest of the equity holder, the monitoring system was set up to limit the agents from self-serving interests. This monitoring process usually takes the form of monetary payments. For this study, since monitoring is a behavioral process, informed people are asked about what is being monitored in their firm and the intensity of the monitoring. First, a CEO compensation-monitoring scale was developed. Second, the scale was used to test the two hypotheses.

The two hypotheses were tested in two different studies. Study 1 involved 175 firms; study 2 involved 243 firms. The chief compensation officers (CCOs) were chosen as the informants because they are the most informed members in a firm about CEO compensations. For study 1, questionnaires were sent out to 500 CCOs. There was a 35 percent response rate. The questionnaires for study 2 were sent out to 500 CCOs. There was only a 28 percent response rate for study 2. In both studies, the researchers looked at the firm's performance, CEO compensation monitoring, ownership structure, and firm size. A difference between these two studies is that the first was a self-reported subjective assessment by the CCOs, whereas the second used a conventional archival performance indicator. The researchers controlled the manufacturing sector in study 2.

A logarithmic multiple regression analysis was used to test hypothesis 1 because it predicted a diminishing return. The firms in both studies were also separated into different groups of high monitoring, median monitoring, and low monitoring.

The results of these studies not only supported both hypotheses, but indicated a nonlinear, asymptotic relationship between CEO compensation and firm performance. What this is saying is that as monitoring increases, managers will stray away from risky decisions that could endanger the equity holder's interest. It was also found that when ownership is more concentrated, additional monitoring is less effective than when it is not as concentrated.

This study has made the important point that monitoring is very important. In order to protect the interests of the equity holders, managers should be closely monitored to ensure that performance is in the best interest of the equity holder and not just the manager.

HUMAN RESOURCE SYSTEMS AND FIRM PERFORMANCE

Do human resource systems affect the bottom line? Although some say that human resource management (HRM) is nothing more than a diverse and fragmented set of "practices," research has proven that when integrated as a whole, HRM practice is closely associated with organizational success.

Researchers Richard Niehaus and Paul M. Swiercz gathered eight different papers that fellow researchers have written. The research of these articles tested assumptions of the link between HRM measures of firm performance. The research on these articles also tested the collective and individual surveys pertaining to the wide and divergent body of work that has been accumulating slowly over the past few years.

Niehaus and his colleague went through the eight articles to see exactly what they had to say about human resource systems. One article displayed three observations, the first being that HRM should be looked at as a whole, and not singling any part of it out. Much of the past HRM work has focused on single practices, so therefore they may want to take a step forward by concentrating on the whole. Another suggestion in this article is that firms that are too aggressive in trying to outsource the responsibilities of HRM could get hurt in the long run in terms of competition. Another important paper that the researchers looked at helped Niehaus and Swiercz out because it focused on two different types of organizations, profit and nonprofit. By using these two different types of organizations, they were able to provide information that supports HRM practices being directly related to organizational performance.

A third article that was used in the research is related to the performance of initial public offerings. This research was very risky. By analyzing companies with an initial placement offering (IPO), you are taking the risk of prematurely analyzing the company before it develops a stable human resource department. Prematurely investigating these companies may not be a good research project because the numbers could be thrown off since the company really has not had time to develop in the market. The research that was done for this study used 136 nonfinancial companies that made their IPO in 1988.

The research that Niehaus and his colleague performed proved that HRM systems do in fact affect the bottom line, but in many different ways. First it can be said that HRM is proven to be an administrative activity rather than a strategically significant function. No longer will HRM be looked at as a difference maker, but rather it will be looked at how HRM can be used to gain a competitive advantage. Results also showed that when pricing stocks for specific companies that are currently offering IPOs, investors tended to ignore these factors when the stock prices were being set. It has been proven that HRM systems that are expected to contribute to firm performance require considerable research in order to make the systems important. Without the research, HRM will only be part of the equation rather than a very important key to the success of companies.

Human resource management plays an important role in every company. It deals with salaries, employment, benefits, compensation, as well as working as teams. When companies focus their attention on only one or two of these, they tend to fail; yet when companies pay their attention on HRM as a whole, they tend to be the most successful. The study of these different papers has proven this statement, and many companies suffer if they do not concentrate on the whole. When dealing with all of the aspects of HRM, companies run smoothly and rarely run into problems.

EMPLOYMENT CHANGES AND FIRM PERFORMANCE

Throughout the 1980s and the 1990s, news of corporate downsizing has been prominent in the media. The phenomenon of employment downsizing has produced fundamental structural changes to the economy and has had a painful impact on the American workforce. A fundamental assumption is that a firm's executives seek to operate efficiently with minimum costs and that they choose to downsize in order to decrease their employment costs. Basically, firms decrease their workforces to improve their performance and increase their competitiveness in their particular market. Ultimately, the market value of a firm's shares would improve due to downsizing. However, recent study has suggested that although firms engage in employment downsizing, they have not significantly shown improvements on stock and asset returns compared to the average companies in their industry. The study has suggested that companies that combined employment downsizing with asset restructuring have shown higher returns on assets and stock returns than other firms.

Researchers Wayne F. Cascio, Clifford E. Young, and James R. Morris, all from the University of Colorado at Denver, used data from companies in the Standard & Poor (S&P) 500 to examine changes in employment in terms of two dependent variables: profitability and return on common stock. The purpose of the research was to determine whether companies that engaged in major employment downsizing were able to improve their financial performance as measured by return on asset (ROA) and total returns on common stock. To do so, they tested the following two null hypotheses. Hypothesis 1—changes in employment will have no effect on profitability in the year of the changes and in two succeeding years. Hypothesis 2 was changes in employment would have no effect on total return on common stock in the year of the changes and in the two succeeding years.

The researchers examined sets of management decisions about employment levels made by all companies included in the S&P 500 over the 12-year period of study, 1981–1992. They also extracted financial data on individual companies to investigate the impact of the changes on the financial performance of firms. Because the composition of the S&P 500 changed over time, the sample size was 537, with 5,479 different occurrences.

With the set sample size, the primary variable of interest in this study was change in employment from one year to the next. Over the period of the study, some companies increased their levels of employment, while others decreased their level of employment or did both. With the data they collected, they calculated and measured the profitability and stock return for all the companies included in the study, along with the industry-aggregate measures of each of the following variables: number of employees (EMP); operating income before depreciation, interest, and taxes (OIBDP); plant and equipment (PPENT); total assets (AT); dividends on common stock (DVPSX); and price of common stock. With the calculated measures, the researchers examined the relationship between profitability and the change in employment, they regressed the change in ROA against the employment–change ratio for both the total sample and for each category, including the asset–change ratio.

The results of the study were mixed regarding the two null hypotheses that were tested. With respect to hypothesis 1, which stated that changes in employment have no effect on profitability, the result was that there was no effect on profitability (ROA). Neither the employment downsizers nor the combination downsizers exhibited ROA improvements that were significantly better than those of either the stable employers or their industries. However, the asset downsizers outperformed both the stable employers and their industries. In conclusion, although some categories of downsizers improved their profitability through downsizing, this effect did not sufficiently justify the rejection of the null hypothesis. With respect to hypothesis 2, which stated that changes in employment have no effect on total return on common stock, the regression result concluded that, for both the employment downsizers and the combination downsizers, there was sufficient evidence to reject it and state that these downsizers performed better than the stable employers. Overall, given the mixed results, downsizing may or may not necessarily generate the benefits sought by management. Managers must make informed decisions to alleviate the painful impact that employment downsizing has produced in our economy.

The study suggests critical implications that senior managers in U.S. corporations are under a considerable amount of pressure from stockholders to improve financial performances. Often, they try to achieve this goal by cutting costs or restructuring assets. Many managers implement strategies of employment downsizing to cut costs without knowing what the outcome will be. The question that needs to be answered is whether such cost cutting translates into higher profits. Managers must be very cautious in implementing a strategy that can impose such traumatic costs on employees. Overall, employment downsizing has been an important phenomenon in American business, yet there is still a great need for additional research about its effects.

THE CORPORATE SOCIAL–FINANCIAL PERFORMANCE RELATIONSHIP

What is the relationship, if any, between social performance and financial performance of business corporations? This question has been a topic of interest for more than half a century. Despite this long record of discussion and analysis, the connection between corporate social and financial performance has not been fully established.

Researchers Lee E. Preston, Professor at the College of Business and Management at the University of Maryland, and Douglas P. O'Bannon, Assistant Professor of Management at Webster University, St. Louis, analyze the relationship between indicators of corporate social and financial performance within a comprehensive theoretical framework. Statistical analysis utilizes reputation and financial data for 67 companies that have been rated in surveys over an 11-year period, 1982–1992, and for which the requisite financial information is also available.

Hypotheses developed are investigated with a combination of data from *Fortune* magazine and *Compustat*. *Fortune* conducted an annual corporate survey since 1982 of several thousand people to reflect the interests of three important stakeholder groups: employees, customers, and community members. *Compustat*, on the other hand, was used as evidence of the financial performance side of the relationship. The researchers tested their hypothesis by computing correlation coefficients between the social and financial performance variables, in both contemporaneous and lead-lag relationships for these 67 firms.

Contemporaneous correlations are relevant both as indicators of the direction of social–financial performance relationships and as reference points against which to compare lead-lag results.

A number of hypotheses were developed in this research. The social impact hypothesis or the stakeholder theory states that favorable performance (meeting the needs of stakeholders) will lead to favorable financial performance, and vice versa. The trade-off hypothesis asserts that social performance is the independent variable and that social accomplishments involve financial costs. A third possibility is the available funds hypothesis, stating causal or lead-lag relationship is from financial to social performance. Another idea is the managerial opportunism hypothesis, which entails pursuit of private managerial goals, which might lead to a negative relationship between financial and social performance. And finally there is the possibility of positive or negative synergies, which determines that a time-pattern of their interaction cannot be detected from statistics.

Out of 270 correlations computed in contemporaneous and lead-lag form, there is not a single negative result. As a result there is no support for trade-off, managerial opportunism, or negative synergy hypotheses. On the contrary, all of the evidence suggests that there is a positive association between social and financial performance in large U.S. corporations and hence this is broadly consistent with the stakeholder theory.

As a result of this study it should be evident that managers should consider the consequences of their behaviors. A direct relationship exists between social and financial performance. Therefore, a positive attitude and friendly behavior in the workplace should lead to better financial performance, which could lead to greater profits. But, a negative attitude and behavior may lead to disappointing financial performance. On the other hand, good financial performance of a company may make a happier work environment too. So, it may be beneficial to work for a successful company since this, in turn, will make you want to work for the company and be a happier individual.

RETIREMENT PROGRAMS AND FIRM PERFORMANCE

Early retirement programs have become a prominent way for companies to restructure their companies. Researchers Davidson, Worrell, and Fox performed this research on companies from the years 1982–1992. Whether or not this is an effective way to improve the financial soundness of the company is the issue they decided to research. Which is the best way to formulate your plans, and at what time you decide to make the announcement of this plan seem to be crucial in the effectiveness of how the equity market will perceive and reward your decision. Obviously by eliminating people in your organization you will eliminate explicit costs at first, but will these cost savings create greater implicit costs or even eliminate the true workers or brains of the operation, thus creating great losses? Recent studies have shown that it is not clear whether or not it is a good decision to cut costs by using early retirement programs.

There are two different ways to categorize the method and reasoning that you use for restructuring your company, named convergence and reorientation. Convergence is more of a defensive reaction that focuses on internal efficiency through cost cutting and fewer employees, which is the main idea behind early retirement plans. Reorientation is a drastic matter where you completely rethink your mission, processes, strategy, and structure your company accordingly. Reorientation would be used more likely in a case of a company that is in serious financial condition. The purpose of this research was to determine market reactions to announcements of early retirement programs using standard event methodology. The researchers found unbiased announcements of early retirement by 51 companies and used these to do the study. They were looking for whether or not the size of the retirements, the financial status before the announcements, and who was being forced to retire mattered in the results.

The first thing that they did was to look at the income statements and profit margins of these 51 companies from the date of the announcement and the 2 years previous. Then they looked for abnormal stock returns in the years preceding the announcement as well. With these figures of abnormal stock returns they were able to calculate CARs (cumulative abnormal returns). CARs were broken down into categories of 240 to 20 days, 20 to 0 days, and a special one of 5 to 2 days prior to the announcement to see when the most market activity was happening. Then these categories were processed into subcategories compared to how many people were being affected at the time the announcement was made (according to the financial status) and who was being affected, such as blue-collar or mainly white-collar workers.

In the 240 to 20 days prior to the announcement, 30 of the 51 companies experienced negative CARs and 31 of the 51 companies stated that cost cutting was their motive for initiating the early retirement program. Half of the companies announced during the Reagan boom, which demonstrated a commitment to growth. The other half announced during the stagnant years of Bush, perhaps making short-sighted attempts to cut costs. The period of 5 to 2 days prior to the announcement is when most of the reaction takes place. Usually the market gets this type of news before the public does. Also, the more extensive that the announcement was publicized the more positive the market's reaction seemed to be. The most outstanding result was that the profit margins of these companies increased from 2.37 percent to 3.38 percent in year 0; also, the return on equity increased on average. It seemed that these programs helped to affect the bottom line in a positive way. There was no significant market reaction for the firms that were in decline the year before announcing. However, there was significant positive impact on companies whose prior year's performance was good.

These implications give knowledge and leverage to firms if they are able to understand what makes some companies successful when going through early retirement program planning. One is now able to look at these figures and realize that the market will reward you more if you show that you are trying to build up strength to your already strong company rather than trying to rebuild a dying one. Therefore, you should announce during a strong financial period rather than wait until the company outlook is depressed. Also, the market seemed to like layoffs in white-collar workers more than in blue-collar workers, making it seem that they believe that the offices is where most of the unneeded fat is. Early retirement programs seemed to be a great idea for thinning out the company and keeping employee morale high; however, it takes good planning and proper execution to make it all come together.

POOR FIRM PERFORMANCE AND CEO'S ADVICE NETWORKS

When faced with poor performance, how does the level of advice seeking from similar and dissimilar executives affect the CEO's corporate strategy? Are managers more likely to look for advice from fellow executives who they see as managing a firm with similar functional background, executives who they have personal friendship ties with, and/or executives from firms within the same industry, or do they look for executives who do not show these characteristics? Research has indicated that although faced with the company performing poorly, top executives often do not initiate significant changes in corporate strategy.

Researchers Michael L. McDonald and James D. Westphal, both of the University of Texas at Austin, selected 600 companies, randomly selected from the Forbes index, to be included in the survey. Questionnaires were sent out, and with a final response rate of 40 percent, 240 companies were included in the sample. Test for nonresponse bias was performed on the sample to ensure that there was no significant difference between respondents and nonrespondents. The research tested the assumptions that managers who are facing a firm with poor performance are more likely to seek advice from CEOs who are similar to them or who they have friendly ties with and how the level of advice from the respective sources affect the manager's level of change in corporate strategy.

In the study the managers were asked to answer questions related to their advice-seeking interactions, with survey questions being drawn from qualitative studies of corporate governance and strategic decision making. For each advice managers listed, they were asked to classify it in regards to functional background, industrial background, and personal relationship. Also included in the survey were questions to assess the respondents' general advice-seeking propensity, such as how many times they had sought advice on strategic issues from a top manager at another company during the past 12 months. Also included in the CEO survey was a separate set of questions as control variables.

Independent of the survey, data was gathered by the researchers about the firm's performance, based on market-to-book value of equity and return on assets, to evaluate whether managers were indeed working for poorly performing companies. To evaluate the effect of the manager's actions, product market diversification and geographic diversification (two important aspects of a firm's corporate strategy) were used to determine the change in corporate strategy.

The results showed that CEOs in the sample sought strategic advice from executives at other firms approximately nine times during the previous year. The majority of these interactions were indeed with CEOs of other companies who came from the same industry (75 percent) as well as with whom the managers had personal ties (74 percent). Fifty-nine percent of managers answered positively in respect to functional background. Managers of poorly performing companies manifested greater propensity to rely on the advice of other firm executives with similar characteristics. The results also proved that for managers of poorly performing firms, the level of advice seeking from similar executives is negatively associated with subsequent change in corporate strategy. The research showed that the higher the level of advice seeking, the lower the subsequent change in corporate strategy.

The study has critical implications for companies that are performing poorly. As the study has shown, firms' responses to economic misfortune can be influenced by social factors. It shows that executives' social network connections can result in strategic inaction due to poor firm performance. As such the advice seeking of CEOs in response to low performance decreases the likelihood of needed changes in corporate strategy, causing even lower subsequent performance and ending in a downward slide in performance. While proving that certain kinds of informal ties can indeed have a negative influence on companies' strategic decisions, it also shows that friendship ties between executives can actually sometimes benefit performance due to increased access to resources. As such, the research should help us to understand the psychological processes that cause managers to react to a firm's poor performance the way they do. That should enable us to devise better control mechanisms to monitor executives' strategic decisions, especially during times of poor performance, to ensure companies' survival during these times.

FIRM PERFORMANCE AND 360-DEGREE FEEDBACK

In the last several years, many organizations base their human resources investment decisions on tradition, fads, or competitors' practices, instead of on sound financial measures. A perfect example of this phenomenon may be 360-degree feedback. A 360-degree feedback program requires that supervisors evaluate employees but employees also evaluate their supervisors. Adopted by a growing number of organizations, 360-degree feedback is widely accepted as an effective performance management tool. However, new research shows that 360-degree feedback programs may hurt more than they help. It does not necessarily mean 360-degree feedback programs should be abandoned. But it does mean organizations should take a second look at their performance management programs to see if they are accomplishing what they are expecting.

Researchers Bruce Pfau and Ira Kay are employed by the global human capital consulting firm Watson Wyatt Worldwide. Watson Wyatt's 2001 Human Capital Index (HCI), an ongoing study of the linkages between specific HR practices and shareholder value at 750 large, publicly traded companies, found that 360-degree feedback programs were associated with a 10.6 percent decrease in shareholder value.

Watson Wyatt's 2001 HCI report revealed that companies using 360-degree feedback programs have lower market value. According to the study, companies that use peer review have a market value that is 4.9 percent lower than similarly situated companies that do not use peer review. Likewise, companies that allow employees to evaluate their managers are valued 5.7 percent lower than similar firms that do not. Taken together, these practices are associated with a 10.6 percent decline in shareholder value.

The HCI study is not the only indicator that 360-degree feedback programs may be failing to match their promise. Researchers and formerly strong advocates of it have begun to raise questions. Jai Ghorpade, a professor of management at San Diego State University, also reported that out of more than 600 feedback studies, one-third found improvements in performance, one-third reported decreases in performance, and the rest reported no impact at all.

Researchers found the roots of the problems. They found that unless everyone participating in a 360-degree feedback program is trained in the art of giving and receiving feedback, the process can lead to uncertainty and conflict among team members. Another issue is that there may be a gap between an organization's business objectives and what 360-degree feedback programs measure. The time and cost associated with 360-degree feedback programs also are stumbling blocks. Finally, reviewers and those being reviewed fail to follow up after feedback.

However, the researchers confirm that there are good reasons to not give up on 360-degree feedback programs despite these drawbacks. The process still holds the potential to deepen employees' understanding of their own performance. And it may be able to help companies create value by better aligning job performance with business strategy.

The researchers demonstrated the right process to implement 360-degree feedback programs in order to help companies transform the program into a value creator, not destroyer. The process includes:

- Implement 360-degree feedback programs for the right reasons.
- Assess the costs of the program.
- Focus on business goals and strategy.
- Do not rely solely on 360-degree feedback programs.
- Get support at all levels of the organization.
- Train people in giving and receiving feedback.
- Create an action plan for each employee based on the feedback.
- Monitor implementation, ask for ideas for improvement, and make adjustments.
- Recognize that a 360-degree feedback program is not a panacea.

This study has critical implications, particularly for companies which have implemented the program. The fact that the programs are associated with a decline in shareholder value should persuade HR managers to revisit their existing or planned 360-degree feedback programs. The existence of such data also should force companies to ask themselves what they hope to gain from feedback reviews, or for that matter, from any HR initiative they undertake.

IMPACT OF E-COMMERCE ANNOUNCEMENTS

When a company makes an e-commerce announcement, does it affect the cumulative abnormal returns to shareholders (CARs)? Is it beneficial for companies to increase their press releases involving e-commerce developments? Are the shareholder returns greater for businesses that engage in e-commerce? How do the returns to conventional, brick-and-mortar firms from e-commerce initiatives compare with returns to the new breed of Internet firms? Will firms that are increasing their e-commerce initiatives and that are investing large sums of money in the increasing online market find it worthwhile?

Mani Subramani and Eric Walden from the University of Minnesota did a survey of 251 e-commerce events broken down into categories of net or conventional firms, business-to-business (B2B) or business-to-consumer (B2C), and involving digital or tangible goods. They were testing four hypotheses: (H1) the abnormal returns attributable to e-commerce announcements are positive; (H2) the abnormal returns attributable to e-commerce announcements of conventional firms are different from those of net firms; (H3) the abnormal returns attributable to B2B e-commerce announcements are different from those of B2C; (H4) the abnormal returns attributable to e-commerce announcements involving tangible goods are different from those involving digital goods.

To calculate the effect of an event, it is necessary to estimate what the return of the stock would have been had the event not occurred. The return of a stock was tied to the overall growth of the firm. For the analysis an estimation period of 120 days was used. The CARs were calculated over two event windows: an 11-day interval, 5 days before the event to 5 days after, and a 21-day interval, 10 days before the event and 10 days after. The abnormal returns are over and above those predicted by the general trend of the market on each day. The strength of their method is from the improbability of random events across different firms on different days coinciding with the announcement of an e-commerce initiative.

The study found that the significance of the CARs are uniformly positive and significant in both time windows and thus provide strong support for H1. While the CARs for conventional firms are uniformly lower than those for net firms, the difference between the CARs are barely significant in the 5-day window and not significant in the 10-day window. This data does not support H2, which states that the CARs for conventional firms would be different from that for net firms. The magnitude of the CARs for B2B and B2C announcements are each large and individually significant, the CARs for B2B are consistently lower than those for B2C. Thus H3 receives weak support. While the CARs for tangible goods are consistently higher than those for digital goods in both time windows, the results related to the significance of the difference between them are different, thus giving weak support to H4.

The results of the study conclude that capital markets react positively to firm announcements of e-commerce initiatives, leading to a significant enhancement of the firm's market value. This positive and significant effect is observed for both conventional and internet firms. The CARs for both B2B, B2C, tangible, and digital goods announcements are both positive and highly significant. The results suggest that at least temporarily value is created for the firm's stockholders.

A skeptical rival hypothesis might be that the results reflect firms' attempts to enhance their market value based on insincere e-commerce announcements to the market. However, evidence from prior studies suggest that financial markets incorporate mechanisms that factor in information on firm credibility in responding to announcements by firms. It is plausible that e-commerce announcements can merely be symbolic moves by firms rather than genuine attempts to initiate e-commerce activities. However, it appears that most announcements are sincere. This study suggests that by keeping the public aware of e-commerce announcements, a business may create value for its stockholders. This also increases the value of the business.

REFERENCES

Cascio, W. F., Young, C. E., & Morris, R. (1997). Financial consequences of employment-change decisions in major U.S. corporations. *Academy of Management Journal, 40*(5), 175–189.

Davidson III, W.N., Worrell, D. L., & Box, J. B. (1996). Early retirement programs and firm performance. *Academy of Management Journal, 39*(4), 970–984.

McDonald, M. L., & Westphal, J. D. (2003). Getting by with the advice of their friends: CEO's advice networks and firms' strategic responses to poor performance. *Administrative Science Quarterly, 48*(2), 1–32.

Niehaus, R., & Swiercz, M. (1996). Do HR systems affect the bottom line? We have the answer. *Academy of Management Journal, 19*(1), 61–69.

Pfau, B., & Kay, I. (2002, June). Does 360 degree feedback negatively affect company performance? *HR Magazine*, pp., 56–59.

Preston, L. E., & O'Bannon, D. P. (1997). The corporate social-financial performance relationship. *Business and Society, 36*(4), 419–429.

Subramani, M., & Walden, E. (2001). The impact of E-commerce announcements on the market value of firms. *Information Systems Research, 12*(2), 135–154.

Tosi, Jr., H. L., & Gomez-Mejia, L. R. (1994). How can CEO's compensation affect a firm's performance? *Academy of Management Journal, 37*(4), 1002–1016.

CHAPTER 19

FUNCTION-TRIGGERED PERFORMANCE

This final chapter, just as the previous one, is about firm performance. There is, however, a difference. Firm performance in this chapter is more likely to be affected by functional causes, such as manufacturing, quality, technology, financial, and marketing.

The first paper evaluates what effect quality practices have on quality, manufacturing, and business performance. The population sampled to provide answers to the above question consisted of supplier firms to the electronics sector in Ireland. A total of 200 usable responses were received for statistical testing. The results show that quality practices positively affect quality performance. Also, quality performance positively affects manufacturing performance. Furthermore, manufacturing performance positively affects customer satisfaction. No relationship was found to exist between customer satisfaction and business performance.

The second paper focuses on which quality dimensions positively affect profitability. The Profit Impact of Market Share (PIMS) database was used for statistical analysis. The focus of the study was on capital goods firms. The results show that quality positively influenced profitability, especially for firms that were the first to enter the market for a product.

The third paper evaluates the effects of technology attributes and sourcing on overall performance. The researchers used the Dow Jones News Retrieval Service for announcements of licensing agreements, technology

Proven Solutions for Improving Supply Chain Performance, pages 267–281

acquisitions, and so on. They then contacted the identified firms and obtained a usable sample of 95 technology arrangements. The results of the study revealed mixed results. If a technology is difficult to imitate, it is important to maintain a tight relationship between buyer and supplier of the technology. If the value of the technology is unclear, then licensing seems appropriate. Other results are also presented.

The fourth paper evaluates the effect of firm characteristics and total quality management (TQM) on financial performance. The researchers used 435 quality award winners as the empirical basis for their study. The results show that smaller firms implement TQM better than larger firms. Also, quality award winners had substantially higher changes in operating income than non-award winners.

The fifth paper studies the linkage between manufacturing process choice and performance. The researchers used company data from 144 U.S. firms. The results showed that the 10 best performing plants respond more quickly to customer orders, focus more on keeping inventory low, and maximize equipment utilization.

The sixth study looks at the performance benefits from just-in-time (JIT) implementation. The researchers surveyed 89 managers from JIT firms to find answers to the question. The results showed that the vast majority of manager respondents were positive about the benefits of JIT implementation. Benefits included quality improvements, inventory reduction, employee flexibility, and time-based responses.

The seventh paper reports on a study of firm valuation of technological versus marketing alliances. The researchers evaluated 119 strategic alliances formed during the 1987–1991 period. The performance criterion measured was the change in market value of the firm. The results indicate that there is a positive impact on stock price when the alliance is announced. However, there was no significant improvement in stock price or market share in the long run.

The eighth and final paper focuses on the effect of incentive pay on performance. The researchers sampled many small businesses and used a case-based approach for evaluation. The results showed that incentive plans need careful planning to work effectively.

Below follow the detailed summaries introduced above. The results show several interesting linkages of management initiatives that can lead to improved performance.

QUALITY PRACTICES, QUALITY PERFORMANCE, MANUFACTURING PERFORMANCE, AND CUSTOMER SATISFACTION

What effect do quality practices have on quality performance, manufacturing performance, customer satisfaction, production cost, and ultimately business performance?

Researchers Brian Fynes of Ireland and Chris Voss of the United Kingdom posed the above question and then developed a survey questionnaire that they sent out to a population of 200 suppliers to the electronics sector in the Republic of Ireland. The results of their subsequent statistical analysis showed considerable support for their hypotheses.

The quality constructs the researchers used were based on existing literature on the subject and consisted of such constructs as design quality, conformance quality, quality practices, external quality-in-use, and relationship strength. Manufacturing performance constructs used were time-to-market, product cost, and customer satisfaction. Overall firm performance was measured by business strength.

The test sample of supplier firms to the electronics sector consisted of about 400 firms. Each one was contacted by phone to identify the responsible person to whom to send the survey questionnaire. The resultant mailing produced about 200 usable completed questionnaires.

The results of the statistical testing revealed that quality practices had a statistically significant and positive effect on conformance quality and design quality.

Design quality, in turn, had a statistically significant effect on conformance quality (positive), quality-in-use (positive), time-to-market (positive), and product cost (negative). The latter result was hypothesized because good design quality should lower cost.

Also, conformance quality had a statistically significant effect on quality-in-use (positive) and product cost (negative). Quality-in-use, in turn, had a statistically significant positive effect on customer satisfaction, and product cost had a statistically significant negative effect on customer satisfaction.

Two relationships were found not to be statistically significant, although the coefficients were in the direction hypothesized. They were time-to-market and customer satisfaction, and customer satisfaction and business performance.

The overall results show that quality practices have a definite and positive effect on quality performance. Also, quality performance has a direct and positive effect on manufacturing performance. And manufacturing performance has a direct and positive effect on customer satisfaction. However, statistically significant, no relationship was found to exist between customer satisfaction and business performance.

WHICH QUALITY DIMENSIONS HAVE THE MOST POSITIVE EFFECT ON PROFITABILITY?

This article focuses on the importance quality has played in recent years in both product and service firms. The authors contend that the business strategy must be aligned with quality goals in order to be successful, but that any study on quality in the past was overly simplistic and unrealistic. They both believe that quality conveys different meanings to different people, and depending on where the company's product is in its life cycle and whether the product is the first of its kind, will change the quality strategy that needs to be implemented.

The study was conducted by researchers Jhinuk Chowdhury and Ajay Menon, who used the Profit Impact of Market Share (PIMS) database from which to pull their sample of data. The database is held at the Strategic Planning Institute and contains managers' evaluations of quality on three quality categories: product-based, service-based, and image-based. The product-based quality consists of durability, reliability, and efficiency, while the service-based category consists of such issues as delivery, competence of the sales force, and technical assistance. The third image-based category refers to the influence of the brand name and customer buying intentions.

The PIMS database is considered the most extensive strategic database in the world and contains information on over 2,900 business units from more than 450 firms during the period from the early 1970s to the mid-1980s.

The particular sample that was used in the study consisted of 431 business units in the area of capital goods. Of this sample, 28 percent represented products in the early stages, and 72 percent were in the late stages of the product life cycle. In regards to the order of market entry, 56 percent of the sample were in the pioneer category with 44 percent in nonpioneer products. Pioneer refers to early entries and nonpioneer refers to late entries.

The sample responses from the database were tested with statistical methods using return on investment (ROI) as the dependent variable. There were two sets of independent variables, the first set used order of market entry (pioneer or nonpioneer), and the second set used the stage in the product life cycle. Each of these independent variables was tested in turn with each of the three dimensions of quality (product, service, and image).

The background theory for this study began as early as 1983 when eight dimensions of quality were identified, from which managers select to establish their quality niche. It was argued that competition based on selected quality dimensions would be more profitable.

Many previous studies have shown the influence of product quality on a firm's return on investment, and that there exist clear strategic variables that affect the quality–performance relationship. The two variables that the researchers focus on are the order of market entry and the stage in the product life cycle. The strength of these two variables rests on the fact that the pioneers have the opportunity to define quality in the market and set the benchmark, and the fact that as the stage of the product life cycle changes, so must the quality strategy.

Results of the study were conclusive, showing that the product dimension of quality influenced ROI more heavily for pioneers than nonpioneers, due to the fact that pioneers are the first to the market and define quality.

The study also showed that the service dimension of quality is stronger for nonpioneers than it is for pioneers. This is attributable to the brand recognition of the pioneer in the market and the need for the nonpioneer to distinguish their product in some other way, for instance, through better service. The researchers found that the image dimension of quality is stronger for pioneers than it is for nonpioneers due to brand recognition.

With regards to the product life cycle, the study found that the product dimension of quality is stronger early in the product life cycle. It was just the opposite for service and image-based quality, which both had a stronger impact on ROI later in the product life cycle.

The implications of this study are very beneficial to managers who need to match their business strategy with quality. Quality does have many dimensions and its focus within a corporation should be changed, depending on the marketing conditions that its products currently face.

TECHNOLOGY ATTRIBUTES, TECHNOLOGY SOURCING AND OVERALL PERFORMANCE

How do imitability, uniqueness, and uncertainty associated with a technology interact with partner interdependence to influence technology sourcing outcomes?

Researchers H. Kevin Steensma and Kevin G. Corley of the University of Washington and Pennsylvania University, respectively, developed a study to find answers to the above research question.

The researchers used the online Dow Jones News Retrieval Service to identify announcements of licensing agreements, technology acquisitions, and related news items. For each identified licensing agreement, joint development, or acquisition, they collected relevant information on the firms associated with each event. For each event they also identified individuals who they contacted and requested their participation in the study. The participation included responding to a survey questionnaire. This data collection process produced 95 technology sourcing arrangements.

The five technology attributes the researchers focused on consisted of technology uniqueness, technology imitability, technological uncertainty, technology dynamism, and organizational interdependence. The information for these variables was obtained through the survey questionnaire. Also considered were the control variables research and development intensity, sales revenues, relatedness of technology, licensing experience, joint development experience, acquisition experience, and firm performance.

The results of the study revealed that if a technology is difficult to imitate, it is desirable to have a tight relationship between the source and the sourcing firm such as an acquisition. In such a case it is not wise to use joint development or licensing.

If there is uncertainty in the market value of the technology, sourcing performance is enhanced by a more loosely coupled relationship such as is found in a licensing arrangement or in joint development.

The researchers found a slightly stronger positive relationship for joint development than for licensing, but the relationship between uniqueness and sourcing performance was negative for acquisitions.

The researchers recommend that tight coupling be used if the know-how is difficult to imitate, that is in case of acquisitions. Loosely coupled partnerships are appropriate if the know-how is relatively easy to imitate, that is in case of licensing or joint development. Finally, loose coupling is recommended for more turbulent and dynamic know-how, that is for licensing or joint development, but not in acquisitions.

THE EFFECTS OF FIRM CHARACTERISTICS AND TOTAL QUALITY MANAGEMENT ON FINANCIAL PERFORMANCE

Total quality management (TQM) has a significant impact on financial performance; however, financial performance is moderated by various firm characteristics. The characteristics that were examined were firm size, the degree of capital intensity, the degree of diversification, the maturity of the TQM implementation, and the timing of effective TQM implementation. It is important to understand how the financial impact of total quality management varies by firm characteristics because the investment of implementing TQM can be costly. Recent research implies that a firm's size can be related to a firm's willingness to adapt to change.

Researchers Kevin B. Hendricks, of the University of Western Ontario and Richard Ivey School of Business, and Vinod R. Singhal, of DuPree College of Management and the Georgia Institute of Technology, have examined the connection between total quality management and financial performance. Their research has shown that effective TQM implementation improves a company's profitability long term. Also, the time and cost to apply TQM varies among firms due to differences in technology and the different markets in which firms operate.

Hendricks and Singhal used the winners of quality awards for their sample selection in their research. Their study of the various quality awards shows that the core concepts and values stressed are most often those that are known to be the building blocks of effective TQM implementation. They concentrated on developing a connection between these winners and their financial performance. For each winner, they identified the year when they won their first award, to determine whether they had a reasonably effective TQM implementation in place a year prior to receiving the award. Hendricks and Singhal used a 5-year time period, following the initial implementation of TQM, and measured the performance changes for each winner.

They used one-to-one comparisons of award winners and controls, which allowed them to estimate the statistical significance of the difference between the growth in performance winners and the control. Their results of these comparisons are based on abnormal growth for industry and size. They used three control samples, with each control sample intended to touch on a specific weakness of the others. Since no matching process is flawless, they focused on the quality of the matches to ensure better results.

The authors reported their hypotheses on the subject of total quality management and how it is related to a firm's financial performance and characteristics. They studied the relation between firm size and inertia, which is the resistance to fundamental changes in managing business. Implementing TQM means putting the firm's focus entirely on the quality of the organization as a whole, and this can entail extreme changes in management and labor relations. Larger firms have a multilayered management system and often it is more difficult for them to adapt, implement, and maintain change than it is for smaller firms. Since there are usually fewer levels of management, smaller firms already have the sense of teamwork and empowerment incorporated into their working environment. This makes it easier for a smaller firm to implement total quality management into their business rather than a larger firm, especially since they are less resistant to change.

The empirical results of this study show the statistics for the sample of 435 award winners. The median winner represents a firm with sales of $917 million, net property plant and equipment per employee of $25,200, and concentration measured by the Herfindahl Index of 0.5 in the year 1990. Another table in the article provides the mean percent changes in the various performance measures for the sample of award winners. The mean change in operating income of the winners is about 39 percent higher than that of the controls. These results imply that firms that have effectively implemented total quality management improve their financial performance. To determine the degree of capital intensity, another table presents the results for lower and higher capital-intensive firms. For lower capital-intensive firms, the mean percent change in operating income is 58.1 percent and sales grew by 33.3 percent compared to a 20.1 percent mean percentage change and an 18.7 percent sales growth for higher capital-intensive firms. These results show that only the improvement for lower capital-intensive firms is statistically significant; and it is implied that lower capital-intensive firms benefit from TQM more than higher capital-intensive firms.

This study shows the association between effective implementation of total quality management and a firm's financial performance and characteristics. It was found that smaller firms implemented TQM better than larger firms. Their advice for management is that managers should set reasonable expectations for their firm to receive maximum benefits from TQM based on the firm's characteristics. It's possible that the quality management practices differ greatly among firms, which is why some do better than others, or it could simply be that total quality management is more beneficial for firms that have specific characteristics.

THE LINKAGE BETWEEN PROCESS CHOICE AND PERFORMANCE DRIVERS

Process choice is a major part of operations strategy and plays a key role in aligning operations decisions with the production environment. Process choice consists of four categories: job shop, batch shop, line flow, and continuous flow shop. The characteristics of the markets served by manufacturing firms are primary determinants of process choice. According to Professors Safizadeh and Ritzman, to monitor and continuously improve operations, evaluation scorecards should pay particular attention to performance drivers, which change depending on the plant's process choice.

The objective of this research is to see how production planning and inventory control decisions manifest themselves in different production environments and to examine the relationship between decisions and operations performance.

The data they used was acquired from 144 firms located in the Midwest and the Northeast through a telephone and mail survey. Also, secondary databases were used for the study.

Their results for aggregate plan, planning horizon, and backlog showed that (1) production line and continuous flow plants base production plans more on forecasts than on actual orders, while the reverse is true at job and batch shops; (2) production line and continuous flow plants experience smaller differences between actual and forecasted demand in both quantity and timing than do job and batch shops; and (3) production line and continuous flow plants have smaller order backlogs and use shorter planning horizons than do job and batch shops.

The results for the batch size rationale showed that production line and continuous flow plants place more emphasis on maximizing equipment utilization and minimizing down time related to setup than do job and batch shops.

The results for inventory level showed that production line and continuous flow plants carry less raw material inventory and work-in-process inventory than do job and batch shops.

Finally, the results for performance drivers showed that 10 of the best performing plants (1) make more frequent changes to respond to customer orders, (2) job and batch shops follow more of a chase strategy, (3) job and batch shops that find ways to reduce inventory in purchased materials improve their operations performance, and (4) the performance of the operations function at production line and continuous flow plants improves when more emphasis is given to minimizing down time for setup and to maximizing equipment utilization.

PERFORMANCE BENEFITS FROM JIT IMPLEMENTATION

Despite an abundance of economic resources, U.S. manufacturers have struggled with increased trade deficits and outsourced operations. With fewer available natural resources, strong market competitors have materialized using superior manufacturing practices in the form of just-in-time production.

Just in time (JIT) is a Japanese-developed manufacturing philosophy that represents production efficiency, emphasizing the achievement of excellence through continuous improvements and the elimination of waste. Illustrated benefits of JIT implementation are improved performance through lower inventory levels, reduced quality costs, and greater customer responsiveness. Nonetheless, the implementation of JIT by U.S. firms has been relatively slow. This lag has been attributed to a lack of understanding of JIT methods, an incompatible workforce and workplace environment, nonsupportive suppliers, and an inadequate performance measurement and incentive system.

This study has two principal objectives: investigate the benefits received from implementation of JIT and examine the dependence of these benefits on the level of commitment in adopting specific JIT practices. Successful JIT implementation should accomplish two major objectives: improve quality and control the timeliness of the production and delivery of products.

Researchers Rosemary R. Fullerton, of Utah State University, and Cheryl S. McWatters, of McGill University, surveyed executives at 89 JIT practicing firms to clearly understand the benefits experienced through JIT adoption and whether a more comprehensive implementation is worthwhile. Respondents to the survey had titles equivalent to Vice President of Operations, Director of Marketing, or Plant Manager. They had an average of 17 years in management experience, including 9 years of management with their current firm. The majority (64 percent) of the respondent firms were from three industries: industrial machinery, electronics, and instrumentation.

The levels of JIT implementation were measured by responses to Likert-scaled questions partitioned into low and high levels. JIT measures were subjected to an exploratory analysis.

The researchers found that approximately 28 percent of the respondents reported significant improvement in operations since implementing JIT. The most consistent benefit from JIT adoption found in this study was a reduction in inventory levels. JIT pulls inventory through production only as orders are demanded. With work-in-process inventories kept at a minimum, production can respond more quickly to errors and changes in demand. Thus, wait, move, and inspection time, which can comprise up to 95 percent of product cost, is reduced.

More than 61percent of the responses were positive, with firms experiencing benefits in all of the measured areas: quality improvements, time-based responses, employee flexibility, accounting simplification, firm profitability, and inventory reductions. Only 5 percent of the responses were negative with respect to no changes after adopting JIT. The negative responses were from firms using a piecemeal approach to the implementation of JIT practices.

Although benefits are reaped at any level of implementation, research confirms that the level of commitment in adopting specific JIT practices determines the benefits experienced by that firm. Managers reaping the highest rewards were the high adopters of either a complete assortment of JIT practices or unique JIT practices and JIT purchasing.

This study has critical implications; evidence supports the concept of JIT as a comprehensive, vital manufacturing strategy that can build and sustain competitive advantage. This study indicates the more comprehensive the adoption of JIT, the greater the level of return and improved competitive performance.

FIRM VALUATION OF TECHNOLOGICAL VERSUS MARKETING ALLIANCES

The benefits that can be realized through common operations such as R&D, manufacturing, distribution, sales, and advertising have been well recognized, but it is usually discussed within the context of combining business units within one company. Does this benefit carry over to independent firms? When companies form strategic alliances, are the alliances perceived as positive or negative? Does it depend on the type of alliance or the details surrounding the alliance? Are stock market reactions to technological alliances different from marketing alliances? The research performed by Das, Sen, and Sengupta suggests that there are differences in the way technological and marketing alliances are perceived in the stock market. By evaluating fluctuations in the stock prices of the companies involved in the alliances within a 7-day period centered around the day on which a strategic alliance announcement was reported in the newspaper, they have suggested predictable events:

1. Alliances will cause greater than normal fluctuations in stocks for the companies involved in the alliances.
2. The fluctuations will be either positive or negative, depending on the profitability and size of the companies involved in the alliances and what type of alliance is formed.
3. The degree of fluctuation will depend upon the type of alliance formed.

Researchers Somnath Das of the University of Illinois at Chicago, Pradyot K. Sen of the State University of New York at Buffalo, and Sanjit Sengupta of San Francisco State University analyzed 119 strategic alliances formed during the period 1987–1991 that were reported by two daily newspapers, the *Wall Street Journal* and the *Financial Times*. The research tested assumptions that firms entering strategic alliances will realize greater than normal increases in their stocks; companies involved in technological alliances will generally realize greater increases in their stocks than companies involved in marketing alliances; the smaller company involved in the alliance will benefit more than the larger, more profitable company; and investor uncertainty will increase following marketing alliances, but will not for technological alliances.

The sample data Das and colleagues collected was obtained from a larger sample of a commercially available database, Information Technology Strategic Alliance. Joint ventures, multi-party alliances, and alliances for which there was no corresponding stock data in Center for Research in Security Prices files were eliminated from the sample. Furthermore, if an earnings or dividend announcement was made within 5 calendar days before or after an alliance announcement, that alliance was eliminated, also due to the uncertainty of knowing what actually caused stock fluctuations. After the exclusions, 119 alliances remained and were categorized by type—technological and marketing alliances. Technological alliances were defined as those sharing R&D, engineering, and manufacturing activities, whereas marketing alliances involve sharing sales, distribution, and customer service. The size of each company was determined from three measures from the COMPUSTAT database: total assets, net sales, and total number of employees. The profitability of each company was calculated to be the ratio of net income to book value of assets.

The companies involved in the 119 selected alliances were analyzed within a 7-day period surrounding the alliance announcement (3 days before, the day of the announcement, and 3 days after the announcement). Differences in the stock price for each company were assumed to reflect the positive or negative reaction to the announcement. Using scientific formulas, average abnormal returns were calculated for the 7-day period. Averages were weighted based on the size of the company.

The results of the research basically support the hypotheses of the researchers. They found that overall, abnormal increases in stock prices occurred when alliances were announced. The average increase, however, was not as significant as anticipated. Thus, this was weak support of their hypothesis that abnormal increases in stock prices would occur upon announcement of an alliance. When broken down by type of alliance, technological alliances did, in fact, yield significant abnormal increases in stock prices. What brought the average down was the fact that abnormal returns for marketing alliances were negative. In any case, the results strongly support another hypothesis that the stock market rewards technological alliances more than marketing alliances. Das and colleagues attributed this differential to the market's perception of technological alliances having more potential for increasing future income than marketing alliances.

The researchers also speculated that larger, more profitable firms would have less to gain from entering an alliance than a smaller, innovative startup company. They expected the market to react less favorably to the larger company than to the smaller one. The results of the study proved their theory to be correct, but only in technological alliances, where the returns were significantly higher for the smaller companies; there was no discernable difference between small and large partners in marketing alliances.

Finally, data from the study suggests that investors are more uncertain about marketing alliances than they are about technological alliances. This result was also consistent with their hypothesis that the amount of variance in abnormal returns increases following the announcement of marketing alliances, whereas there was no change in variance of abnormal returns for technological alliances.

Taking the results of this study as gospel of what will and will not affect the value of a firm when entering an alliance with another firm is not wise. There are too many factors that play into the results that are uncertain; even the researchers themselves caution one to interpret their findings with care, acknowledging limitations of a small sample size of data and lack of detailed information about what the alliances were actually about. They speculate that different circumstances regarding an alliance could very possibly alter the market's reaction to the companies involved in the alliance. Their sample data is inherently heterogeneous and aggregating the sample could also have caused a netting-out of different effects. More detailed categorization of alliances needs to be completed in order to make a definitive statement about added/decreased value due to forming an alliance.

Finally, a positive stock market reaction in an alliance does not necessarily translate into subsequent positive performance in terms of return on investment or market share of a company in the same way that initial positive market reactions to mergers and acquisitions does not guarantee consistent good performance of those firms from that point on. Thus, this study cannot be used to predict what alliances will add value to a firm and those that will not. In spite of the limitations of this study, it documents interesting evidence of changes in stock market values due to the formation of strategic alliances of companies, and provides some explanation of the causes for those differences.

INCENTIVE PAY AND PERFORMANCE

When companies decide how to motivate employees, bonuses based on performance or profits are options. One problem with these plans is that they must be designed in the correct way. If they are not, employees may actually be demotivated and the company may actually show less profits than before the plan was implemented. This is an even larger problem with smaller companies that do not earn large profits. This problem is amplified when revenues are earned through long-term contracts, which is the case in this research paper.

This study was done by Nerys Fuller-Love and R.W. Scapens. They studied the effects of a performance-based incentive plan in a small shipyard company. They were looking for a decrease in costs (increased profits) if ships, and smaller tasks, were completed quicker, on schedule, and in high-quality fashion. They also observed the effects of the bonus plan in respect to management's control.

The researchers used a case-based approach instead of a sample of many small businesses because it gives them the opportunity to go into more detail than would otherwise be impossible, and because this is a unique environment. Their research consisted of interviews with the owner-manager, production manager, and employees, and investigated details on the job cards used, amounts paid, bonus rate, and number of hours allocated to the tasks.

The interview with the owner was done in order to find out the reason for wanting a performance-based pay plan. In a small business the owner can motivate the employees while he is on the shop floor. However, in larger businesses the owner or manager can no longer spend as much time on the shop floor and the employees may then be less motivated.

Many of the findings in this paper are intuitive and make sense. The reason the research helps is because it substantiates those thoughts. Interviews were conducted before the plan was implemented, while changes were made, and at the end of the study. Conducting interviews throughout the stages gives an idea what was happening to the company as certain parts of the plan were tested.

One problem is that it is hard to foresee all the tasks that are required when the project is as big as building a ship. The problem this creates is that tasks will not be allocated in the beginning and will result in more hours necessary than planned. This led to failing to meet the delivery date and going over budget, two of the things this bonus plan was created to fix. This would have been slightly easier if a system would have been in place prior to implementation of the bonus plan. However, with a project this large it is unlikely that all tasks would have been accounted for, but it could have been much closer.

Another problem is that the bonus rate was too high, which is also largely due to the lack of information and monitoring of costs and processes. An interview with an employee verified this as well. Bonuses were paid on the percent of time it was early or late.

For the most part, the employees liked the bonus plan. However, it is not fair to all employees. Employees working on indirect jobs were not entitled to receive a bonus. Another problem related to this is also due to the lack of information. Since the jobs were set with standard hours, some employees received a higher bonus since certain jobs were allocated more hours than were normally required while others were allocated only slightly more than normally required.

This study shows that incentive plans need careful planning to work effectively. One way the researchers tried to improve the plan was to allocate less time to the beginning tasks. The tasks should have allocated hours closer to what is actually required. This would make the plan fairer to employees and would not cost the company as much money. In addition, the bonus rate should not be constant. First, the rate should vary based on the number of hours over or under the normal for each task. This is similar to how they did it, except it should be closer to the bonus rate when the task is completed close to the standard time and should vary, increasingly, as the variance increases. Second, this same idea can be used for the beginning through the end of the processes by increasing the bonus rate toward the end of the project. Of course, this would only work if all employees performed work at the beginning and at the end.

REFERENCES

Chowdhury, J., & Menon, A. (1995). Multidimensional components of quality and strategic business unit performance: A PIMS test. *Journal of Managerial Issues, 7*(17), 449–451.

Das, S., Sen, P. K., & Sangupta, S. (1998). Impact of strategic alliances on firm valuation. *Academy of Management Journal, 41*(1), 27–41.

Fuller-Love, N., & Scapens, R. W. (1997). Performance related pay: A case study of a small business. *International Small Business Journal, 15*(4), 48–63.

Fullerton, R. T., & McWatters, C. S. (2001). The production performance benefits from JIT implementation, *Journal of Operations Management, 19*(1), 81–96.

Fynes, B., & Voss, C. (2002). The moderating effect of buyer-supplier relationships on quality practices and performance. *International Journal of Operations and Production Management, 22*(6), 589–613.

Hendricks, K. B., & Singhal, V. R. (2001). Firm characteristics, total quality management, and financial performance. *Journal of Operations Management, 14*(2), 269–285.

Safizadeh, M., & Ritzman, L. P. (1997). Linking performance drivers in production planning and inventory control to process choice. *Journal of Operation Management 15*(4), 389–403.

Steensma, K., & Corley, K. G. (2000). On the performance of technology-sourcing partnership: The interaction between partner interdependence and technology attributes. *Academy of Management Journal, 43*(6), 1045–1067.

Printed in the United Kingdom
by Lightning Source UK Ltd.
110010UKS00001B/7